CHASING
THE
DREAMS

A traveller remembers

HAMISH BROWN

SANDSTONE PRESS

Published in Great Britain by
Sandstone Press Ltd
Suite One, Willow House
Stoneyfield Business Park
Inverness
IV2 7PA
Scotland

www.sandstonepress.com

The publisher acknowledges support from Creative Scotland
towards publication of this volume.

ISBN: 978-1-912240-78-4
ISBNe: 978-1-912240-79-1

Cover design by Raspberry Creative Type
Typeset by Iolaire, Newtonmore
Printed and bound by Totem, Poland

Your young men shall see visions
and your old men shall dream dreams.

Acts 2:17

Dreams are more potent than reason.

W. H. Murray

CONTENTS

Just So; Stories

FOREWORD

A previous collection, *Walking the Song*, I called a potpourri, a collection mainly of articles which had appeared in print over the length of an active life. *Chasing the Dreams* is very much in the same vein, describing more places and experiences that caught my imagination and have stayed clear in my 'shaky edifice of memory'. Most mountaineers are curious about life in general, with many strands to the rope that belays them to the world. Pieces selected have largely been left as they appeared though I have added a few notes where helpful. Sections this time end with a poem, and the last section is different. Fortunately, I have always kept logs (diaries) so can check on facts but I just wish I'd taken more to heart Dr Johnson's admonition to Boswell, '... when we travel again let us look better about us.'

As with *Song*, *Dreams* is set out in sections of related themes and interests, topical and geographical. There is considerable autobiographical content as, perforce, I'm describing the curious I've seen, enjoyed, or suffered. In my experience, the fabled city of dreams is always over the horizon, never just round the corner. Dreams have to be chased. It is the chasing that is life. As Robert Service sang, '... it isn't the gold that I'm wanting, / So much as just finding the gold'.

In the longer Scottish-based accounts the Ordnance Survey Landranger map number is given at the start so, if wanted, readers can follow wanderings in detail; and I've a sketch map for one Atlas narrative. Heights and distances set a problem because of our half-baked attempt at going metric but generally British locations will have heights in either feet or metres and distances in miles while furth of Britain is all metric.

If there is less 'straight' mountaineering content in *Dreams* this is largely from responses to *Song* where many said it was the stories of people and places and various 'happenings' which were most interesting. ('One climb described is very like any other climb described.') There's a touch of the nostalgic, remembering a more innocent world, a less-endangered, unpressurised existence and I was also fortunate in seeing many of the world's great sites / sights (Victoria Falls, Taj Mahal, Machu Picchu) before the advent of Tourism, with a capital T. Tourism always wears such big boots. We have become an affluent society, in thrall to such trite interests, while our needy seas and landscapes face a general insensitivity, and the continuing rapacity of commercial interests. Two of my first realisations of this when younger were the unbelievable plan to dam the Nevis gorge to make more electricity (which roused Tom Weir to the conservation battle of his life) and the National Trust for Scotland surrendering St Kilda – now a double World Heritage Site – to the military. Today's most blatant scam is seeing vast tracks of scenic landscape blighted with windfarms in so many, many *wrong* places.

All through my lifetime this duck-nibbling destruction of landscape quality has gone on; constant rear-guard actions no match for the big guns of moneyed self-interests. We know we need the rainforests yet continue to destroy them, we need the oceans but continue to misuse them, we are even filling the sky overhead with junk. What right have we to seek other worlds when we have miscarried on the one we have? Thirty years ago I suggested we were 'a failed species on the way out'. Maybe the world will flourish again when we have gone.

At school I was once called 'Curiosity Kid' (one regular, much-enjoyed schools' 'Nature Question Time' programme on the 'wireless' was entirely given over to answering the questions I'd sent in) and I am glad never to have lost an interest in this very fascinating and very beautiful world, however we, humankind, seek to destroy it and each other. I've walked songs and chased dreams. Norman McCaig wrote 'There's a Schiehallion wherever you go, / the thing is, to climb it.' Dreams have to be chased. Beware, however, once you have the sniff of desert, mountain or sea air, you may be sneezing for the rest of your life.

Chasing the Dreams is the result of being fortunate enough to spend most of a lifetime roaming wilder places (mostly mountains), at home in Scotland and many far corners of the world, from Arctic to Mediterranean ranges, America, Africa and the East. Fortuitously, thirteen years, which is the total from fifty-three visits, have been to the Berber people's world of the Atlas Mountains. There is something, beyond telling, in having another place in the world, another people and culture nobler than one's own in which to find solace and escape the inconsequential pressures and hamster-wheel captivity of life in our Western world. It is desirable to have a well-filled past; it is all the future we eventually have to hold.

> *Happy the man, and happy he alone,*
> *He who can call today his own,*
> *He who, secure within, can say,*
> *Tomorrow, do thy worst for I have lived*
>   *today.*

John Dryden

TRAMPING IN SCOTLAND

THE FIRST MUNRO ON SKI

I find exercise ... unbearable. I much prefer to set off and suffer the first few weeks.

Wally Herbert

This piece was written over fifty years ago and I came on it only recently – and marvelled at my youthful enthusiasm. That first Munro, Stuc a'Chroin, was climbed with ordinary ski equipment: no touring bindings with heel uplift, no skins, nothing to help. There is nothing quite like 'the first fine careless rapture' of confident youth so I have left the text unaltered. A note of warning however: our teaching ourselves to ski was not a good idea. There are technical tricks we never discovered, and we picked up some bad habits. When I realised this I went on a course at Glenmore Lodge to be 'sorted out' (by instructor Clive Freshwater who would later open the Loch Insh Outdoor Centre). I would go on to gain my ski instructor's certificate and enjoy ski-mountaineering in the Pyrenees, Alps and Atlas. So, if you'd like to learn to ski, do so under proper instructors!

Another matter that this piece, never intended for publication, almost flaunts, is the abundant availability of snow.

Our recalling good snowy winters those decades ago is not just the gilding of memory – they happened. I kept a note of hills climbed on Christmas Day and New Year's Day and they invariably tell of deep snow flounders in the far North West, of lochs frozen solid, of lower landscapes and roads burdened with snow. Once competent enough on skis I determined that skiing was the only way to 'bag' winter Munros. But after some years the number of such outings began to drop, for starting points became higher and higher as the snow base rose, and it became far too big a hassle to gain a reward. Struggling up through the heather carrying skis was not in the contract. Oh, but what glory days they were! When it was good it was purest bliss, as I tell in 'The Ring of Tarf' a little further on. You need to be mental to trump any denial of climate change by now.

From extensive reading at this time I knew of mountain skiing in the Alps or in Polar regions, but what about in Scotland? After a deep snow flounder over a summit above Drumochter I came on the sweeping curves of ski tracks on the slopes below me. Ah! – it *was* done in Scotland. Skiing could complete an enthusiast's winter triptych: Munros, Climbing, *Skiing*.

A harsh winter promptly brought snow down to sea level in Fife (February 1963) and, after a first morning on a local golf course, we lugged our skis up Largo Law (just under 1000 feet). Icy, crusted conditions ensured plenty of thrills and spills, and a dramatic encounter with the top wires of a fence when heading down and suddenly realising that skis did not have brakes. We had a few encounters of a prickly kind when ending up in gorse bushes. Fit climbers as we thought ourselves, we suffered aches and pains and stiffness on a new level after that.

Our next outing was to the Ochils, where we camped

at Paradise above Dollar, on a level with Castle Campbell. On good slopes there we learned kick-turns then, in the afternoon, headed up the 2000 foot White Wisp in conditions all too familiar to tourers: spindrift blasting across the snow and stinging our faces when we cowered in the stronger hits. On the bald summit we crouched for long minutes, gasping and blinded, stunned by the brutal assault of the storm. We edged down the lip of the corrie for shelter and noted the length of the burn below was choked with avalanche debris. Over half a mile of circling windslab snow had been detached; as we skied along we trembled at the possibility of setting off another lot. Vanishing in and out of clouds, we again zigzagged down and round the hill. This first taste of the heights was good, we felt, but being able to turn properly would be an asset. Kick-turns as our only option had limitations, and were apt to become sit-down turns on steeper, deeper snow.

We had another brilliant day just along from Buckhaven, the perfect powder snow lying six inches deep on the braes. We actually managed turns – of a sort. When we made a whole series down to the beach there was a glow of satisfaction. I recalled entries in Alpine hut books that told of exploits like Chamonix to Zermatt. Someday perhaps ... Meanwhile, we'd had Largo Law, just under 1,000 feet, Whitewisp, just over 2,000 feet. Surely the next step was a Munro on skis.

In the meantime two of my pupils, together, and I, alone, set off to hitch north on a Friday for a rendezvous on the edge of Rannoch Moor. We had our eyes on a climb on Saturday, and on Sunday, when our local club's hired bus arrived, we planned the historic Upper Couloir of Stob Ghabhar.

None of us managed further than Strathyre. I perforce spent a tentless night out in the forest near the village: an unforgettable bivouac, so still a night that a candle on a spruce frond lit up the scene in magical fashion. On a li-lo, and with two skimpy summer sleeping bags, I was cosy enough and lay reading awhile. (Somehow, to my embarrassment, the *Sunday Post* got hold of this incident and made a song and dance about it.)

In the morning, with no opening of roads ahead, I thumbed a lift southwards – all the way to Edinburgh in one go – and returned to Fife by train. A phone call confirmed that the Kirkcaldy Mountaineering Club bus would still set off on the Sunday and would simply stop when forced to and let us loose wherever. I could take my skis, I decided. (Later I heard the two lads supposedly meeting up with me the day before had spent the weekend camping and roaming the Ochils.)

The bus stuck at Lochearnhead; Glen Ogle was still blocked. A mass assault on the Ben Vorlich/Stuc a'Chroin pair was mooted and so, by chance, here was the opportunity for my first Munro on skis.

What climber does not revel in rhythm? Here it was then: on and on up Glenample, across the burn, gradually ascending and traversing the hillside. Only occasionally was a turn necessary, only occasionally a herring-bone pattern to break the long clean line. Hard work, but joyous, satisfying. Above Glenample shieling I heard the dogs barking and saw the dots of our bus group crossing to the cottages far below. Who had the laugh now? (Most regarded skis as very suspect).

The Allt a'Choire Fhuadaraich was crossed and for the steep climb up Creag Dubh (the *Black Crag*) I dismounted – and at once sank in to the knees. Those 500 feet are best forgotten. I had to rest continually with heart pounding furiously. Gradually I reached the stage of cursing skis and climbing and myself for ever putting on a pair of boots. On top of the shoulder I lay on some bare rocks with legs shaking uncontrollably and the sweat freezing my shirt tail into a board. I lay flat out, crunching sugary sweets until muscles and nerves slowly returned to normal. The others could catch up if they liked. To hell with it!

Skis on again for the continuing ascent. Several times I had to rest, twice I tried to walk only to find it even more strenuous. Gradually the height was gained, and spirits could do nothing but follow as Ben More and Stobinian rose over the intervening hills as great white pyramids.

The view from the hard-won summit was superlative: Lowlands and Highlands completely white-washed. I sat by the cairn eating and staring round, naming off range after range of peaks from Arran to Nevis to the Cairngorms – they were all there – all old friends, all climbed, and loved and longed for again. The Stuc had always been kind: this was the fifth perfect stay on its top in two years. I dozed off for half an hour until the cold woke me again. I fastened on the bindings and pushed off – and went flat on my back. Ice!

I felt a mixture of meanness and wickedness in a satisfying sort of way as I sped across Coire Chroisg to where the others were still plodding up. After a brief exchange I swung away across the corrie again – back and forwards – long runs and sweeping turns, all with exaggerated aplomb. Some turns were not exactly smooth but I managed not to fall and spoil it all. With the others on the top ridge I swung along to Creag Dubh again. Here the slope was steep and broken by crags and frozen waterfalls and burns. Its descent was highly exciting. At the foot, long slopes of soft snow gave endless swinging routes. The air rushed past with a roaring and popping in the ears. Rather frightening. Very wonderful. Then into the banked hollow of the burn: a mild Cresta run to twist and turn down for a mile. When it became too hectic it was simple to turn up the bank and lose momentum.

About the 1,500 ft contour I skirted round under Creagan

nan Gabhar and the aim was changed to losing as little height as possible while running down Glenample. Apart from the crossing of the farm burns it was a continuous glide of one-and-a-half miles. In front lay Loch Earn and the creamy hills of Glen Ogle, behind the unwavering track from the crags and the white ridges lifting against an Alpine-blue sky: utter silence but for the soft swish of the skis; utter content; singing solitude; tired muscles relaxing. Yes, every agony was worthwhile. I laughed and sang and then turned for a last *schuss* down into the trees and over the burn for the path again. Lingering pauses were made beside snow-ringed pools. Only a solitary hare moved in the warm afternoon hush. I walked back to the bus in a dream. Tomorrow the agony!

Three hours later the others came back. Till then I sat in the hotel enjoying cup after cup of hot, sweet tea. The armchair was soft and relaxing. The view was across to the hills we had been on. Slowly they turned pink and the shadows rose with dusk over their slopes. The first star shone out above a lemon-washed crest. As Ben Johnson noted, '... in short measure life may perfect be.'

EASTER: MULL AFLAME

> Of course there are dragons in the mountains.
> That is their attraction and their fear.

OSLR 48, 49

'Where do you want off?' the driver asked as we sped down Glen More in the Iona Ferry bus from Craignure. 'At the bridge, please' – but I should have said 'right now,' for framed in the glen was the bold, angular bulk of Ben

More of Mull, sovereign Munro in all the isles – other than extravagant Skye. The hill lay sharp as if chiselled, a blaze of blue beyond; a picture of perfection.

We were dropped off at the Teanga Brideag bridge, after a wee chat, for on Mull bus drivers are friendly. He said the weather might last, even if Mull had 'used up half the annual good days this one week.' The bus had picked us up in eastern Glen More where we had left my campervan for our exit from the hills once Mull had given Colin his first Munro and I had climbed my penultimate Corbett. There had been frost on the van's windscreen when we left Fishnish at 07.30. We left a note with the Craignure police in case someone began to worry about the van, parked for several days.

As the bus sped off for Loch Sgridain and the Ross of Mull to the Iona ferry, we were panting up the Brideag Burn, thankful to be going over only the first bosses of hill to pitch our camp near where I had first camped on the island a score of years before. That, too, had been during an Easter heatwave, with a school group, while now the sun smote down on a sturdy, fit young nephew, enthusiastic for any ploy on land or sea. The heat was tempered by mercy, however, as, despite the sun, a bitter wind blew. For walking this was an unusual perfection: no rain, no midges, no sweat. Storm, the dog, may have wished for a shorter coat; he was a Shetland Collie.

The slopes were deep-littered in tawny dry grass which we collected in armfuls to lay under our tent groundsheets. Boulders from the burn provided stools. We brewed, and with the tea we ate the last of a Christmas cake. Migrant wheatears flew past the site. A first wood anemone was in flower in a rocky nook above a deep pool of startling clarity.

I recounted to Colin how, on that first visit, everyone dived and splashed in the water and then wandered slowly upstream from tempting pool to delectable waterfall to better pool. My snooze by the tents had been broken an hour or two later by shouts and yells as down the hillside came what looked like a gang of naked savages. The slopes were just sprouting new growth after extensive burning and proved very sharp to bare feet, hence the war dances. They were also sending up clouds of black soot – a good excuse for another swim.

On that visit we also had an unforgettable close encounter of a midgy kind. The sweltering day had brought them to the boil and, as we were dependent on public transport and were camping, flight was impossible. We camped on a breezy knoll above the burn, saved largely by anabatic and katabatic winds. The cleft with the burn, entirely windless, held a seething stew of midges. One could reach an arm into the buzz and in seconds it would be covered in a black tactile skin of insects. Draw the arm out again and they fell off like blowing coal dust. It was a shivery fascination to do this, for at the back of one's mind was the vision of doom if the kindly breezes should go. On that visit, however, the breezes sent for reinforcements, and a gale drove us to Tobermory youth hostel, a cosy eighteenth-century building on the seafront. At the storm's climax we went to Calgary Bay to see immense rollers smashing ashore, spray flying inland for hundreds of yards, and the waterfalls standing on end. Today's ascent with Colin would be quite different. We set off at 11.00 – the last time I checked my watch. When there's plenty time, forget time.

Ben More is a big tent-shaped block from many angles, with the lower cone of A'Chioch lying to the east along a narrow ridge. The hill often appears to be smoking like a volcano (which it once was) or looks black and forbidding, for the rock is mainly basalt, rising from great skirts of scree.

Not to be underestimated: Loch na Keal or Loch Scridain, the usual starting points, are sea lochs, so you climb all of Ben More's 3,169 ft (966 m). The hard work is rewarded by hauling out to as fine a hill view as you'll enjoy in Britain, ranging from Ireland in the south to the Torridons in the north, and with the Outer Hebrides down the western horizon. Cuillin, Rum, Ardgour, Nevis, Etive, Cruachan, Arran, Jura, all these and other mainland or island hills will be displayed on the days of gifted glory.

Ben More is the top favourite of all Munros that are kept for 'the last' by those who have been ticking off the list. The next favourite is the Inaccessible Pinnacle – perhaps from being 'the hardest Munro' – but Ben More is kept for the last for geographical reasons and, I'm sure, a touch of the romantic. Being on an island does mean a certain amount of extra organisation is required to reach Mull, so Ben More is often only given consideration well on in a walker's Munroing, at which stage the thought is planted 'This would be a splendid Munro to finish on'. Oddly, it was my first Munro when I set off to do all the Munros in a single expedition. That was a heatwave April as well, with the girls in bikinis – and regretting it by the time we got back to our camp by Loch Scridain. They were all too literally 'in the pink' by then.

I have just checked my record for weather in case I'm also conveying the idea that the weather in Mull is always sunny. I find notes of ascents with 'traverse in thick mist,' 'severe gales,' 'thick, wet clag,' so the weather is fairly average. But when it is good, it is very, very good.

Colin and I cut the corner a bit before the head of the valley as we wanted to follow up a side-stream descending from the pap of A'Chioch – water would be welcome up high with such thirsty walking. Hills began rising all around. Mull is surprisingly hilly and feels big enough that you can forget you are on an island.

I'm sure the majority of the people who climb Ben More simply walk up the NW slope from Dhiseig (Dhisig), a pity for the finest approach is undoubtedly along the eastern ridge from A'Chioch. I'd recommend our line from Glen More, or by Glen Clachaig from Loch Ba to the north-east. A'Chioch is a cone of 'chaotic rubbish' to quote one of my lads, but any contouring traverse to avoid the bump gives much harder work. Colin romped up its unstable slopes. Once on the connecting ridge to Ben More the going becomes 'interesting'. We followed a white hare to begin with, Storm tracking it along the edge of nothing in a way we found rather nerve-wracking, on a sort of Carn Mor Dearg Arête type of ridge. Ben More's steep north face was still deeply snow covered, scarred with fallen cornices, and the rocks crowning it were grey-bearded with overnight frost. By this approach Ben More feels like a real mountain.

Approaching the top, we could hear voices above us and Storm shot off to bark insults at the summit trespassers. For a 'remoter' Munro, Ben More was remarkably busy. A couple from Derbyshire and a lad from Edinburgh exchanged greetings and exclamations of delight. Storm rolled on the snow. Never a demonstrative lad, Colin just grinned, and dug out an Easter egg saved for the occasion of topping his first Munro. I wonder whether he could have any idea that he would later come to live and work out here in the West. In 2004, as part of the *Boots Across Scotland* event (described in a later section), he climbed Ben More again as his chosen hill. We stayed on the sunny summit for half an hour. By then, another man and dog and a cheery Croydon school party had arrived. A swirl of seagulls was speculating about our being a food source.

Those who have kept Ben More for their last Munro will be delighted at the choice if they enjoy such a fine day as we did; but they may not know of a bad-weather hazard shared with the Skye Munros: the summit rocks are magnetic and the compass erratic. This is quite amusing (or quite alarming) for we are so brainwashed into believing 'the compass never lies' that we are shocked when it does. A careful bearing off the summit of Ben More will take you down on a quite unscheduled line! The effect is bad only on the summit. Knowing this in advance, one just takes care: there are well-defined ridges and corrie edges which help with navigation. A trick I learnt for Skye conditions was to make tiny two-pebble cairns up the last clouded climb – so the way off was well-indicated, while the markers were easily enough kicked over in passing during the descent.

We scampered off, down to the A'Chioch col again, then turned down into Coir' Odhar and across to follow ridge rather than valley back to the tents. We managed to stalk five hinds to about fifty yards, and shortly afterwards Storm set up two hares which careered off to panic another group of hinds. For a while the whole hillside seemed to be moving.

We came upon some big whalebacks of rough granite, but they were too easy-angled to be of scrambling interest. The basalt is useless, too, and the red granite outcrops of Fionnphort are too small, so Mull is not much of a rock-climber's island. We arrived back at the tents ready for a brew and all too soon the shadows crept down. I kept moving up the hillside with my book to stay in the sun, while Colin started cooking, another fun part of the outdoor world he was into. The day grew bitterly cold, and after supper we soon burrowed into our sleeping bags, enjoying 'the rush of the burn and hill bliss' as my log noted.

Mull offers excellent trekking routes and the next day we

had a good sample. We were heading for a bothy, so as we'd be motoring this way at the end of our sortie, we stashed the tents and other odds and ends beside the next burn up Glen More, hiding them with the plentiful dry grass. This Allt Ghillecaluim came down in many little falls and the old path up its banks was visible only occasionally as we sweated up Coir' a'Mhaim (many old paths in Mull are no longer maintained). There was a long levelling-out with the burn slowly shrinking till it vanished and we emerged on to the fine col of Mam Breapadail (c.1,250 ft, 380 m) with its whisper of wind and sky-scraper cumulus above.

This was no gentle watershed crossing: the ground fell away before us into Coire Mor with Devil's Beef Tub steepness and Glen Cannel seemed miles below, yet we soon zigzagged down to brew where several streams joined, each draining an equally fine corrie, an impressive heart to the mountains of Mull at the head of the flat-floored Glen Cannel. A purply haze crept over the ridges and only when we smelled it did we recognise it as moor-burning. The shepherds were busy using the dry spell.

A mile down the glen was a ruined farm, Gortenbuie, while across the valley lay long-abandoned burial grounds – the 'dead centre of Mull' Colin reckoned. There were no graves visible. People no longer live in these remote spots; the shepherds come in by Land Rover and return to comfy homes on the coast at night. The gain is sometimes ours as we acquire a bothy here and there. We headed off for one now, crossing the burn by the skeletal beams of a 1910 bridge.

On the way we passed a 'bird-cone' which had been much used by a buzzard (we'd put one up), for it was well whitewashed and surrounded by animal skulls, vertebrae, fluff and feathers. These cones seem to be a phenomenon peculiar to the islands. Usually they are coastal, but here they were central and in profusion. A slight knoll makes a perch, the birds' droppings encourage growth, dust is caught by the growth and the process builds up a solid green cone. On Jura I have seen them five feet high.

We cut up and round, eastwards and then northwards, with birch wood [now, alas, a conifer plantation – Glen Forsa, too is now constipated with conifers from end to end] leading to a pass at just over 500 ft (151 m) and then down to neat Tomsleibhe bothy, where a squabble of crows rather grudgingly welcomed us. Glen Forsa was busy with men and dogs driving sheep out of danger, so after a lunchtime brew Colin, Storm and I headed south up Glen Lean behind the bothy for Beinn Talaidh (Talla). Some dead sheep lay in the burn: 'Never mind, Colin; just extra protein'. We more or less kept to the stream itself – 'burning up' as I called it – till near the top the burn ran in a small gorge which might offer us some scrambling. Back, nearly at valley level, we had found some aluminium rods which I hoped might be parts of a meteorological balloon, but after finding some other bits and pieces we realised there had been a plane crash somewhere nearby. The pieces of wreckage became steadily more numerous as we boulder-hopped up the burn, with bits of complicated machinery appearing as well as mangled shards of the aircraft's skin. A big strut lay on the bank. Then ahead we saw a pile of grey material, as if a lorry had tipped a load of rubbish into the gorge. The crash site was above, high on the hill, so the wreckage must have been pushed down into the gorge. There must have been mice living in the wreckage, for Storm was soon all but invisible – just his tail waving from a jagged hole. There was a propeller showing and one big and one small wheel. Colin thought we were seeing two engines, but it was all so broken up it was difficult to recognise anything. He found one 'sliding part' of stainless steel that glittered with surprising fresh-ness, but much of the wreckage was thoroughly embedded in the rocky banks. What we saw was sickening, not just an impersonal TV report; this was real.

We climbed on in silence, but the gully walls had converged to a narrow gut down which shot the small but wetting stream. The escape was an ungardened Jericho Wall, and we scrambled up a loose-enough exit line, which certainly took our minds off the crashed aircraft. Storm rushed off and was soon tail flag-waving in another hole. It looked like a rabbit burrow, but this was 1,700 ft up and all we saw were hares in various stages of transition from winter to summer colouring. There are either high-level rabbits on Mull, or hares that burrow.

The east flank of Talaidh is steep with plenty of rock poking through so any distraction was welcome as we zigzagged on. Eventually we came up against the summit screes, but just as we were about to tackle them I noted a faint track going off at a slant to the right. Whether it was made by man, sheep or deer we did not debate. We used it thankfully, crossed a rim of snow, and were soon scurrying, Colin ahead, along the easy-angled final shaly stretch to the cylindrical concrete trig pillar of Beinn Talaidh. I'd ticked my Corbett [now, alas, reclassified as a Graham, only just failing to make 2,500 feet].

The glory had departed: steely greys and denim blues filled in the picture, like a poster done by a child with a limited range of felt-tip pens. As a viewpoint, Talaidh matched Ben More ('stunning' in the SMC guide). This is very often true of many Corbetts and lesser summits. They may not be so high, but often being more isolated, they can provide grandstand views. Indeed, Beinn Talaidh is possibly Gaelic for *hill of the view*.

Dun da Ghaoithe, Mull's undisputed Corbett at 2,513 ft (766 m), stands across Glen Forsa in the eastern block of hills. This hill, *fort of two winds*, can be climbed in a pleasant circuit from Craignure or by taking the Iona bus round to Glen More and returning over the Corbett. I pointed out several other challenging hills south of the Glen More road, such as Ben Buie (one of my favourites), while perhaps as rewarding as any ascent, the coastal paths give a rich variety of walks. In some ways one wants a canoe or a boat for Mull as well. One of my friends actually kept Ben More as his last Munro simply so he could sail to the island for the celebratory completing.

For this Easter visit we had hired a caravan near Fishnish and Colin's gran, my mother, was ensconced there during our sortie in the hills. (Travelling to and from Mull she had slept in the campervan while we two slept in tents.) After our return to Fishnish we all went to explore Duart Castle, walk the Carsaig coast, voyage out on the *Iolaire* from Fhionnphort to Staffa for Fingal's Cave, and visit Mull's Little Theatre for a reading of poems and prose plus a Chekhov skit; activities enjoyed alike by Colin, a busy 12-year-old, and mother, a lively 79.

For two or three years a wagtail chose to nest on the Fishnish-Lochaline ferry and successfully raised broods – and became quite a tourist attraction. Now Mull is busier than ever with the lure of nesting sea eagles which can be seen from viewing hides but may be encountered anywhere. An adult eagle on one occasion took off from the road verge and passed only feet from my van's windscreen. They are impressively big. I braked hard!

Our chat on top of Talaidh was cut short by an inconsiderate flurry of snow. We scuttled off down the long easy north ridge, huge slopes to the west; westwards the whole of Glen Cannel seemed to be in flames with arcs of fire zipping up the hills and rolling great clouds of smoke into the air. Looked at from lower down, it seemed like the setting for some epic war film. Red deer pranced around in obvious distrust of this strange, fiery world. Thankfully our transverse glen had not been set alight.

Tomsleibhe bothy was once a small farmstead with signs of other ruined buildings around it. First mentioned in a 1494 charter, it survived the Clearances of Glen Forsa to become the home of a shepherd. A tight little stone cottage with a slate roof, there are three rooms inside, the walls are whitewashed, there's an original fireplace (we lit a fire just to dry off sweaty garments), essential large table etc. Lying off popular routes, it seems to keep vandal-free. And full marks to the MBA enthusiasts who look after the bothy (it was re-roofed in 2016). Supper I recorded: a tin of chicken supreme, then a bolognese, apple flakes, and soup (in that order) and plenty more to drink. All that time we were aware of those fires in front and behind, flickering and dying and flaring up again. We had one of those gloamings 'when birds are shapes on coloured sky/and beat their flights without a cry'. Even after dark the gold eyes of fire glanced along the slopes of Glen Forsa. We had stars after dark, a naming of stars, a touch of infinity. The Andromeda galaxy, our nearest, could just be seen by eye, yet the light we were seeing began its journey to us two and a half million years ago.

Frequent notes in the bothy book mentioned the crashed aircraft. (Most such sites are cleared.) One writer said he had turned down a lift on that very flight while stationed in Iceland. The crash date was 1st February 1945, the plane a Dakota on a Canada-Prestwick flight. When we went into the church hall in Salen two days later, a framed citation told us a few more details. Surprisingly, while three crew died, there had been five survivors; one managed to make his way off the hill in deep snow. Local rescuers set out in 'the worst conditions in living memory'. Dr Flora MacDonald was given an MBE, there were three BEMs awarded and various other commendations for the rescuers. A piece of the Dakota's cockpit hangs in the Tobermory museum. (A twisted propeller from the plane has now been set up in Glen Forsa as a monument to the tragedy.)

The bothy book also had many entries complaining about heat. 'The guide says Mull is one of the wettest of islands. Rubbish!' I wonder if that writer stayed on the island long enough to realise the guide's veracity. I can only think most of the visitors came to Mull *because* the weather was good – at the time. Sadly, most entries also pointed out the brief nature of visits: the minimum required to grab Ben More – minimalist Munro-bagging. There had been couples there the previous two nights. Colin stuffed bags full of soft grass as padding on the bed-shelf.

When I looked out of the skylight in the morning, it was to discover that the meteorological fire brigade had arrived in the night and dampened down everything. We rose at our usual '06.30 up, 07.30 off' to exit while the rain held off. Only as we were passing southwards under the eastern slopes of Beinn Bheag, Talaidh's lesser neighbour, did we discover that both sides of Glen Forsa had been fired. Our boots were soon black and messy while the dog's under-parts were many times worse. At one stage he slipped and covered his face in clinging black soot.

We washed the dog once we ran out of the burnt area and made the campervan we'd left in Glen More just before the rain came on. No matter how many days of good weather you may have on Mull, it is still one of the wettest islands in the west. One day Colin will realise how lucky he was. (He knows. He and his wife now live in Appin, with Mull in their view.)

A buzzard flew up from a wayside telegraph pole. The island seems to have scores of the birds, and Colin wondered where they had perched before man erected these uprights. We drove up over the Glen More pass through boiling cloud. The rain eased. Then we saw where the early smoke of yesterday had come from. All the eastern flanks of Ben More were black. I groaned. Somewhere up there lay our cache of tents and other odds and ends. As we approached we could see some of the items peering through the black fur of burnt grass. The Ultimate Tramp tent was melted into a lump of green goo and the gas cartridges had no doubt added their contribution to the conflagration but, when ready to weep, under it all, unharmed, I found my cherished old Challis tent. I would have sacrificed a dozen others for it – my friend of the months of the Munros-in-one trip, of part of the Groat's End Walk, of visits to Atlas and Arctic and to the Nanda Devi Sanctuary!

I'd been rather wondering why whole hillsides were being burned, a practice I'd not seen elsewhere. Selective burning of heather is common enough but here whole hill-sides of grass were ablaze. Moorburn is, shall we say, a hot topic, its value open to question and its practice too often less careful than might be desired. Mull obviously has its own tradition – perhaps a practice unlikely to rage out of control, given the usual weather on the island.

As we were loading the van the Iona Ferry bus drew up. The driver asked if we had had a good trip. 'Great, just great,' we replied. He looked at the wall of rain sweeping up Loch Scridain. 'You were lucky'. But that new storm was nothing to some I've met on Mull. I described my worst night ever in a campervan. Parked on the Ross of Mull, I had to hold my supper pan on the wobbling cooker (gimbals are not part of a camping car's standard equipment) and I hardly slept as I feared the van was going to be blown over the cliff where I was perched. I was frightened enough to climb out of bed to drive on to find a less exposed spot, one not far from a place called Pottie – which I thought appropriate. If you must have it bad there is a certain satisfaction in having it memorably so.

But my memories of Mull are many and varied: finding a way on to Erraid island, the sunset bonfire by Loch Scridain at the start of my walk over all the Munros, Glen More echoing to the curdling cries of curlews, the *Captain Scott*'s anchor dragging in Tobermory Bay in the middle of the night, a ceilidh in the pub at Salen after we'd walked across the island, otter sightings at Dhiseig… To me, these are all part of the joys of being in the mountains, or on an island. On Mull you have the best of many worlds – and for this Easter visit, we added on a variant new memory: Mull aflame.

ACROSS SUTHERLAND AND CAITHNESS

> Once we had accepted the conditions of travel, the time and distance involved, we had found in the simplicity of our daily routine a feeling of peace and of well-being such as perhaps no other form of travel can give.
>
> Eric Shipton: *Mountains of Tartary*

OSLR 15, 16, 17

Kipling's 'go fever' is most readily cured by going and the going is usually most rewarded by longer ventures. One needs time to physically and spiritually tune in again. Treks then fill the blanks most suitably, taking days into weeks and weeks into rewards. One picks up nature's rhythm again.

June 22: Suileag; North of Suilven

Yesterday the radio moaned about Britain's wettest solstice in a quarter of a century but there was no rain in Sutherland. It had been a rather frantic day: climbing Ben Hope early (before the gale) and laying food caches for the coast-to-coast trek as we zig-zagged up and down endless single track roads (with or without passing places) before ending at Inverkirkaig to meet up for a sociable night with Stan Bradshaw. Stan and I had last been together climbing Toubkal, but here it was Suilven that filled our talk and caught our eyes as we leant on the wind for a pre-nightcap dander out to the point looking over the Minch to the black-browed Hebrides. Summer pipers (nothing 'common' about these heralds of the spring) flitted about and buzzed the dog who was much more interested in rabbits than baby birds.

The gale was still galloping over the bony wilderness this morning and I rather trembled to be setting off to walk across the 'wildest and best' of Scotland. Most big winds end in big wets. Beyond Suilven is a country of perpetual savageness – without needing any weather tantrums added. However, I look forward to a journey long enough to reckon in days rather than miles. I parked the car behind the Lochinver police station as arranged, shouldered the pack and we were off. Five minutes later we (dog and I) left map-red road and wended up a gorge, hemmed in by trees and crags, a secret wood which would probably be our last. Trees, if met at all, would be ranked conifers, puddle-footing in the bogs of Sutherland and Caithness out of which rose the astonishing shapes of our northern peaks: Suilven, Canisp, Assynt, Leoid, Hee, Klibreck, the Griams, Morven, 'lonely, brooding mountains that seemed to be awaiting the resumption of creation' (Prebble).

Linking that lot on foot has been a long dream. Now (in 1985) it is happening. As I write in this welcomed bothy I look out at Suilven, most stunning of them all. It suddenly stood before us as we topped a wee pass from the River Inver into this bigger, rougher, brawling world of rock, water and wind. It is an exaggerated hulk of hill – like some bulging bodybuilder – but its flexed biceps leave no doubt as to the punch it could pack. We prefer to look rather than touch today. A gale in the glen will mean a hurricane up there. My last visit outside Suileag found golden light flooding the glen below us, the slope with bobbing scuts of cotton grass and the knolls casting long shadows, the sun spotlighting a dozen deer splashing across the narrows of a lochan. A cuckoo is clocking its monotonous call across the strath while, eastwards, comes the solitary sorrow-chasing-sorrow sound of a curlew calling.

June 23: Green Garden Country

There was no harm in dreaming, as long as we won through to Inchnadamph today where the first food cache waited for us. The hardness of a planned journey like this is the necessity for covering the miles rather than climbing any feet upwards. It was not a good night – the first sleeping hard seldom is – but I was up and down like a yo-yo: Storm pounced on a mouse at 4 a.m., my bladder called me out at 5 a.m., the alarm went off at 6 a.m. (I listened to the wind and the rain and snuggled back in the sleeping bag) and at 7 a.m. the water carrier decided to fall over and pour out half a gallon. I got up in self-defence!

We eventually set off at 9.30 a.m. when the rain had stopped. A good path took us along under the moorland pedestal of Suilven. The peak was hidden in a turmoil of cloud. It would have to wait. Loch na Gainimh was not quite a mile long but the waves were crashing ashore and white horses rode its grey waste. Rocky bumps, scattered lochans – this is wilderness indeed, yet a good made-path allowed us to tramp east at a great rate. A narrow gut of gorge, the Ghlinne Dorcha, *the Dark Glen*, led through to Lochan Fada, *the Fair Loch*, and from half way along it we began to contour upwards steadily to gain the lower levels of Canisp which we had felt rather than seen. A cheery waterfall spilling over a crag above a wind-free hollow called for an early lunch brew.

As soon as we crept up to the lip of the fall we entered a new, wide-horizoned world. Storm was led off by a grouse doing a broken wing act. Several deer tiptoed across the skyline and a fleeting shadow suddenly resolved into a swooping golden eagle – just 100 yards away. When I turned to follow its flight I saw Suilven was jagging out from the clouds. Cameras, quick! By the time we'd wended on through a quartz wilderness onto a ridge, Canisp couldn't be denied. The rucksack was left and we sped up, pushed by the wind. The final cone never did clear but Suilven was there, grey on greys, shot silver now and then by touches of sun. We were quite sorry to swing round and down the quartz miles to the River Lonan that drains down to Inchnadamph and Loch Assynt. We twice saw cuckoos flying up the glen. They may be coming scarce in the south of England but in the west of Scotland they are plentiful – more cursed than loved.

Just two days ago I'd left a food dump by the Allt nan Uamh near the Fish Hatchery and while still half-a-mile off I could hear a strident bell ringing from the hatchery. It went on and on: an alarm of some kind shrilling to a Sabbath-silent world. I cursed it for all the nearby wind-free camping places were within sound of it. The din could go on all night! So I had to go upstream and camp in the tight valley – a bit of a wind tunnel. Tins and fresh vegetables ensured a good meal. Later we wandered up to see the resurgence of the river. The natural line is suddenly dry; all the water pours out of the side wall of the glen, very weird, but the whole area is riddled with burns which vanish and appear in peculiar fashion. The 1:50,000 map only hints at some. It is the best of Scotland for the modern caveman. The evening cheered up for the sun went down over Canisp, shining in the tent door and countering the chill wind off the big Assynt hills of tomorrow. When I wrote the first paragraph this morning it was in a spirit of gloom. Now I feel much better. The first 'empty quarter' has been passed, even a hill climbed – and the sun shines for the last drink of the night.

June 24: The Ascent to Assynt

Today in many ways was the crux of the crossing and having it now behind is both a relief to the soul and a glad resting of the soles. Ben More Assynt, 3274ft/998m, is the highest summit of the crossing and the descent off it led, not to the security of a road but into one of the bleakest of wastelands imaginable. The tent stands 300 metres up on a green shelf of grass by a burn whose waters actually flow to the East coast yet we are closer to the western sea here than we were two nights ago under Suilven, for two big fiords, bridged spectacularly now at Kylesku, cut deep into the grey hills: Loch Glencoul and Loch Glendhu. Everything drains into them, except for this vast hollow, fifteen miles round, which drains south to forgotten Glen Cassley and eventually into the east coast Kyle of Sutherland. I've heard this country described as 'land God forgot to finish'. I'm particularly glad to be over the main drain for a dozen years ago I came off Ben More Assynt in a monsoon deluge that had the rivers rising into dramatic spate. I had to ford the Cassley waist deep – half an hour later it would have been impassable. At one stage I thought that desperate day was going to be repeated.

The brilliance of sun, and no wind, woke me at 5 a.m. but I snoozed till 6 a.m. and set off at 7 a.m.. What a difference that last hour would have made. Early hours should always be grabbed if not for necessity, then for the 'fierce joy of living,' and the balm of coolness and an earlier arrival. And early in the day we see most wildlife. The first hour in the sun was a sweat-bath across heather moors pockmarked with sink-hole craters. I changed into shorts while Storm investigated a badger sett but we eventually hit the river we wanted. It was a good sized burn, but all at once it swung up against a crag and vanished gurgling into the ground. Perhaps it is the one which pops out two miles away to pass last night's campsite?

We had a brew at the rucksack and in just the twenty minutes of relaxing the sky changed from ninety per cent blue to one hundred per cent cloudy while a wall of wet was advancing up Loch Assynt. 'Too bright too soon will rain by noon.' The rain came as a saturating smir, still without wind, so I just draped my waterproof over my pack. We wended up to the Bealach Breabag, under Conival, one of the finest passes in Scotland, both as a through-route and for its structure and scenery and its flowers: cornel, thrift, mantles, globeflower, roseroot, starry saxifrage, violets, thyme, even daisies and dandelions were about our feet as we edged under cliffs for the mossy gap and the red screes beyond.

The SE Ridge of Conival sweeps up in craggy steps but I wanted something new so carried on round into Garbh Choire, *the rough corrie*. A name like that usually means it and here the headwall is a shambles of scree while the scoured bottom just fails to have a glacier-scooped lochan. We sheltered under a boulder for lunch, then zig-zagged up steep grass east of the screes to gain the lofty ridge connecting Conival and its bigger brother Ben More of Assynt. The pair were visited in turn. Without the drag of the rucksack I seemed to float over the mist-slippery quartz. Storm exploded a grenade of ptarmigan chicks.

We bailed off down the other side of the linking ridge and, coming out of the mist, set one lot of deer after another high-stepping along the slopes. It was three miles down to the river but another was added because of the constant bog and water deviations. There was a ration of ups in the downhill too. A *sair pech*, and a *slaistery dander* (Scots vocabulary has words like that for every gloom.) A similar crossing would be easier in winter with everything frozen underfoot. The centre of that vast hollow is covered by two lochs: Gorm Loch More and Fionn Loch Mor. They were neither *gorm* nor *fionn*, just *liath*, and connected by a river a third of a mile long which might or might not be fordable but almost at once I found a spot where it was possible to boulder-hop across. That deserved tea as a relief: sweet, milky Earl Grey.

The lochs drain down Glen Cassley and, unsurprisingly, this area is noted for having the lowest-selling map of the OS Explorer series (Sheet 440). My Landranger 15 shows a 20 grid-square area of nothing but lochs, lochans, river and bog.

All the rimming hills were covered in cloud and the drizzle had saturated the grass. We began the long haul up the Fionn Allt towards our escape pass of the morrow and found our secret sward a mile up. I write up my log with a dipper bobbing on the rocks of the burn and I can hear a diver flying overhead. Black moorland fades away into grey mist. The rough ridges of fatigue will ensure sound sleep.

June 25: By Beinn Leoid and Ben Hee

A mix of soft moss and grey stone led us up to Beinn Leoid. Inside the wall round the trig point was a flourish of delicate wood sorrel. Outside were whole mats and rugs of thrift, including one white one. As we charged down out of the mist we set some deer scampering. All day, every day, there were deer, too many to record, far too many for the good of the land. We had tea by Loch Dubh after the path contoured down off the pass. Beinn Leoid refused to clear. The hill still would not clear as we traversed along to break over a ridge to pick up a stalkers' path down to the deep gash of the next motorable glen, the A838. The houses of Kinloch stood solitary with Loch More and Arkle beyond. The tiny, single-tracked road seemed an apology for mechanical intrusion. What a fastness this area must have been in the bad old days, though perhaps then there would be houses and shielings where now I walked in a deserted world.

A string through Storm's collar and we ambled up the A838 to Loch Merkland. We have now walked right across and off Sheet 15. Sheet 16 we unearthed from roadside boulders. Mice had been at the cache in just the few days it had been there and a carton of juice had drained away. As it was too early to camp (2 p.m.) I ate a tin of raspberries, a tin of custard and some other weighty goodies before shouldering a heavy pack again. After a couple of miles of road I swung off up an estate track through the Bealach nam Meirleach, *The Robbers Pass*, and then round the skirts of Ben Hee for an hour to camp at Loch Coire na Saidhe Duib below its NE cliffs. A peat bank acted as a wind break for the loch was lively. Ben Hee is a huge pile of bulging tops. If the weather allows we can sclim it the morn's morn.

The wind dropped after supper and now I write with an anti-midge coil on 'just in case'. Earlier the air sizzled with flights of insects, midge-sized, but harmless. A fish plops in the loch occasionally and the water is edged with spearwort in flower. The view is out to Klibreck and the Griams – three days of walking to the next horizon. Grey and raw as November, the rain only persists now when we are snug in bed. Today really has given a surge eastwards, the jumble of peaks is behind, the more spacious landscape ahead. Apart from a couple of cars passing on the A838 I have not seen anyone since Lochinver. You could not walk four days so alone in many countries. When lecturing about solitary expeditions the most frequent questions I am asked are, 'Do you not feel lonely?' and 'Do you not get bored?' which, to me, shows what a thrall modern life has become – and how much more so today with so many trapped by their little unreality screens.

31

June 26: Ben Hee and Ben Klibreck

A northern farmer was once asked what the climate was like 'up there'. The reply was a shake of the head. 'I don't know much about climate now but it's certain we get plenty of weather.' Today gave a pretty good sample of weather. I doubt if it stayed the same for more than an hour or two at a time.

The day began sunny and bright so after half a breakfast and the first midge bite we romped off, unladen, for Ben Hee. A path led from the loch's outflow up to a bold buttress but we cut up its flank under a line of cliffs to have a look at the climbing potential. Ben Hee had twin summits and the lower had to be traversed to reach the higher. The cloud rolled in as we rounded the impressive ridge to the top. It seemed to be a personal spite for I had hardly finished the second half of my breakfast when it cleared again. It was steam-drying rather than turning wet however, and Klibreck churned out cloud like a volcano. A four-mile path along the flank of the ridge, Druim nam Bad, led to the wee road from Altnaharra to Ben Hope. 'Bad' was probably the right word; the symbol for bog was spread over fifteen grid squares! Conditions were grilling-hot but windless and grey.

Ben Hope and Ben Loyal had come into view yesterday afternoon. First one, then the other dominated the view today as we gained miles eastwards. Klibreck is a huge sprawl with a certain abstract symmetry. The four miles of road saw it clearing at last to fill the view ahead. I had hidden a parcel near Altnaharra Hotel so I sat on a knoll to organise again. I posted home a packet of maps, finished films, and a colourful feather I'd found (probably from the breast of a cock pheasant). Adding two days' food would make my rucksack heavier but I was fitter than at the start. I phoned home to give a progress report – the only one family would receive. I noticed a bit of graffiti on a shed wall: 'I like it here. Please safe (*sic*) the endangered species – us.' Setting off I actually passed someone with a dog. He said, 'Aye, how goes it?' and I replied, 'Fine'. Too hot to chat. It was very hot and we crossed the moors towards the wall of Klibreck in a lather of sweat. Sixty deer were traversing high on the hill.

Originally I had planned to stay overnight at Altnaharra. As the only 'place' of the journey it even had the temptation of a hotel but it was too early in the afternoon so we wended on. When I found we were on the lower slopes of Klibreck, well, we climbed it, because it was there, between us and the east coast, a menace of a Munro, a black cloud-gatherer that might be foul on the morrow. We had the summit clear, just; it clouded over five minutes after we left the top. Today's weather was in such a hurry it kept tripping over itself.

I was determined to have a midge-free camp so high on Klibreck seemed a safe place. On the last zig (or zag) of path there was a fortuitous gush of water so I filled my carrier. This yellow object was useful for locating my belongings in the mist, for I'd left my kit over a mile from the top. A wee bump remained before we dropped to the col before The Whip, the last bump of the Klibreck collection. The tent was just up in time. A shower came scudding over from Ben Armine. It soon passed then the wind changed to blow in the tent door. You can't win! Just have the patience of trees. We are pitched high above Loch Naver and beyond the moors behind it rises the carbuncled mass of Ben Loyal;

a view of sweeping grandeur. If my every joint aches it is worth it. In the end the sun put gold leaf on the western horizon, one of those magic 'blinks' to end the day.

June 27: Step We Wetly on We Go

I was ready for off at 7.30 a.m. when the heavens opened. 'Soon go off,' I told the dog and we '*cooried doon*' awhile. It did not go off for over two hours by which time I felt very cold. I heated some soup and then took down the tent. We groped our way through tearing cloud down hillsides which were exploding rivers out of springs and pools. The option of staying put was not practicable as I was low in fuel for my stove. We came below cloud level and across Loch Choire could see all the burns were white-foaming torrents. This at once revised my plans; no river-crossing would be safe for many hours. Loch Choire exits as the River Mallart and I'd planned to go down its left bank on a path and ford where it turned north to Loch Naver. We would then head east outside a strangle of spruce plantation to the succession of lochs beyond which lay my cache under Ben Griam Mor. As fording was out of the question I just hoped a bridge shown would let us on to the right bank.

Our feet were saturated by the time we reached the valley. For most of the day the rain was a dreary dribble – enough to keep waterproofs on and so swelter along. The deluge on high had been fun but squelching miles of spongy bog were simply tedious and exhausting. A mere stream flowing in before the forest forced us to backtrack a quarter of a mile before we could leap across. I had a coffee to cheer me up and spiced Moroccan sardines were warming. Saturated ploughed land was as near as I could describe the next mile.

It took nearly an hour. Beyond that the same again should have led to a track but on topping a rise it was to see the landscape all under trees. Rude things were said about the Forestry Commission and the Ordnance omission, though hardly the fault of the latter. Strangely, I once had a nightmare bit of navigation searching for a Borders bothy in the dark because the map showed a forest – and there wasn't one, not then anyway. The only interesting moment was when a strange deer trotted past us. It never saw us and went by in graceful bounds. It was neither red deer nor roe. I hope it originated in the tundra rather than arid regions. Maybe it had webbed feet.

We sloshed up drains and over the corrugations and were relieved to see the track still existed. A mile on there was a deer fence across the path. No stile. Storm found it an awkward climb. Two miles on and with a car seen on the B871 ahead, I had a look at the map and, horrors, found my compass had gone. I left the rucksack and walked back to the deer fence without finding it. An hour later I was back at the rucksack feeling pretty dank in spirit. No compass might mean no Caithness flourish to end the Sunderland days. I felt tired and bad tempered. We cringed in the lee of a bridge and drank tea till the stove ran out of fuel. Four or five miles of road walking at that stage was cruel. It was like the opening sentence of John Buchan's first novel: 'Before me stretched a black heath over which the mist blew in gusts, and through whose midst the road crept like an adder'.

The weather at last hung itself out to dry. Ben Griam Mor cleared and our food and fuel lay by the roadside below it. Away beyond a fang bit into the grey – mighty Morven. A biscuit tin of perishables and a carrier bag of tinned food had been hidden in roadside rubble (Altnaharra's had been in a nettle patch!) and just two hundred yards away was some close-cropped heath on an alluvial bank: the perfect nook for a safe, dry pitch, in such a world of wet and wilderness quite enough to revive the spirits.

The view back over loch after loch to the black cloud-draped Klibreck group was like something from the Arctic. The weather felt that way too: a cold drizzle and a chill wind. The sleeping bag was relished. Supper in bed. You don't have that sort of service in a hotel. Today we walked off Sheet 16. Sheet 17, from the cache, is the last. The evening went in studying it. Just how would we tackle Morven without a compass? Tomorrow will tell. This is proving as tough a crossing as I expected. It surprises people when I tell them this sort of thing is much harder than trekking in Atlas or Andes or Himalayas – and is as rewarding for that very reason. When conditions deign to smile, when feet are dry and belly full, why, it is the best there is.

28 JUNE: MORVEN AHOY!

'Slow and easy goes far in a day,' Moleskin Joe says in *Children of the Dead End* and I applied this quite consciously today. It works! Mind you the weather helped: our first reasonable day. What a delight to dry everything before setting off. A gentle mile saw us up to a wide col under Ben Griam Mor and away over a roll of hills a real peaky peak jabbed into the sky. It could only be Morven but it looked so far away – fourteen miles as the fly crows. Would we ever climb it? Rather than mash my feet on the B871 down to the Kildonan road, dog and I headed east over the moors. The Eileag Burn had grassy verges in a sea of brown bog, the natural, easy route to follow despite many books saying we must never follow streams. Where the burn became broad and deep before golden-edged Loch Arichline Storm had an escapade. A duck went scooting off along the water followed by eight or so young ones. The dog thought this most interesting and scampered along the vertical bank watching the birds rather than where he was going. There was a bite out of the bank and Storm, not seeing the drop, in best Disney style, shot off the edge. He came up sputtering and indignant.

There was still enough water running off the hills to follow down and cross a high pedestrian suspension bridge outside Kinbrace. Between it and the road I managed to go over the top of both boots. Storm's turn to laugh. The cache nearby was rather a big one but we left a biscuit tin of goodies by the road (in a passing place) in hope that someone would find the offering. As we were about to tuck in to lunch a figure wended off the moor. He turned out to be a Halifax lad, the first person I actually chatted to properly since the Bradshaws at the start.

There was only the one range of hills between us and the sea but their initial slopes held a weird splatting of a hundred lochans and a hundred symbols for bog. No planning authority would have allowed such a disorderly landscape. We made a gentle route up to skirt them all and when Morven suddenly appeared again it was near and big: a great matronly boob shape (the Pap of Glencoe is nubile in comparison) which dominated everything around. We could see back as far as Klibreck and Ben Loyal and here and there sweeps of rain hazed the clarity of a day of towering cumulus and a ration of blue. At one stage I turned a step into a frantic leap (quite an effort with a hefty pack) otherwise I would have stood on an adder. All across I've been a bit worried about them for Storm's sake. He spends most of his time chuntering along with nose to ground and could so easily run into one. It was a testimony to a better day that this handsome sluggard was out. He made no threat when I waved and when I stamped he simply tried to curl up into a bowline. Nobody has been able to explain why some areas have adders and others don't. There is no obvious common denominator for their presence.

At the end of the great upland morass a green burn channel gave a camp site on the 350m contour, and neatly framed Morven behind Small Mount, a barren swelling in the ridge. We are as close as that, and the tent is pitched a couple of hundred yards into Caithness. Two deer came up the burn and were greatly puzzled by the tent. My supper was a mix of tinned mince, carrots and green peas (emptied into a poly bag at the cache) to which I added some spices and some couscous; it was *haute cuisine* one might claim.

29 JUNE: MORVEN THE MIGHTY

Morven the Magnificent. That sounds like a title to some awful Hollywood movie. The peak, however, deserves the title: it is an extraordinary place. Two or three miles of skirting along the intermediary bumps brought us to the col below the peak. I had some coffee and tried not to look at the peak but Morven stayed fiercely steep: a conical pile of conglomerate sandstone which gave a shock to the acid sterility of the normal vegetation. Cloudberry, alpine ladies mantle, blaeberry, azalea, fir club moss, St John's wort, even rowans were growing on a feet-deep pile of moss and heather.

Few summits make one feel so airborne, or spread the world so like a map below. I could, one way, see the Cairngorms, in the opposite, Dunnet Head and Orkney but, better yet, west, beyond Klibreck and Hee, beyond Assynt, there were the paps of Suilven. 'My beginning was in my end,' to misquote. It was cold enough to bone a skeleton with sweeping showers veiling half a dozen areas at once. We left when I could no longer stand the chill. Deer tracks skirted the huge cone of hill and then a peat-held stream took us to an estate road at a place called Wag which then ran down the Langwell Valley in easy fashion. I found several pipit nests and a baby snipe which Storm nuzzled in curiosity. Many young, grouse for instance, have no scent as a survival aid.

The sky grew black and I turned off up a stream just in time to raise the tent before the rain exploded on us. It gave a burst at full blast for half an hour and saw the day away in dreich rawness. Scaraben is my view through the rain and for once we lie on ordinary grass. A wren reels outside the tent – such quantity of sound from so small a mite. Rain brought out a platoon of big black slugs which I had to keep ejecting from trying to enter the tent. I didn't fancy one of those in my sleeping bag. The rain hardly stopped all night, whiles *pianissimo*, whiles *fortissimo*.

30 June: Berriedale the Bountiful

Today was a brief coda, filling the walk across Northern Scotland into a full, very satisfying, symphony. The third sheet of map has nearly been crossed. There was no hurry to rise after a night of wet and cold but at seven the sun shone hotly into our calm nook of hills. The wren still sang. The burn was high and inky dark. There was a blue sky patched with a braid of clouds.

The Langwell Valley grew richer with every step, the banks with old alders and the flanks bright with birch woods. I was wondering about the site of a ruined broch only to discover I was standing on top of it. We crossed one of the many footbridges, with deer grazing on both banks, and crossed back at a simple but graceful 1866 cast iron bridge, which I hope will long be treated as the treasure it is. The whole glen had been unusually tidy and, entering the real policies of the estate, it became apparent that a great deal of attention had been given to both landscape and buildings. It was particularly heartening to see a large area of newly planted oaks while the drive down to the A9 (next day) was a delight of many species – and many planted in the last forty years. The first thing I came on was a big walled garden and as it was all labelled, presumably open to the public. The door was not locked so I went in and wandered round while Storm sat by the rucksack. It was formally divided up by tall hedges but each section was different. There were even practical things like cabbages being grown! A new heath and alpine area was my favourite. A garden was a strong contrast after such barren days of walking. I was about to shoulder my rucksack when someone appeared – and we greeted each other warmly for Francis had been one of a party of us who had once wandered through Skye and the Outer Isles one autumn. He then lived in Leeds but had been delighted to move to Langwell as head gardener. I was about to knock on a door to check if he was still there. (He became a regular on our Atlas Mountains flower-hunting trips and, retired, created his own Berriedale garden, and regularly wins prizes at Scottish Rock Garden Club shows.)

That really ended the crossing, with a bit of a bang, for I was suddenly being fed and spoilt, would sleep in a bed and on the morrow was borne off to Lochinver by Francis to retrieve my car. However, before anything else, I insisted Storm and I *walked* down to the sea at Berriedale. The crossing of the A9 at the foot of those thundering braes was the most dangerous moment of the entire route! An old castle perched on a cliff noisy with kittiwakes and the sea sparkled cheerily. A last cuckoo was heard. I took a piece of beach sandstone as a souvenir; it was marked with the fossil ripple marks of some other, multi-millennia-ago, seashore. A sentence from Edward Whymper can sum up the hike: 'Toil he must who goes mountaineering; but out of toil comes strength (not merely muscular energy, more than that), an awakening of all the facilities; and from the strength comes pleasure' – or as the Good Book says, '... tribulation worketh patience, and patience, experience, and experience, hope'.

WITH *BOOTS* TO THE MAIDEN

Mountains ... an escape from an existence that is useful but purposeless to one that is useless but purposeful.
Simon Thompson: Unjustifiable Risk

OSLR 19

For those aiming to climb all the Munros there is a truism that, once over the two hundred mark, those left to 'bag' are generally in awkward places, usually somewhere beyond the Great Glen. A local friend in Fife was in that situation, so when the *Boots* event for Midsummer Day 1992 was planned, she immediately put in in her bid for A'Mhaighdean (pron Ah-vyé-jèn), one of the triumvirate of 'remotest Munros' (along with Lurg Mhor and Seana Bhraigh). The SMC *Munros* Bible uses terms like 'one of the most spectacular viewpoints in Britain ... among the most highly prized

41

Munros ... worth saving for a fine day'. The last of course becomes a gamble when any event is pinned down to a particular day. We were duly allocated A'Mhaighdean.

Over the years various groups have organised attempts to climb all the Munros on the same day, usually failing from having inadequate manpower. In May 1988 *Boots Across Scotland* had a go. About 2,000 people were involved, so many Munros even had double coverage. The event nearly succeeded. The day before was brilliant, the day after was brilliant, the vital day was diabolical, so a few summits were not attained, wisely no doubt. After all, the idea of the day was to raise sponsorship money for those who had come to grief on the hill or for those who give time and effort in our rescue teams. Our fierce freedoms and joys can be shattered in a moment (as they can, anywhere, by like bad luck) so we go very aware into the wilds. Our feet are shod with chance and mischance and even a pebble might decide our fate.

Big Davy Pearson was one who was unlucky. After a horrendous fall down the Trilleachan Slabs he was glad to be alive, but was confined to a wheelchair. He owed his life to the Glen Coe Mountain Rescue Team and Stobhill Hospital – and these were seen as worthy of support by Gordon Pearson, who had this idea of a sponsored Munro effort to raise money. That was the genesis of *Boots Across Scotland* and the 1988 attempt to have someone on top of all the Munros at the same time.

The initial target of £20,000 was left far behind as a grand £75,000 rolled in, and many worthy people and causes were aided. I recall one instance where a blind and severely disabled girl was helped up Ben Nevis. Seeing her standing with the sun and wind on her face was a magic not to be forgotten.

One spin-off from *Boots* was a series of entertaining yet important safety lectures by the guide Mick Tighe. I was lucky enough to make the evening at Glenrothes, and most enjoyable it was. This is one of the secrets of *Boots* I feel: it touches everyone. Munroing is utterly non-elitist, all about the good news of the hills. Over 3,000 people attended these lectures, learnt much and will pass on what they learnt. Many boots will stand on the Munros as a result.

Nephew Colin and I canoed down Loch Ericht on that 1988 occasion and climbed Beinn Bheoil from our base at Ben Alder bothy. Both visibility and temperature were about zero on the summit. Adding Ben Alder was more serious and I could understand some people not making their chosen summit. Having the canoes allowed us to climb the 'elusive' Corbett of Stob an Aonaich Mhoir on the east side of Loch Ericht before paddling off to Dalwhinnie. Roll on 1992, and another chance for good venturing.

At our midgy camp by Loch Maree in the North-West of Scotland, Val and I heard the weekend forecast: Scotland would be hot and sunny except for the north and west where conditions would be cloudy with the possibility of rain at times. We could not kid ourselves we were other than north-west and the clouds were the colour of charity shop pewter. Why, oh why, had we picked A'Mhaighdean? The answer of course was that for something so special we wanted a special hill. A'Mhaighdean (*the Maiden*) is a 'coy bitch' as I once heard her described, 'Not easy to pick up'. The hill stands in that wild country north of Loch Maree, chivvied by lochs and rough miles, a real 'macho, male landscape'. Even experienced hill-goers feel like fumbling adolescents faced with that bared beauty.

Midsummer Day though? That would be different. Little darkness. Blazing sun maybe. Why not canoe over

Loch Maree and slip over for a bivvy on the summit itself, with an incomparable view to top and tail the day? Val, my companion for the event, had not canoed before and her first experiments, during my absence in Morocco, were not propitious. After five minutes afloat she turned turtle. After seven minutes she did so again. After ten minutes she decided walking was preferable. So it came about that we two and her dog, Joss, willy-nilly set off to hoof it in to Lochan Fada. We would camp there and fight the bogs to the Munro for the 1-2 p.m. *Boots* deadline on the summit, return to camp, then out and home next day. Why are forecasts always right when the forecast is bad?

From Incheril, Val, Joss and I walked along the two miles of flat ground that are thought once to have been under Loch Maree's waters, the wending river on our left, and steep craggy slopes pushing down to us on the right. At the foot of Gleann Bianasdail there are faint traces of the old iron smelting works that depended on the local oakwoods, while six miles on there is the appropriately named Furnace. This path continues right along Loch Maree to Gairloch; before the road was built on the SW side of the loch this was the rugged route the postman had to walk, carrying mails from the Gairloch area and the Outer Hebrides. Following the postman's route was one of my 'bucket list' ploys that never happened – but then, the bucket was always full and running over, as it should always be. But this whole area is full of walking routes 'without compare' in Tom Weir's view; made paths, cunningly constructed, which have lasted for generations, finding their way in to the battlements of A'Mhaighdean. That block of land, from Beinn Lair over to A'Mhaighdean and Ruadh Stac Mor, is beyond comparison, a compression of cliff-girt steeps and deep-set lochs. Nobody lives between Kinlochewe and the

A832 Dundonnell road; there are no hydro schemes nor hideous big tracks scarring the landscape. Thank goodness there was a good sturdy bridge over the river coming out of Gleann Bianasdail.

That glen path is good too. Half-way up, those heading for Slioch break off up Coire na Sleaghaich, the only entrance for this mountain, *the Spear*, which is not barred by defensive tiers and buttresses of red Torridonian sandstone. This is not tame country. The Ochils of my boyhood couldn't be more different, though an anagram of the same six letters, Slioch.

Conditions going up the glen, a fault line, were 'gey dreich,' but that proved to be the best of the weather for the *Boots* weekend. Unlike 1988, however, it was not universal: south of the Great Glen the days were hot, sunny and marvellously clear. Our view backwards was to the grey shawl and green skirts of Beinn Eighe; ahead the top of the glen is a slot of gorge, and the path rises steadily, switching the view to the Mullach Coire Fhearchair muddle of Munros, the Mullach the highest of all these hills of many lochs, the only one topping 1,000 m (1,019 m on the map). The track follows a tributary burn down to the outflow of Lochan Fada. We found a rare patch of grass and pitched our tent under the glassy eyes of shaggy goats with big sweeping horns. The dog was not sure about these wild-looking animals, well known on Slioch and round about.

Lochan Fada is a chilly, atmospheric place, worthy of a Gothic novel. It is almost four miles long and gouged out by past glaciers to make it 248 ft (76 m) deep. There are two outflows: the way we had come, and from the eastern corner, where there are two small linear lochs set in a mile of indeterminate country (once an extension of the loch) before the waters descend Gleann na Muice to the Heights of Kinlochewe. This is the result of late-Glacial scourings and dammings and how ultimately the meltwater wins a way out. One dictionary definition of an island I noted said, 'a piece of land surrounded by water'. Does that make this hunk of Kinlochewe Forest rising to Beinn a'Mhuinidh an island?[1]

A lochan is a small loch so why are these juvenile exit waters called *lochs* and the big brother *Lochan* Fada? And everyone seems to call this the head of the loch when it should be the foot. It is a bleak spot anyway, made more so by the lonely call of a golden plover coming across the wave-shivery waters. At least it was blowing wet rather than weeping wet, so there were no midges – and still not blowing enough to blow the tent away. The midges here are man-eaters, woman-eaters, dog-eaters... There is a perverse enjoyment in being tested; the too easy days are the ones we forget.

Two other *Boots* teams went by. At 6 p.m. the drizzle was driving past. We slept. At 6 a.m. the drizzle was still driving past. It had obviously listened to the forecast. We procrastinated but, perforce, had 'to boot up and go'. This boggy world, dry for weeks, was mopping up the wet with glee and doing nasty things with it. After an hour along the south-west shore of Lochan Fada our boots had mopped a ration of the wet too. There was a trace of track along strata of red sandstone about the 350m level. Slioch is that more cheerful colour among the grim greys of the gneiss. Bits of deer/goat trod and steady tramping took us reasonably easily to the far end of the loch, a shoreline without a tideline of the usual plastic rubbish. (Query: How do people appreciate our beauty spots? They leave their cans, papers and fag ends.)

We paused to eat our pieces, wedged between the great

cliffs of Beinn Lair and the Tharsuinn Caol battlement thrust of our objective. Beinn Tharsuinn Caol is a very narrow, very rocky but perfectly walkable crest, quite unlike anywhere else I know. A bit Aonach Eagach-like but with the deep-set Gorm Loch separating it from A'Mhaighdean. Not that we were going to see much of this wonderland, as the swirling cloud level was about 300m and the whole world was reduced to nuances of grey. We lingered. We chatted. Joss went to sleep. There is always the past, some of it pretty bloody, among our mountains. I tried to recall the story of how Gairloch came to be MacKenzie lands.

Apparently it was MacLeod territory originally and they shared a fanatical enmity with the MacKenzies. When the oldest of the three sons of the late MacLeod chief married a Mackenzie and bore children, the rage of the other brothers overflowed and they murdered their brother and his children. No MacKenzie blood was to pollute the succession. The widow had to produce the bloody garments of the two boys to be believed when she fled to her MacKenzie home and the outrage was reported to the King in Edinburgh who then issued orders that the MacLeods were to be dispossessed and outlawed. The lands became MacKenzie country.[2]

Of course Gairloch is much more associated with a more pacifist Mackenzie, and an admirable book by him. Osgood Mackenzie's *A Hundred Years in the Highlands* gives a fascinating account of this area under a remarkable man who would create the Inverewe Gardens among other things. When the Potato Famine arrived in the mid-1840s it was his mother's doing that road-building was introduced to give employment in the area (our A832 along Loch Maree). She saw that Gaelic-speaking schools were set up. He was a notable Gaelic scholar. He obviously cared for people and the landscape, yet was so of his times in some ways. His game book figures for 1868 make sorry reading: Grouse, 1,313; black game, 33; partridges, 49; golden plover, 110; wild duck, 35; snipe, 53; rock pigeons, 91; hares, 184; a total of 1,900 head without mentioning geese, teal, ptarmigan and roe. He writes: 'What a big pile it would make if all the black game I shot between 1855 and 1900 were gathered in one heap. Now alas! There are none, and why, who can tell?'

Surprise, surprise. The statistics of 'vermin' killed would be horrendous in our eyes. A keeper, further up at Gruinard, once boasted of shooting dead three golden eagles and two chicks on a nest, all 'before breakfast'. All this slaughtering plus the felling of forests and overgrazing has reduced much of our landscape to wet desert. Nature always finds its balance, including that between prey and predator. Man has kicked the balance into touch. Time we blew the whistle.

'We'd better be going,' I suggested. We stood up stiffly and Joss gave his silvered coat a good shake over us. A snipe went ricocheting off as we turned the end of the loch to tackle as steep a slope as you'll ever find. On the map the contours could not have been closer. We drifted up steadily, into the murk, the dog content to walk at our heels. When I now and then looked back at Val I was given a grin (or was it a grimace?) from under her cagoule hood. Some may wonder why we had followed the south side of Lochan Fada for this longer route and steep ascent – after all, the contours were much kindlier-looking on the north shore and all the way up A'Mhaighdean. Well, I had been that northern way before, and had sworn 'Never again!' Peat as porridge and the contortions of the contours reflect the complex reality.

However I did once have an unexpectedly easy walk this way, during a 1964 Hogmanay at the Ling Hut in Glen Torridon. A friend with the only car ran me up as far as the Heights of Kinlochewe where I slept in the stable (the signature of Jock Nimlin on a wall) and headed off up Gleann na Muice next day, the route chosen by Munro for climbing A'Mhaighdean. Lochan Fada was frozen solid and made a ridiculously easy highway. I just wished I had skates with me! I headed out by Gleann Bianasdail and then faced the hike back down Glen Torridon to the Ling – a night of scudding clouds and the road flowing with spindrift. A massive but magical day.

Being determined not to miss the magical hour for *Boots* we had ended up far too early, so we slittered up the wide, gentler-angled grassy slopes that reach to A'Mhaighdean without meeting any of its defensive cliffs. We had a bit of a flower hunt for the alpines which sensibly grow 'with their heads down' at Munro altitude, we procrastinated (again) over lunch in the lee of a boulder, and were discovered by another Fife trio who were also a *Boots* party for A'Mhaighdean. They were from Freuchie, and two nights before had been in the pub with the lad who had sold Joss to Val! Several others of our BFMC were also involved in *Boots*, and nephew Colin was heading for Ben More in Mull with a friend.

Arriving this way onto the summit of A'Mhaighdean is apt to leave one's 'gask flabbered' as I once heard it, for the view opens instantly at a cliff edge, onto a heart-stopping scene. So it was rather anti-climactic to stand there with no view at all. This was my ninth ascent of A'Mhaighdean and views were graciously granted me on four occasions. Most of the visits were while making the circuit of 'The Six' from Shenavall, but I had camped beside Lochan Fada before, hence our quicker entrance; I knew of the rare grassy spot that would take a tent.

Even in the murk we could just peer down – it felt vertically – to Gorm Loch Mor as if from some ultra-high diving board. At our level there were just walls of mist. The summit view, when there is one, takes in the whole three miles of Beinn Lair's north cliffs plus Meall Mheinnidh and Beinn Airigh Charr (and on to distant Skye). What about a Four Peaks Race over that lot? Westing, the Fionn Loch and the Dubh Loch are the main eye-catchers, the two separated only by a man-made causeway taking the pony track to Carnmore. ³ The stable at Carnmore is an open estate bothy and perfectly placed for climbing on the big cliffs above. Each generational wave of pioneer climbers seems to rediscover this area's potential. After excessive rain the causeway can be submerged to reunite the *fair* and the *black* lochs. In the 1870s Osgood Mackenzie (him again) pursued a legal case to decide whether they were to be defined as one loch but the House of Lords overturned the decision, so the Dubh Loch is legally a separate loch. (Could we see the House of Lords one day pronouncing on what was and wasn't a Munro?)

The summit of A'Mhaighdean is surprisingly flat, a tent-shape from afar, a real contrast to neighbouring Ruadh Stac Mor; ruadh is *red* as is the sandstone, while grey A'Mhaighdean is the highest summit of Lewisian gneiss, some of the oldest rock in the world. Could anywhere else feel older? What were the feelings of James Hutton when he first realised the true timescale of rocks – 'no vestige of a beginning, no prospect of an end'? How little of it will *Homo sapiens* occupy?

We bade goodbye to the A'Mhaighdean supplementary *Boots* folk and headed down the rocky flank to the col to

Ruadh Stac Mor and used the lee of a boulder there for another lunch, hoping for a weather improvement. The boulder had once provided a delightful bivouac spot on a round of 'the Six' from Corrie Hallie. There was a space below the boulder and the front was built up with rocks, perfect for making a one-man sleeping space. I had all the gear to make this an enjoyable night out – and I had the first Munroist dog Kitchy for hot water bottle. Quite a blizzard blew up in the night (13.11.74) and it was curious to see the snow blasting past only a couple of feet away yet lying snug and dry. A'Mhaighdean was an icy maiden next day.

Peeved at no change of weather, Val and I and Joss carried on up through the clarty clouds to the stone-built trig of Ruadh Stac Mor, as the name implied: *red, peaky, big*. On the summit screes we met its *Boots* delegation descending, so at least these two Munros had been comprehensively 'bagged,' even if one or two other summits in the NW were to prove too challenging on the day. We didn't linger and soon caught up the Ruadh Stac Mor party to continue high up along on the slopes of Beinn Tarsuinn for drier ground (relative term) than the bogs and braes by Lochan Fada. At the loch's end we crunched a small sandy shoreline and wondered if many other walkers had been on the two end beaches on the same day. Passing the site where the Freuchie lads had camped, we were soon back to our camp and its neighbourhood goats. This whole area I always associate with bird song (well, bird noise) for there are greenshank, dunlin, golden plover, snipe, divers, even cuckoos all contributing, all very much birds of the wild and lonely places, many with the pibroching voices of melancholy.

Looking in the SMC's *Munros* once home I was surprised it doesn't give approaches from Kinlochewe for A'Mhaighdean, though such routes had been taken by Hugh

Munro, by the Rev. A. E. Robertson (via Gleann Bianas-dail) and by generations since. Robertson usually treated the Sabbath as a day of rest, so his ascent of A'Mhaighdean on a Sunday (29.5.1898) was a near-unique happening – for which he received 'copious rain all day'. Oddly, Munro also climbed the hill on a Sunday (Easter 1900) – for which he in turn received 'the worst of a very wet week'.

At that time of the first OS survey, the proprietors of these mountains thwarted the surveyors' efforts to map this area with their usual rigour. So A'Mhaighdean was shown with a top contour of 2,750ft. Exploratory SMC pioneers knew better, and gave it at 3,100ft (945m.; today it is 967m). Munro's companions that day were Lawson and Ling, the latter the greatest explorer of climbs in the North-West, who would climb on 'the black, frowning northern preci-pice of Beinn Lair'; which they looked at through the rain and sleet on top of A'Mhaighdean. Only now can we be certain of the Munro heights in this area. Ruadh Stac Mor, which is paired with A'Mhaighdean, only gained 3,000ft recognition along with Beinn a'Chlaidheimh in the 70s, the latter however, with today's certainties, being sent back to the rank of Corbett. Beinn Tarsuinn, 3,074 ft (937 m today) , similarly slighted by the OS, failed to appear in the original *Tables*, but the SMC stalwarts with their aneroid barometers were sure of its being above the Plimsoll line and my precious 1953 *Tables* had it as a footnote; everyone then dutifully completed on 277 (the 276 plus Tarsuinn). Ah well, *tout passe*.

The weather was still wet for our walk out. Val sighed, 'Wouldn't it be nice if we actually had a climate in Scotland instead of a rag-bag of weathers?' South of the Great Glen *Boots* had had perfect weather. On Mullach Clach a'Bhlair above Glen Feshie there was a very special gathering, thanks to the landowner, a good driver and willing friends. Big Davy (could he ever have dreamt what a world of pleasure his misfortune has led to?), a girl with ME, a girl with motor neurone disease and a man with no legs all made the Munro. The last played his fiddle and the company had a dance! A boy with spina bifida went up on his pony. That was what *Boots* was about.

---

1 Another example I came on starts at a lochan high in the hills between Loch Duich, Loch Long and Glen Elchaig; OSLR 33, NG 936261.

2 That version was not bad for a fifty-year-old memory (I'm always fascinated about how memory works – or doesn't). I've since found the story told in Seton Gordon's *Highways and Byways in the West Highlands*. It dates to the late fifteenth century. Allan MacLean was laird of Gairloch and was murdered by his brothers as he snoozed on a knoll, still pointed out today. The widow took a bloodied shirt to her father, Mackenzie of Seaforth at Braham Castle, who sent his brother Hector Roy to the King, who then issued him the commission of fire and sword.

3 In his early book *Highland Days*, which brims with youthful enthusiasm and the excitement of exploration, Tom Weir records visiting Carnmore while it was still occupied by a family, the MacRaes, with whom he found shelter when his tent blew away. The eldest lad, a teenager who had attained the School Certificate, was the officially appointed schoolteacher to the other children. Supplies were rowed up the loch twice a year. This happy, contented family were dispersed by World War Two and nobody has lived there since.

A SALTING OF SNOW

'Just a salting of snow'
the shepherd said,
an odd way of putting it
for salt and snow we usually see
in the mess of busy streets.

But it was aptly right
with the fawn haunches of the Ochils
spread with the salt-snow
and nicely grilling in a winter sun
set at a low number.

We raised the dust of it
as we tramped white turf
the short day through.
Just a salting of snow,
but enough to flavour
the day so the ordinary
turned into a feast.

BY ANY METHOD

> *Early years are remembered in gleams only.*
> **George Mackay Brown**

My pedestrian wanderings have carried me all over the mountainy regions, the most basic progression of all, and the easiest to lose in a world that runs on wheels. Canoeing, too, is a grand adjunct to mountain travel and Scotland has lochs, rivers and coastline for a lifetime of canoe expeditions. I try and do something with the canoe each year, apart from yet another trip to Inchkeith which is my home circuit.

My canoe normally causes raised eyebrows among the plastic-paddling generation of today, being a sturdy, fifty-year-old kit-built canvas-on-wood frame job, solid as a stollen. It cost me £5 and has been down most Scottish rivers, on many lochs, and on long sea expeditions. I know if it goes over that I can right it and climb back in, even in a gale, and even with what feels like a ton of camping and hill gear on board.

Like any antique she takes some looking after, but many coats of paint have added to her weight and watertight state. But she always wants something else. This year I added a hinged back-rest and several hooks for shock cords across the deck to carry spare paddles and other gear, including a collapsible trolley for portages. As I can only just carry the canoe when empty, this trolley would be a boon for longer trips. Its acquisition could really be blamed on this particular journey – the Caledonian Canal – which would give a considerable number of carries to avoid all the locks.

A trial run to Inchkeith to test the latest alterations seemed wise. I trundled the canoe down to the shore on the trolley, but as it bumped hard on to the sand off a wall, one of the trolley supports bashed a six-inch hole in the canvas. Twenty-four hours later, with a repaired canoe and a modified trolley, I tried again. The dog went too of course, a great puffin-spotter and gannet-counter, but during a leg-stretch on the island I kept him close in case he could be contaminated by the hundreds of dead and dying gulls that make Inchkeith such a place of sorrow. Everything seemed to work satisfactorily and we plowtered back to the home sands. As we landed I heard one paddling child yell up the beach: 'Hey Maw, see the canoe. The man's got a dug and a pram in it!'

As I was joining forces with nephew Colin and a friend of his, impecunious school lads, we had planned to camp, hostel or use bothies. The dog, perforce, was left behind. At the last moment so were the tents, a big saving of weight and bulk, for you fight every ounce of the way just as you do on foot or cycling. We worked the route so we could manage with just bothies and hostels, and hoped we could get by 'in the flaws of fine weather we call our summer' (RLS).

Nephew Colin had a slick two-man Canadian canoe which was a descendant, many times removed, from anything Hiawatha knew, being all plastic and aluminium. It was very good of him and his pal Roddy to condescend to accompany me in my ancient craft. Being young, Colin missed the point when someone at Loch Lochy youth hostel smirked and asked me, 'Do you call your canoe *Rob Roy*?' [1]

It could be argued that the Caledonian Canal was Thomas Telford's greatest masterpiece of engineering. It was begun in 1803 and completed in 1822. It was a national enterprise rather than a private commercial venture, and has always been operated by the Government. Naturally the Government also looked for a return on its investment, but National Security was a big incentive: to transfer shipping coast-to-coast without risking the Pentland Firth. The defeat of Napoleon removed this danger and for the next century the main users were fishing boats. Telford also saw the work as helping to alleviate the poverty of the Highlanders, a people for whom he had much sympathy (he designed a standard small church which was built throughout the Highlands, in remote areas where needed).

The canal is about 60 miles long, with a third of that being in man-made canal, the rest using the natural waterways of the lochs that line up through the Great Glen's huge fault line. 'There are 15 locks to the summit from Corpach, and 16 from Inverness, each raising any ship for 8ft.' I quote, for my modest arithmetic is rather puzzled by those statistics. Is the sea really 8ft higher at Loch Linnhe than at the Beauly Firth?

The definitive book on the canal, still in print, is A. D. Cameron's *The Caledonian Canal* – a social, historical and engineering saga of great interest. Telford was attempting a work years ahead of its time. He often had to invent the machinery to do the job, and how to operate the canal. It was a great undertaking but – sounds familiar – it took longer and cost more than originally estimated. It was completed just in time to be obsolete.

The Great Glen has several youth hostels: Glen Nevis, Loch Lochy [2], Alltsaigh (Loch Ness) and Inverness, but the first and last of these are usually mobbed in summer by the international hitchers. The first day saw our canoes taken north on my campervan and a cache of food laid by a loch west of the Great Glen. We spent the night at Loch Lochy youth hostel in the Great Glen, and early the next day went to Corpach harbour office for our permits before launching. Corpach, near Fort William, is where the canal meets the western sea in Loch Linnhe. We watched a puffer being loaded. Rather than start at the sea lock and shortly after have the huge flights of seven locks, 'Neptune's Staircase,' to carry round, we started above them, at Banavie. Our journey would end with the canal entering the Beauly Firth at Inverness.

It was a place of memories for me, especially as we saw the Sea Cadet training ship *Royalist* going down the locks. She and the *Eye of the Wind* had been alongside there a few years previously: two tall ships in the canal, an unusual sight. On that occasion I had taken some of the crew of *Eye of the Wind* for an overnight climb of Ben Nevis so they could see the sunrise – a smiling sunrise.

The brooding Ben was crisp and clear this morning too. We took to the oily dark waters beside a big Danish schooner *Opal* which greeted us by starting her engines, which then blew out a series of smoke rings with every putt-putt of the motors.

After an hour's paddling along the smooth canal we landed for a few minutes to rest arms and bottoms (the parts which feel the work of canoeing), then to explore where the big River Loy flows *under* the canal. This arch and the pedestrian one beside it are in the reverse shape of the canal's arch above, the U of the canal being the same as the Ω of the underpass and stream. The midges soon had us back on the water. *Opal* passed. A fishing boat passed. At Gairlochy (locks and swing bridge) we used the trolley wheels for our 'portage,' in turn, and were sitting having a picnic when the boats passed again – with some interesting double takes. However, our rate of progress was about 4½ mph so even the holiday cruisers, at 6 mph, quickly over-hauled us. As we paddled out into Loch Lochy there was a brief puppy storm. This reach was originally the river but a new cutting was made for the river and this goes down to Mucomir power station, then under a fine Telford bridge to join the Spean.

Conditions were rougher than the lads had met previously, but in the middle of a big loch there are fairly limited options. The prospect of drowning, as much as hanging, 'concentrates the mind wonderfully'. We battled on for two hours to eventually land on the west shore where intended. It was hot enough for Roddy to spend much of the time in the loch, while Colin and I trundled my canoe off on a two-mile portage to Loch Arkaig. 'At least there are no midges underwater.'

Colin walked back with the wheels to Loch Lochy, along the *Mile Dorcha*, the Dark Mile, while I meanwhile looked at the drought-reduced Chia-aig waterfall (which appeared in the film *Rob Roy*), and retrieved our cache from the forest. This had been tied in a waterproof bag and hung from a tree, not, as one of the lads suggested, to keep it from bears, but to keep it from equally destructive mice. I still had time for a paddle (a heron went rowing overhead, and tiny trout nibbled my toes), and then to have a dixie of tea ready for the boys' return.

In the time we had taken for our double portage the wind had risen considerably. The gale hit us on the starboard bow and reduced a two-mile paddle to an exhausting hour-long battle, along a lee shore. We had rather splashy going, but were glad not to be among white horses out in the middle of the loch. It was a relief to reach land. We ran on to a bank of water lobelia and leapt out into knee-deep mud. Never was a bothy more welcome. We carried our gear over to Invermallie and set about the serious business of eating the evening away – easy enough for teenagers after a long first day's canoeing. The free-ranging garrons tried their best to join us inside. They didn't seem to like midges either.

The midges had been behind our decision to find buildings for the night, rather than camp. There was one other person in the bothy who was on his fourth day of walking from Ardnamurchan to Stonehaven, then the next night it was someone heading to Skye. He was complaining at the lack of birds, yet sitting outside the bothy we'd seen sand martin, pipits, wagtail, warblers, chaffinch, hoodie, a merganser family, and heard woodpecker, cuckoo and an owl woodwinding in the night. (Also on the trip, but I'll not mention where, we first heard and then found a nesting osprey.)

The next day was spent on a traverse of Beinn Bhan. The summit gave a long view of our route and nodded across to Ben Nevis. The heather was already in bloom and we guzzled blaeberries on the way down. In the night we were woken with a start as the garrons went galloping past.

The midges also plagued our departure from Invermallie next morning, but by the time we had reversed the portages to Loch Lochy, the wind had fangs. The rain drooled. Clouds had camped on the hills. The wind was more or less behind us and we surged and surfed along in fine style. After an hour we were so chilled we landed to don waterproofs and brewed some tea. Any idea of climbing the Munros above the loch was abandoned. The clouds were being ripped up by the gale, and the rain was swabbing the hills.

From the loch we had views quite different from those we knew from motoring the Great Glen – such as the railway viaduct above Letterfinlay. To clear the jut of Kilfinnan Point into the Ceann Loch (*Head Loch*) we were paddling hard with our right hands only. The wheels behind me were apt to make the canoe yaw. Then suddenly we were landing in a scattering of ducks and noisy oystercatcher comment.

We reached Laggan Locks far too early: a good excuse to guzzle and fester in the tearoom. The café walls had pictures of the canal in early days and quite by chance, on a previous visit in 1976 I saw the locks empty for repairs – only the second time ever. The huge arched hole emphasised the scale of the canal. It was built for ships. We canoeists did not count at all and had to carry round. The difficult cutting from here up to Loch Oich is the highest reach on the Caledonian Canal at 106 ft. A mile on up the tree-hidden canal we landed, just one field away from the comforts of friendly Loch Lochy youth hostel. A dapper landscape.

My first Braehead canoeing trip in the Great Glen had been based there decades before and the same kindly warden, Mrs Fraser, was there to greet another generation.[3] Someone on a canoe course at the SYHA summed up their hefty day to Fort Augustus and back as 'Rain. Rain all day and then a gale coming back. It was great!' A twelve-year-old had been one of the party and still buzzed with energy. I noted our pair retired early to bed. There were plenty of drookit cyclists as well as canoeists but Mrs Fraser and her cheery assistant made everyone at home. The fire alarm went off three times in the night (accidentally) but Colin and Roddy did not even hear it.

The weather cheered up for the A82 swing bridge and

into Loch Oich. We stopped at the Well of the Heads, that uniquely blood-thirsty memorial that comes up to port not long after the swing bridge. While many know something of the tale of murder and revenge and the seven renegade heads being washed in the well before delivery to the chief at Glengarry Castle, few realise the well still exists. It is under the road, but there is a passage in to it from the shore of Loch Oich. We landed beside it, but ice-cream in the shop rather than historic interest motivated the landfall.

Dredging Loch Oich set Telford some problems, and Alastair MacDonell of Glengarry was a thorn in the flesh. This is the chief still famous because of the resplendent portrait by Raeburn in the National Gallery of Scotland. He did not like a canal passing his castle. We had a look at its ruins.

There was hardly any water flowing over the weir into the River Oich so there was no temptation to run it. We once did with some school lads from Fife and as we swept past the lawns of a mansion house a hi-falutin' voice trilled 'What do you think you're doing?' to which the blockhead at the rear returned the perfect rejoinder 'Canoeing!' – and vanished round the bend. (From Fort Augustus we could see the river would have been impossible to run.)

Before Fort Augustus two locks, Cullochy and Kyltra, break the placid canal miles. At Kyltra the keeper once allowed us to pick rhubarb from his garden for the time it took *Eye of the Wind* to pass through the lock. Rhubarb rained down on the decks. Fort Augustus greeted us with a pipe band, it being gala day. The Lochaber Pipe Band, a traction engine and various other oddities ensured a crowd of people, through which we wheeled our canoes to the pepper-pot lighthouse at the south end of Loch Ness. The pipe band still marched and played and when the Tannoy music from the Abbey grounds began, poor Colin winced at the competitive cacophony (he was then pipe major of his school's band).

We felt remote onlookers at all these festivities, being set apart for tougher challenges as it were – which took all our concentration and effort. Being water-borne set us aside from the bustle of life on road and in village. The five locks of Fort Augustus run down through the village, so the two worlds of town and canal meet rather brutally.

It was sunny again, with just a flirting breeze, and two more Danish schooners arrived: *Jens Kroch* from Loch Ness, and *Grena* – when the festivities finally allowed the swing bridge to open. *Grena* tied up opposite us and one figure stripped off and had a splash-bath on deck. A rich Glasgow voice in the picnic spot next to us screeched, 'Wid ye credit that? She's nae got ony claes oan at aa!' to which came the reply 'Dinna be daft, hen. Ah've nivver seen you tak a shoor wi yir claes oan!' The boys probably thought I was choking on my sardine sandwich.

The new OS map now noted Cherry Island (Loch Ness's only island, given the name by Cromwell's soldiers) as being a prehistoric lake dwelling, a crannog. I'd long suspected this. We soon picked up a strong tailwind. Any help up Loch Ness was welcomed for there is a certain scenic monotony. We twice landed just to ease numb bums and weary shoulders, before reaching Alltsaigh (Loch Ness) youth hostel, an old favourite which looks over the loch so it is like being on board ship.[4]

Mrs Maclean signed us in for two nights, for on the following day we had only eight miles to cover instead of today's score. We would leave the canoes at Drumnadrochit Bay and bus back to the hostel, then reverse the procedure the next day. The canoes were actually left near Urquhart Castle, out of sight, and our paddles and jackets were hidden in the bracken. It felt odd to then go and catch a bus.

The castle has had one of the stormiest of histories and little enough remains, but the towers and battlements set on the knoll over Loch Ness make it a magnet for the tourists. We paddled around to take photographs from the loch. The only other landmark on the short day had been the cairn in memory of John Cobb, holder of the land speed record, who died in 1952 trying to achieve a new water record on Loch Ness. Off Urquhart Castle the loch reaches its greatest depth, over 800 feet, which is deeper than the North Sea.

The rest of Loch Ness gave us our only discourteous wind – bang on the bow – so it was hard work with little to catch the imagination. 'Non-scenery' someone called it. A couple of miles before the end we passed the spot where a Wellington bomber ditched in the loch in 1940. Swimming the length of Loch Ness is one of the sport's famous challenges, first done in eighteen-and-a-half hours in 1966 by the teenager Brenda Sherratt.

We were glad to rest at Lochend, below the house that has an inland lighthouse attached upstairs. The tour boats seemed to be busy: *Jacobite Lady* and *Jacobite Chieftain* and *Scott II* passing us there. The last set up a big wash just as the Canadian was being launched. Two big waves caught Colin right below the chin and ran down inside his life jacket; the only wetting of the trip while involved with the canoes.

Loch Dochfour is small and pretty and we could actually hear the weir where the River Ness left it. Dochgarroch was our last lock, the only change in level from away back at

Fort Augustus. The finishing flight of locks at Muirtown seven miles on we would avoid by completing the trip above them. Dochgarroch was lifeless apart from two children fishing with the traditional bent pins. A notice on the lock-keeper's cottage said 'Gone to lunch, back at 1.30'. We were obviously nearing civilisation. You could tell by the cans floating in the canal.

This was another length that proved difficult to construct; for some 500 yards the bottom was lined with locally-woven cloth which was then plastered in a clay-based 'puddle' to make a waterproof barrier that is still effective over 150 years later. Telford is such a ubiquitous figure in Scotland with his record of roads, bridges, 30 churches and manses, harbours and canals that we tend to forget just how long ago he lived. It was the period of the Napoleonic Wars that saw the Caledonian Canal built.

Tomnahurich Hill appeared: 'one of the most picturesque burial grounds in the country' as the guide book declared. Many years ago one old Highlander was so taken by the setting he declared, 'That is where I'd like to be buried, if I'm spared.' Below the hill the A82 crossed the canal by a swing bridge, and it was there that we hauled out our canoes for the last time. Nearby lay the municipal camp site where we had been warned that spaces to pitch were often scarce – and we wanted to be sure. All that remained of the canal (walked later) was an urban Inverness mile to the last locks, then the Muirtown Basin and sea lock into the Beauly Firth, near where it becomes the large Moray Firth. Maybe it was as well we checked in quickly. Only a few pitches remained free. We hurried my canoe in, then I left the lads to deal with the Canadian while I caught a Fort William bus back to Loch Lochy YH where I'd left my campervan. Once back, we pitched a tent for the boys, and the thunderstorm broke that somehow seemed appropriate to end our 67 mile journey and also the 67 days of that hot summer.

---

1 John 'Rob Roy' MacGregor was a Victorian canoeist who made some remarkable journeys in his 'Rob Roy,' as you can gather from the books of the trips: *A Thousand Miles in the Rob Roy Canoe* (1866), *The Rob Roy on the Baltic* (1867), *The Rob Roy on the Jordan, Nile, Red Sea and Gennesareth* (1869).

2 Loch Lochy youth hostel later closed as an SYHA hostel but now operates as the attractive, privately run Great Glen Hostel.

3 When I was struck down with flu during one Braehead trip we were allowed to stay in over a wet day and the boys found a hay barn an excellent place to play. The next day, being fair, I sent them off to climb Ben Tee by themselves. Imagine that being considered these days!

4 Staying in Alltsigh as a teenage cyclist I stabled my steed in the cycle shed down near the snuffling water's edge. Torrential rain fell in the night, guttering the hillsides, and flooding the road. On going to collect my bike I found I had to paddle to reach the shed door. Loch Ness had risen a foot overnight, what must have been a staggeringly large volume of water, Loch Ness being the largest, in volume anyway. That additional volume had fallen from the skies overnight. I was impressed. Loch Ness contains more water than all the lakes of England and Wales combined.

As there are often arguments over the term 'largest' or 'biggest' when talking of Scottish lochs (Volume? Deepest? Longest?), here is how the honours are shared out by the 'Big Four':

The Largest in Area (km^2) is Loch Lomond 71 (27.45 sq.mls), followed by Loch Ness 56, Loch Awe 39, Loch Morar 27, Loch Tay 26.

The Greatest in Volume (million m^3) is Loch Ness 7895 (263,162 mn. cu. Ft.), followed by Loch Lomond 2784, Loch Morar 2445, Loch Tay 1697, Loch Awe 1305.

The Longest Loch (km) is Loch Awe 41 (25.45 mls), followed by Loch Ness 39, Loch Lomond 36 (Loch Morar, 19, is 9th).

The Deepest Loch (m) is Loch Morar 310 (1,017 ft), followed by Loch Ness 230, Loch Lomond 190 (Loch Awe 94 is 15th).

You could tabulate their positions:

L.Ness	2	1	2	2	(7)
L.Lomond	1	2	3	3	(9)
L.Morar	4	3	9	1	(17)
L.Awe	3	5	1	15	(24)

Loch Awe is unusual in that its outflow changed from one end of the loch to the other thanks to ice-age scouring.

A SEA ROUTE TO THE HILLS

> Hills and seas neither love nor hate us
> But they have the notion yet to try and break us.
>
> **Anon**

I was woken with the cry of 'Lee-oh' and thereafter was rolled over on my angled bunk to end up against the side of the ship. Through the wooden hull I could hear the sound of the water rushing past. It was a moon-bright night and I could imagine the ship, all sails set, ghosting through between Ardtornish Castle to starb'd and the mountains of Mull to port like some spectre from another age. I snuggled down and was asleep almost at once.

It wasn't always like that, of course. I can remember fearsome hours feeling like death from seasickness, the hot-cold misery between decks when trying to explain how Primus stoves worked to equally green trainees who 24 hours later would be camping at 2,000 feet on Arran in a winter gale. The agony and the ecstasy; concentrated, uncompromising, inescapable. There aren't many escape routes off a sailing ship, and the weather doesn't furl its sails very often.

Strange how this suddenly re-entered my thoughts. The

radio had played music from Khachaturian's *Spartacus* which included the theme music to the 1970s TV serial *The Onedin Line*, as evocative a reminder as salt spray on the face. Then I happened to open an old log book and found myself reading about Course 38 on the *Captain Scott*, an October 1975 that saw us crossing the Minch twice, sailing through most of the Inner Isles and visiting the Clyde, with shore expeditions on Arran and round Suilven. My Nelson Watch, grand lads, carried off 'The Captain's Prize' and 'The Ensign' at the end. I still have letters from some of them which ring with the sheer magic of the time together. One tends to forget the seasickness or the 60 mph winds driving rain through the tents on the Saddle between Glen Rosa and Glen Sannox – I baled my tent at the rate of two pints per hour. A day later I chanced on a dusty file on a high shelf that had all my notes and all the literature of the three such courses I'd been on as a temporary expedition officer. This file is now all parcelled up ready to be deposited in the National Library archives so before it disappears, I decided to write about some of those memories. Tall ships offered real adventure – none of the 'simulated adventure' beloved of the educationalists these days – and most were better for it.

In the 'struggling Seventies' nobody in Britain would pay the price of half a mile of motorway to buy the training schooner *Captain Scott*, so she was snapped up by an Eastern buyer and now sails the Gulf as *Youth of Oman*. I've since sailed on several other tall ships – in the Channel, France and to Morocco – but there was something especially splendid about the western seaboard of Scotland. In January, October and November we certainly did not lack for wind.

On one of the courses we had a tough time on Ben Nevis

for a first shore expedition, a tougher time on Arran for the second, after gales had driven us over to Ulster, then after a long sail up the Minch, the third shore expedition was for three days in the Cape Wrath area which gave everything from sun blinks to blizzards by way of thunder and lightning. Weary lads regained the ship in Loch Eriboll having traversed from Loch Inchard.

Our watch, over three days on duty, with all sail hoisted, then sailed the ship along the north coast towards the Pentland Firth. One by one we had to hand the sails as the wind strengthened. Talk about tiredness. Off watch, one lad fell asleep while still climbing into his bunk! Sails went on again. We'd no sooner slept an hour than the call came for 'All hands on deck!' We quickly struck all sail. The chain rattling out to anchor in Dunnet Bay didn't even wake those sleeping with their heads inches away from the chain locker.

The ship was heading for the annual refit in Buckie where she was built, but we had to put into Invergordon. I can recall taking down the yards with several inches of new snow on them. Often on that trip, to climb the rigging we had to grip the rope (or wire) long enough to thaw the ice before risking any pull on it. Up there, seasick, in a gale, at night, rounding Ardnamurchan, you were playing for keeps. One of the ex-trainees' letters picked out that experience, too: 'Writing my report for the bank is very difficult. You have to be aboard to realise what went on. I find it difficult sometimes to believe I did what's in my own log.' He then described something of the above. 'Even though I was exhausted, what a feeling of achievement, finding reserves of energy to do what was asked of us.'

The *Captain Scott* was the dream-reality of Commander Victor Clark RN. He won a DSC in the Battle of Narvik, commanded a destroyer in the Atlantic, was in at the chase of the *Bismarck* and was sunk off Singapore in the *Repulse*. Raids behind enemy lines earned him a bar to his DSC but the Japanese caught him and he spent years in a POW camp [a full account of his heroic activities at this time appears in my book *East of West, West of East* (Sandstone Press, 2018)]. Retiring in 1953, he set off in a 33-foot ketch on the then longest-ever small craft circumnavigation of the globe, only returning in 1959. I'd read his book *On the Wind of a Dream* (Hutchinson 1960) with interest. He then had years trying to create a sea-based Outward Bound-type set-up which led to the *Captain Scott* being built for the purpose. Until compulsory retirement at 65 he was her master. He then 'settled down,' married and raised a family! I can recall one lad being terrified at the prospect of going up 'over the yards' and Victor challenging him, 'If I can do it, will you?' – and then shinning off upwards.

What the trainees seldom knew was how much of a challenge it was to the temporary crew, at least until we 'learnt the ropes' a bit ourselves. Under the Master was the Mate, Expedition Officer, Bo'sun, Engineer, Cook, Second Expedition Officer, and for any month-long-course, four temporary instructors/watch officers – and the three watches of about 12 trainees. The pressures were tremendous, for besides sailing the ship there had to be training and preparation for three three-day shore expeditions – on the first the instructors led, on the second the trainees organised it with instructors handy, and on the last they were on their own.

Two of the temporary crew were 'goats' (mountaineers) who had to operate this side of things and be able to learn and pass on all about the sailing routine, too – a frantic life is putting it mildly. You had to be slightly mad to enjoy it, and

I loved it! The Expedition Officer on all three full courses I went on was John Hinde, who had been in charge of the RAF Kinloss Mountain Rescue Team and later worked at Outward Bound Locheil, where the ship was based some of the time. John had the perfect laid-back personality to cope.

Those of us who go to the hills regularly tend to forget how beyond the conception of the ordinary person such a lifestyle is: ninety-nine per cent of the population have never faced a night under canvas, far less carried tents on a self-planned expedition round Suilven in winter after just a couple of practice runs; ninety-nine per cent of the population has never sailed a ship of any size, far less in the Minches in autumn gales as part of a disciplined team whose greatest treat would be an hour's sleep. The element of shock is something not met with very often these days, more's the pity, for it is the quiet waters that have crocodiles.

Most young people today are unfit and cosseted yet, given the chance, most react favourably to challenges such as the *Captain Scott*. But only a proportion of the population finds its own way to the wilds. The hills and the sea are more needed than ever these days as a restorative escape from the artificiality of life. We need to 'impel' youngsters into experiences.

One of my fondest memories was sailing across the Minch from Stornoway to Lochinver and coming on deck in a bruised-grey dawn to see Suilven and other hills rising like prehistoric monsters in the east. We spent three days wandering there and climbed Suilven, Cul Mor and Canisp from remote and piercingly-beautiful camp sites. And how it rang with Wordsworth's 'two mighty voices' – the sea and the mountains.

I've reached the hills by many means over the years but none has quite captured the sheer romanticism of the *Captain Scott*. As we worked up on the snowy yards at Invergordon at the end of that course one lad said, 'Instead of taking the yards down, couldn't we just put to sea and sail round the world? The skipper knows the way.' I think most of us would have gone.

CYCLING THE FOUR

Forget the destination; enjoy the journey.

Arab saying

Having walked between the Four Country summits of Scotland, England, Wales and Ireland in 1979, I thought linking them by cycling could be fun and set off to do this in June-July 1982. To use our predominantly sou'westerly winds to best advantage I would start with Carrauntoohil and to ease travelling buy a bike in Ireland. Airports were a bit puzzled at all my cycle panniers – and no bike.

I had cycled across Ireland once before, as a schoolboy, and did it in one day to make the Dublin Horse Show where Capt Harry Llewellyn on 'Foxhunter' was dominating the jumping world. That run was across the deadly flat centre of the country and I arrived at my aunt's house in Dun Laoghaire with a bad attack of the 'knock'. She thought the remedy for this might be a tot of whiskey and it was a decade thereafter before the very smell of the spirit didn't set my stomach heaving.

I'd a good day on Ireland's highest range (Macgillycuddy's Reeks) for starting this latest ploy: up by Lough Callee and in turn out and back for the various summits of

Caher and Beenkeragh, so Carrauntoohil, Ireland's highest (1039m) was visited twice. Caher, a black jag, gave the only view through a blanket of dirty cloud. I rejoiced to see St Patrick's Cabbage (a speciality), big butterworts, roseroot, campions and thrift, the flowers of high hills. My log was brief, 'Abandon the green people-less heights to bomb down the over-worn Ladder. Very marshy at the bottom. Regain the route at Lough Callee and so back to the hostel. Place to myself. Welcome turf fire. Bullfinches. Wet and windy night.'

Even from the train I'd caught the sweet scent of the turf (peat) reek, something always special. The Irish 3000-ders are a joy, the four groups of haughty hills very different in character but all rising above the green, green of fields, dotted with cottages and hamlets, that reek drifting to the tops, along with children's voices – a lived-in landscape, in many ways superior to the Scottish Highlands which are such a man-made wasteland. The Irish mountain land-scapes sing, the Scottish hills lament.

There's not much really to tell of the cycle ride back to Dun Laoghaire except to say I fought *headwinds* all the way and spent a great deal of time under trees, in cafés or any other shelter while showers (mostly *fortissimo*) went through. So much for the regular SW winds that were going to assist me. My log girned, 'Bum numb, palms red, knees aching'. Elsewhere on that setting off day a son was born to a Princess Diana.

My route went through Blackwater country, Mallow, Fermoy, Lismore, Waterford, Arthurstown, Arklow, Mizen Head, Wicklow Head, and Bray. Torrential rain and gale force winds ('swearing winds' a local called them) were the norm. New Goretex waterproofs and Bogtrotters on my feet kept me surprisingly dry. At one B&B the bedside

Gideon Bible opened at the words '... the waters prevailed exceedingly upon the earth...' (Gen. 7:18). Lismore was the home of Dervla Murphy (visited on a drier occasion) whose first book, *Full Tilt*, had described her epic cycling alone to India. I went up into the hills to overnight at Tiglin YH. The gutters in Bray flowed like rivers. With hindsight I wonder why I didn't just sit out this spell of diabolical weather. Time wasn't important; I was just being bloody-minded I suppose. I crossed to Holyhead. The ship's choice of film was *Chariots of Fire*.

I found the Holyhead post office and sent home a parcel of the tent (which I'd not used), the Irish maps, films, and odds and ends, then dawdled (dry, with a wind from behind) across clover-scented Anglesey and Telford's Bridge over the Menai Straits to Bangor YH.

Not wasting dry conditions I was off early for 'quite a grind' to Llanberis for 8.30 then the pass, 'hard graft' and to the YH 'in a lather'. I booked in and went for a tea across the road before heading off up the Pyg Track, freshly re-made, up to Bwlch Moch, walking slowly to let walking muscles get into gear after all the cycling, then enjoyed a dry scramble up to Crib Goch. Down off Crib y Ddysgl I saw a train, *Wyddfa*, come puffing up to disgorge its customers at the summit of Snowdon (Yr Wyddfa, 1085m), there to join the mob already milling around. I counted one party of 56 approaching. Clouds were touching some tops so, after a quick cup of tea in the café (so ridiculous a feature it had to be sampled), I fled, steeply down to the Bwlch Ciliau. A helicopter came and hovered just over my head on the summit of Lliwedd for no obvious reason and for many minutes, giving me an annoying downdraft while picnicking. The pilots were grinning – so I threw a stone at them and enjoyed their change of expression. Then two jet fighters belted through Bwlch Ciliau and Bwlch Glas one after the other, a very tight turn. Maybe they were all in high spirits just back from the Falklands War. What with people and engines, this was the noisiest day I've ever had on the British hills. I went out to Gallt y Wenallt to complete the circuit then back to make down by Cwm Dyli to the Miners' Track. The hostel swarmed with school parties, rampaging and noisy. Child-warfare.

Next day, because the hills were there, and because I'd always come from the north to traverse the Glyders, I took the chance to climb them from the south and had my first completely dry day. My route started up by gull-noisy Llyn Cwmffynon then a rising line to gain another Miners' Track to the crest of the range where a transverse path led to the Bwlch Tryfan and thence up Tryfan, that joy of a hill. I had it to myself if you don't count Adam and Eve. Mountain blackbirds (ring ouzels) were chacking and there had been pipits, wagtails, wheatears and ravens. I envied tents down by Llyn Bochlwyd. Nobody was about but there were figures on the Castle of the Winds. I met a lamb only a couple of days old. Glyder Fawr was the day's highest point (just) and by then there were people everywhere. It was pleasant to come off hard rock underfoot for Y Garn and then on for Foel-Goch and finally Elidir Fawr, the last of the group's 3000-ers. Heading for this summit I heard odd bird calls which took a while to register but when a group of black birds flew up in a noisy explosion I let out a yell of glee. A chuckle of choughs! Descending through the old Dinorwic Quarries was a novel experience. 'Bit more than Ballachulish,' then it was 'Time for tea in Pete's Eats, shop in the Co-op, and bus back to the hostel.'

Moel Siabod had often looked good so I couldn't resist it *en passant*. There was no problem crossing the river and 'the ascent was utterly unexciting: grass nearly all the way, no birds, nothing of note and no views as Snowdonia was hidden in cloud,' which soon brought wet, so there was another day of cycling with showers, many and heavy, with café refuges in Pentrefoelas and Cerrigydrudion, lots of ups and downs, and after cowering under a tree for another splenetic storm the long whiz down to Ruthin. Cycling after two weeks was fairly painless, physically at least. Nansen wrote of '... the same wonderful feeling in the muscles as one stretches limbs after a strenuous day. It is a sense of well-being that animals enjoy, the joy of suppleness unimpaired'.

At Ruthin I had a few days staying with Ann Roberts, the widow of Eric, a climbing friend who had been very active in the Eastern Alps, writing several guidebooks. He had climbed Nanda Devi and died in an avalanche on Annapurna. In 1979 I'd stayed with Ann on my *Groats End Walk* (the first foot-link of our Four Country summits) for my August 13 birthday. Then, on October 25, I stayed with her again when heading home from Land's End, and she told me about Eric being killed. Ann had first heard the news on the radio!

Ann was away but had left notes all over the house. A pile of mail was also waiting for me and new maps and some proofs to correct. I did relax and watch the Wimbledon finals: Navratilova beating Evert, and McEnroe beating Connors after a four hour epic. I'd a couple more days off once Ann returned.

The weather had decided to be friendly, and pleasant byways took me to Chester for too brief explorations and a youth hostel night again. I enjoyed a surprisingly dapper Wirral and found myself landing off the ferry in front of Liverpool's Liver Building just before noon. The Maritime

Museum filled the time before the *Manx Maid* ferry set off. My ticket to Man was made out for 'one passenger and dog'.

I explored the Isle of Man fairly extensively, something well worth doing if at all interested in historical and pre-history sites – and historic railways. Many hill list-tickers I suspect 'bag' Snaefell and that's all. I visited the 1854 Laxey Wheel, the largest such in the world, before taking the train up Snaefell (621 m, 2,034 ft), the island's highest point. Good views but not to 'all the countries'. I've never had that on the Isle of Man, but did so unexpectedly once from the Mull of Galloway: Ireland's mountainy horizon over the sea, England's Lakeland clear and the Isle of Man puzzling till I realised its impossibly big hills were actually distant Snowdonia. I had several days cycling round historic sites and riding on Manx's variety of steam and/or electric trains. I kept meeting tanker lorries on the road which bore the threatening logo, 'CHRISTIANS FOR FUEL'. To explore I had three nights in B&Bs: at Castleton, Port Erin, and Peel – cycling between them.

The *Manx Viking* took me over to Heysham, arriving in the dark with my front light not working and, while searching for digs, the rear light went as well. I went into the first hotel I met in Morecambe and fell into bed at 11.45 p.m. I couldn't resist buying a few of the most kitsch post-cards to send to various climbing friends: 'What the hell's he doing in *Morecambe*?' I escaped the place after a conveyor-belt breakfast. Carnforth Railway Museum was fascinating though a BR strike had marooned the *Flying Scotsman* at Carlisle. After dawdling through Silverdale I called in to Milnthorpe for a coffee with Cicerone publisher Walt Unsworth before a very hot ride up to touristy Windermere for the ferry. After crossing, a 1-in-8 hill was cruel. There was a magnificent view up Langdale before dropping down to find Elterwater YH sharp on opening time. Full. So were two B&Bs. I cycled in a fury on to Ambleside YH. Full. A row of B&Bs all declared 'only doubles'. 'Much as I love the Lake District, unbeatable scenery, oh dear, the mobs that clog it in the lemming season,' my log bleated, 'I long for the lonely miles of home hills.' How values change: I thought £9 was expensive for the B&B I eventually found.

Another sizzling day, so the B&B kept my panniers and I went for the hills in trainers, shorts and refreshments in a jacket tied around my waist. I decided if I broke a leg I'd be found in five minutes. I enjoyed cycling up Langdale, and went by Rossett Gill over to Angle Tarn – at 10 a.m. free of visitors – but after dripping up to Esk Hause, folk were approaching from every direction and on Scafell Pike (977 m) the top of England was crowded. Ah well, that was number 3. I worked my way down to near Mickledore then round and up Scafell by Foxes Tarn.

Back at Angle Tarn 'the sky was going to explode' as I heard a youth put it. I took time however to kick off trainers and plunge straight in. Shorts and shirt were dry again by the time I reached my bike. The 'explosion' came during supper in busy, noisy Ambleside YH and it rained all the next day. I sensibly festered, met Syd Prentice for coffee, did some overdue writing, and read Kes (Barry Hines) in the evening. I then cycled via Windermere to Kendal for a merry night with old friends, Harry and Molly Griffin, lights out at 2 a.m. Next day, with Harry striding ahead, I yawned my way up Carlin Gill for a Howgills walk, 'burning up' the Black Force gorge. 'Hills like the thighs of Renoir's women!' A rising traverse led to Fell Head and there was only one dip to the Calf (676 m), the highest of these characterful hills. Sadly, it was raining hard by then, a rain that roared rather than purred. We returned west down Long Rigg Beck and back to Harry's car on the Fair Mile Road, for us a two-and-a-half-mile wet road. We talked till midnight. I was nearly gaga by then. Keeping up with oldies is exhausting. At our last meeting when I was praising Mahler, Harry went over to his piano and just played me some. He was then in his eighties.

The quieter, shady side of Thirlmere was enjoyed and the quivering (late Turner-like) views from Castlerigg Stone Circle seemed to take in every Lakeland summit of note. The Keswick YH entrance lay along a boardwalk above the River Greta. A balcony over the river was welcomely cool. A friend Simon Glover joined me for tea. A cricket match was being played over on the green and above the trees the bulk of Skiddaw was being sunset-washed.

Any thought of a hill on the morrow vanished in another roasting day. Far too hot. Minor roads and plenty of stops for liquid took me to Carlisle where I spent a couple of hours in the brutally-built castle, then took the bike for a bit of an MOT. The rear wheel was dragging as slightly buckled. Another youth hostel night. The MOT cost £4 and I was on the road at 8.30 a.m. next day and feeling a bit like a horse, exercised all day, who picks up again when turned towards home. I put in 76 miles despite the heat, to finish at an empty Kendoon YH. Trite Gretna marked being into Scotland.

A day of ups and downs followed, both physically and metaphorically. Car-kill (*roads* don't kill) along the way accounted for adder, sheep, blackbird and sparrow. And could have been me as well. I stopped near the Green Well of Scotland to have a circular walk round the grassy bumps to the west, a mere enclosure in the constipated conifer country of the south-west: Garryhorn Rig, Knockower,

Coran of Portmark, Bow, Meaul and Cairnsgarroch and Craighit, a real gargle of names. The A713 rose to 1300 ft before descending to Dalmellington; tired legs then for the final swoop into Ayr. I explored a bit then, coming to a junction, a car 'breenged' across my front so I had to turn violently to avoid being hit and the gritty camber twisted my wheel right around and I went into orbit. My log recorded, 'Went over handlebars (conscious of "Oohs!" from the crowd at the lights). Front wheel wrecked – a Tate Modern exhibit. Despite the flight and several forward rolls I wasn't run over and hadn't even broken skin. No time to tense, so a skiff rather than a splat. A sweltering search in the busy town found a cycle shop so the bike went in overnight.' Mail at the hostel included the six new maps sheets which would see me to the end. On bedding, the peaks of Arran stood black and proud against a scarlet sky.

I collected my bike and paid £9.50 for the new wheel and other repairs. Prestwick, Troon, Irvine, Saltcoats were passed in the morning, keeping mainly to minor roads, and the *Clansman* took me to Brodick to cycle round the Arran coast to Lochranza with its finely-posed castle. I made the last ten minutes to the attractive YH pushing my steed – the first and only puncture of the trip. Someone recognised me from our meeting at the Eas a' Coul Aulin (Scotland's highest waterfall) the previous Hogmanay. I repaired the puncture once the evening cooled and the midges had gone to bed.

The ferry *Rhum* took me to Kintyre's Claonaig for another day of weather perfection, the sky a blue-eyed stare, the wind hiding. I went by the Crinan Canal, the brightest gem among British canals, and spent the rest of the day exploring the plethora of prehistoric sites in this Kilmartin area: Dunadd, Baluachraig, Nether Largie, Templewood, Ri Cruin, etc.

Kilmartin to Oban was 33 miles, starting in full water-proofs again for a persistent drizzle. The knobbly nature of Mid Argyll, with the complex of sea lochs and views out to islands and mountains, made for a scenic run. The rain stopped. The sun put its brand on the day again. I guzzled wild raspberries. Oban, teeming, was a shock. More mail was waiting at the YH – and the key for the CIC Hut on Ben Nevis.

The *Canna* went to Kerrera in the morning and returned with a load of sheep. Once the boat was hosed down, we were off to Lismore, passing the *Caledonia* coming in, and a good view to the spread of the town crowned by the folly of McCaig's Tower. The ferry landed me half-way up Lismore at Achnacroish, so I had sorties south and back to look at sites (castles, graveyards, brochs, crosses) and then north for the wee ferry from Port Ramsay across to Appin. There was a statutory stop to photograph Castle Stalker with the background of the Kingairloch Corbetts across Loch Linnhe before, genuinely like a horse returning home, I hardly paused in cycling round Appin, over Ballachulish and up the lochside to Fort William, reaching Glen Nevis YH at 7.30 p.m. My cycling miles for linking the Four worked out at 827 miles in a desultory 40 days. I felt quite sad that the regular routine was broken. (I did not become greatly attached to my cycle, as one can, and sold it to my brother not long after.)

The morrow was, neatly, my fiftieth ascent of Ben Nevis. My first ascent had been on a cycling and wandering trip, aged 14, meeting thick cloud, and being fascinated on top to see the water in the turn-ups of my trousers had frozen: this in mid-summer. By the time I pulled up to the track I was sweating mightily and had a good break by the lochan. At 9 o'clock. people were beginning to dribble by. I was heading for the CIC Hut and a German lad had followed me round to the Allt a'Mhuillin only to see the cliffs and ask, 'Is this really the way up Ben Nevis?' He had no gear and no map and compass, however he was young and fit, the weather settled, so after a brew in the hut I sent him on to go up from the Arête. 'How will I then find my way down?' Easy.'Hundreds ascending will indicate the route for you.' The cliffs were busy; there were ropes on Centurion, Caligula and Bullroar when I eventually daundered up Ledge Route to gain the plateau and rim round to the summit, the anti-climax to 'Cycling the Four': Ben Nevis (1,334 m). Descending to the Arête I met someone who had started his day in the Lairig Leacach bothy and had traversed Grey Corries, Aonachs and Carn Mor Dearg. Now that was the way to finish something on the Ben! I wandered on to Carn Mor Dearg and back to descend Coire Leis to the CIC Hut. That felt the finish, especially when given an Alpine sunset and a night of breathless, blissful *silence*. I was home. I woke, cheery as Bach in the morning, knowing the game was won – and over.

'And the end of all our exploring

Will be to arrive where we started.' (T. S. Eliot)

THE RING OF TARF

> Success is getting what you want. Happiness
> is liking what you get.
>
> **H.J.Brown, jnr.**

OSLR 43

I'm sure others, like me, made early mountaineering ski days with ordinary *piste* equipment. My third day on skis, as described earlier, was doing Stuc a'Chroin, but what an effort that was with the wrong gear (and lacking real skills: it was all 'long traverses and sit-down turns'). The necessary gear was soon acquired, the biggest change being proper boots, bindings that allowed heel lift, and 'skins' that went on the soles to allow uphill progress – something that looked quite unbelievable when I first saw it. A brief explanation for the unconverted and a necessary preamble for what follows: these (artificial) skins were put on with the hairy 'lay' facing back so when the skis were slid forward there was no friction, but any tendency to run back down at the end of a stride was stopped by the skin rucking up (like stroking a cat the wrong way). There is naturally a limit to the angle of climbing and sometimes a slope may be too icy. There are actually ski crampons (*harscheisen*) which can then be attached to the skis. Once, on Beinn Mheadhoin in the Cairngorms, the slope was so icy and hard that my metal blades buckled.

This was gear for the ski-mountaineer; for touring in the Norwegian style light 'skinny' skis were used and various waxes applied to the soles for going uphill and to counter various snow surfaces. Changing waxes, or taking skins off and on, is a bit of a bane (cold fingers struggling in spindrift) but has been simplified over the years with skinny skis having 'fish-scale' soles instead, and skins are now stuck rather than buckled on. In good conditions both are equally suitable on the hills. However the summits are frequently too icy, the slopes of our hills often too steep, and the valley bottoms seldom have good snow cover for *langlauf* use.

Our trip from the Tilt involved two of us, one on skinny skis and the other on mountain skis. We ended the day more or less together and argued the pros and cons all evening. I reckon it was a draw but given nasty conditions (the normal in Scotland) the mountain skis have the edge – in more ways than the literal. Both types of touring can be enjoyed wherever there is snow. There are days when the Pentlands can provide ski-touring as good as anywhere, that is *langlauf* skiing, where travel on skis is sought rather than ascending peaks (Scottish or Alpine). In Norway everyone seemed to ski. Miles across high and lonely plateaux I found myself being passed by whole families – baby being pulled on a mini-*pulk* (sledge). Once or twice I met such families digging into the snow seemingly at random only to hear they had their 'summer houses' there and were trying to find the trap-door in the roof. They spend their weekends ski-touring from 'home'.

Ski-touring carries you loping over the landscape as fast as a man can run and even with a pack on your back you will travel further and faster than is possible on foot. It is the way to go winter backpacking – given the snow, the damnable decider.

Glen Tilt is very much the gateway to a whole range of Munros and Corbetts either side of the great fault line and is one of the classic through routes to Deeside. The road up is private, but a push bike can save miles of walking (legally a cycle is not a vehicle but 'an aid to pedestrianism'.) I have taken a party of boys cycling from Blair Atholl to Braemar; rough stuff some of it, but saner than the Lairig Ghru. At one point, the footpath was so deep-set that my pedal caught the bank and I went, as one of my mates poetically put it, 'arse over Tilt'. The bouncing left me on the bank and the bike in the river.

The geography is a bit strange, for high up the glen at the 1886 Belford Bridge the incoming Tarf Water is by far the bigger flow while the Tilt is much reduced on to its tiny Loch Tilt source. At one time these waters flowed north-eastwards to the Geldie and Dee but glaciers forced what is called a 'river capture'. So it is the Tarf Water that drains a huge area of desolation, with the Munros and Corbetts forming its rim, that makes for the special character of the Ring of Tarf. The whole drainage system takes up much of the OS Landranger 43 map. While walking on the rim is pleasurable, the hollow heart of the Tarf gives a lesson in purgatorial progress: wet, peaty, a roughness to destroy all rhythm and turning the miles longer. In spring it echoes to the calls of curlews and waders, in winter it is the home of ptarmigan and little else. I once had a summer view of this spaciousness spoilt by the thoughtless pitching of a bright orange tent in it: a visual carbuncle. Winter makes travel easier by freezing all the wet, and a good snow cover makes it one of the best areas for ski-touring. And there's the Tarf Hotel to welcome stravaigers in the heart of this 'Great White Silence'.

It was near the end of one February that Mike and I grabbed the chance for this ski-tour. We had a bitter cold night in my campervan in Blair Atholl and were off early up those miles of Glen Tilt to Gilbert's Bridge. Scores of deer were down below the snowline. On the hillside we found a whole ruined village which is not indicated on the map, though it shows many other odd ruins. Later, I could not find out anything from reading up the area. The bridge shown on the map on the stream which is the union of the Allt Diridh and the Allt Mhairc is a sturdy stone structure but small in span as the gorge leans in to make almost a natural bridge. The lonely bridge appeared as incongruous as a ship left in a field.

When there was snow enough we put on our skis: Mike had Norwegian touring skis and I had mountain skis. At the end of several hours we would arrive at our destination more or less at the same time. Neither was a convert to the other's style.

We both zig-zagged up Sron a'Chro at the maximum angle possible; concentrated work with our packs so when the gradient eased off and we rested the change of scene was dramatic. We had a dark trench below us, Glen Tilt, while all around lay a world of Polar whiteness. The humps of Beinn a'Ghlo looked like the ermine pelts of huge beasts – Polar bears perhaps. Beinn a'Ghlo's Braigh Coire Chruinn-bhalgain is surely the most lengthy Munro name, but the Corbetts can produce a whole clutch, with Sgurr Cos na Breachd-laoigh, Beinn Liath Mhor a'Ghuibhais Li, or Meallan Liath Coire Mhic Dhughaill; mercifully not on Beinn a'Ghlo.

We had chosen this way up so that we could use our skis as quickly as possible. Walkers generally go on up past Marble Lodge and up the Balaneasie ridge, or the stream before it. A stalker's path leads up from Forest Lodge. Our route had been the descent route when Queen Victoria, a modest Munroist, climbed Carn a'Chlamain. We had nearly three miles of rolling plateau around to the summit where we sat below the crest, out of the wind, to admire the Polar view. Everything in view was white.

The reward of uphill effort is the run down and we had three miles of that to step out of our bindings at the Tarf Bothy. Later we sat outside enjoying tea in the sun. The bothy was still in good state then, but later vandalism meant a big restoration in 2012. An AA hotel sign hung on a gable! There were actually beds (no mattresses) and we had a comfortable night snug in our sleeping bags. Mike had what was then a new idea in stoves, a Trangia, and keeping up his eastern interests, a Russian panoramic camera. A picture of the bothy that he took with it is pinned to my study door.

The photo was taken the next day after we had crossed the Tarf and bagged An Sgarsoch and Carn an Fhidhleir (*Eeler*), the two Munros that rim the Tarf on the north and beyond which lies the moat of the Feshie-Geldie rivers. Most ascents are made from the Dee-Geldie track. How gentle these summits are can be seen in An Sgarsoch at one time having a cattle/horse fair on its summit. Carn an Fhidhleir's summit is the meeting place of the old counties of Perth, Inverness and Aberdeen. A surface of ling, berry and moss below the snow makes them a treat for skiing. Which is why we were back at the bothy for lunch and floundering about still on skis, taking photographs. We drank plenty to counteract the fierce dehydration from sun on snow. Our fast descent led to a fox crossing our bows only about fifteen yards ahead, his lope turning to racing in a stride.

Conditions like this might not last overnight, so we had a crazy idea to add Beinn Dearg, traverse it, and overnight at the wee Allt Scheicheachan bothy in Glen Bruar. This we did: curving up by the Tarf, skiing across a frozen and hidden Loch Mhairc and steadily up the *red hill* which, for once, belied its name. (It is a vast carbuncle of pink granite breaking through the brown skin of ling.) We skied right to the summit.

From there we could look to familiar neighbours – Schiehallion the nearest. The fangs of Cruachan seemed to be gnawing a bloody sunset. The cold came pulsing in as day ebbed. We rasped a route down into the shadows of the west, eventually linking runnels among the ling to end at the door of the welcome bothy. Bliss is when the effort of the ascents is balanced by the pleasure of the descents. The aches of a ten-hour day were forgotten in huge eating and much drinking of tea. We were abed by 8.30 p.m. – and slept for ten hours.

We walked down by the ancient Minigaig track to Old Blair. A walk-out at the end of any tour, in any land, has a sorrow in it. Few winter rounds have been as satisfying however – or proved the value of skis so effectively. On foot in that deep snow coverage it would have taken two long days of struggle for the one done on ski. We had hard work, but pleasurable.

On another winter occasion some of us climbed Chalamain and a friend Jim and I (plus the dog) went on to add Dearg. This proved an epic flounder on foot in such mutinous weather. I had to carry the dog (thank goodness he was a small Sheltie and not an Alsatian) as he was balling up so badly he could not walk. We fled from a thunderstorm on Dearg and then ran out of daylight and fought bogs, drifts, blizzard and night down Gleann Diridh to reach Glen Tilt utterly exhausted, which only emphasised the gain to be had by using skis. Another classic example of skis' superiority occurred when Martin Moran was making his winter continuous round of the Munros. A group of us connected with Intermediate Technology accompanied Martin and his wife Joy up the outlying Munro of the Creag Meagaidh hills. Nick and Rick Crane were of the party and so were Alan Hinks and Chris Bonington. Chris had had his skis stolen overnight and in the deep snow conditions prevailing reached the summit of Carn Liath long after all the rest of us who were on skis. He also missed a marvellous descent run. Martin, on skis, circuited all the Munros. For years I'd try to make any ascent of any Munro on skis, but this became less and less as long, snowy winters seem to be a thing of the past. But they were all memorable escapades, winter snow aye the icing on the seasonable cake.

LAST RUN: COIRE NA CISTE

The swing in the wind,
In the drift of snow;
Dappled delight,
Sunshine below.

The song in the heart,
In the thrust of limb,
Weaving wonder –
Sharp as a hymn.

The joy of the schuss,
In the taste of fear,
Stolen seconds
With life made clear.

The sun in the loch –
So soon away!
Mountain mirrored
At end of day.

OF OTHER DAYS

To Knoydart With Billy

Some time ago I chanced on this tale that first appeared sixty-two years ago in the *Dollar Magazine*, the magazine produced by the school there since 1902 and which, in various guises, still continues today. I'm grateful to the magazine as my very first article appeared in its pages – not quite that long ago! The story is well worth re-telling. We all have had our fiascos, haven't we? And it is interesting to see what has changed, and what hasn't, of places we hold special.

A trio, identified only by nicknames, were seeking to renew some of their earlier hill enthusiasms, and decided the answer was to engage a garron to carry their gear and so make possible an ambitious visit to Knoydart. They would start at Strathan at the west end of Loch Arkaig, follow the Mam na Cloich Airde to Loch Nevis, then over by Glen Meadail to Inverie, and return by Barrisdale, Loch Hourn, Loch Quoich, Glen Kingie, to their cars parked at the Strathan start. My first thought was 'poor garron'. They had been promised 'a fine quiet pony'. The writer gave his friends the titles, Pony Man and Cook.

'The road from Achnarry (*sic*) runs along Loch Arkaig. The scenery is magnificent and the road surface easily the worst in Scotland. These 14 miles seemed to take ages, but at long last the car bounced around a corner and there was the shepherd's house and the single-room tin school, and a cattle float.' Billy was introduced at once,' indeed a fine quiet beast' who was just cropping the grass contentedly.

'A sheep fank and old shed, surrounded by a high fence, was handy for our first night, the tent erected with a view to those shapely peaks Streap and Sgurr nan Coireachan, towering above Glen Pean. The arranging of stores was made in the shed. We had four shaped waterproof bags for this purpose. It really looked as if we had twice as much as any garron could carry. Billy came into the shed to see what was going on and promptly started to eat a loaf of bread.

'Next morning mist was well down and we packed as a fine rain started, becoming quite heavy as the saddle was positioned and the bags arranged. On top were the small tent, cooking utensils, Billy's oats and the etceteras.

'The pass through Glen Dessarry to Loch Nevis is about 12 miles over the Mam na Cloich Airde: it rises from 100 to 1000 feet, then drops to sea level. In olden days cattle were driven through regularly, and how those drovers managed was beyond our understanding. It was a pleasant walk to the summit but there we struck very wet bog. In pouring rain we tried to pick a way through over firm ground, progressing slowly, when Billy suddenly got bogged right up to his houghs. It looked as if the load would have to come off, but with a tremendous effort and loud squelching Billy shot out. Billy also distinguished himself struggling over nasty rocks and a three-foot drop. The track appeared again, more or less level for a mile but to our dismay then climbing in steep zigzags, which took a long time.

'Then came a most horrible-looking descent which appeared impossible for a laden animal, but Billy very cleverly picked his way down the steepest and most slippery slopes without any trouble. We emerged from the mist, and there was Loch Nevis. It was now 7 p.m. and we had been walking since 10 a.m. with little food or rest. There was a half-ruined house at the head of the loch and our one thought was shelter and a meal. Then the blow came.

'A normally small stream crossing the track had become a raging torrent. We stood dejectedly in the pouring rain then, without a word, one of the party plunged in and crossed, soaked well above the waist. We need not have worried about Billy. He picked his way across carefully and charged up the bank, knocking over two of the party on the way. The semi-ruin came into sight and even in its dilapidated condition was a sight for sore eyes.

'The place is called Sourlies and for many years here lived a charming old couple, the McPhersons. No road of course and the nearest town is Mallaig from which, twice a week, weather permitting, chugs a motorboat with mail and the necessities of life. When John died Mrs McPherson had no way of contacting anyone and built a bonfire to make a smoke which eventually was seen. The Pony Man had stayed there and had asked John, 'Don't you find it very lonely sometimes?' The reply was "No, no, there is always something happening. If the tide is not coming in, it is going out."

'Billy had his oats in the stable which was in better condition than the house and had plenty of hay to munch or lie on. The party got a fire going, had a large meal and a large nightcap, and so to bed in rather damp sleeping bags. The next day was fine and warm. Billy was completely draped with drying clothes, only his face showing, but appeared quite happy and often stopped to munch extra-tasty grass. The floor of the valley here is a mass of sea pinks. Sgurr na Ciche, one of the shapeliest of mountains, towered in front as we followed the Carnoch River. The track started to climb steeply but we stopped often and lay in the sun while Billy cropped peacefully. At this point the Pony Man's shoe sole came off, so the Cook was given the halter and set off proudly. The garron climbed hard for about 50 paces, pushing one hard in the back, then would stop dead and was not to be persuaded to move till he was ready. The matter of the shoe, the views, delayed the rearguard and the Cook found himself alone on high and not too sure, the scenery awe-inspiring and drops from the narrow track considerable. He realised he knew more about primus stoves and frying pans than garrons.'

The track descended at an easier gradient, they forded the River Meadail and after walking through some trees came to a bridge. A large herd of Highland cattle, from small calves to a ferocious-looking bull were curious, so they hurried to cross. Billy proved uncooperative. 'We spoke nicely to him, coaxed him, took his load off, promised double rations but he would not budge.' However, the sight of a loaf of bread saw the pony wallop over to what proved a delightful camping spot.

Billy was securely tethered to a tree but in the middle of supper there was a clatter on the bridge. Billy was loose. There was a gate on the far side of the bridge so the garron turned back and headed off upstream, crossed, and set off full speed for home, followed by the herd of Highland cattle. So there they were 'with supplies for three humans and one pony for five days, plus deer saddle, a farrier's kit, tent, cooking gear, etc, and no road, no house for miles'. Cynically, someone raised his night-time dram, 'To Billy: a fine quiet beast'.

'Over breakfast a sheepdog entered the tent, followed by

its owner, a tall lean man. He, MacPhee, had walked over the day before the 24 miles from Strathan to Inverie to visit his brother, and was now heading back the same distance again: this an annual social call'. He assured them Billy would manage fine and the Strathan shepherd would catch him, or he himself would pick the pony up on his way. He also suggested some possible assistance; 'Mr Reddie, the factor at Inverie, is a very kind gentleman and you could ask him for help.' The shepherd then excused himself 'as he was not quite so young and it would be late before he arrived at Strathan. Off he started, as if on a two-mile walk, over what had taken us two days.'

So, if they could borrow a pony to shift their gear to Inverie, and if there was a boat calling on Wednesday, they could travel to Mallaig and train to Spean Bridge and somehow cover the 29 miles to Strathan where they hoped they would find the errant Billy. They set off for Inverie.

'Inverie is a delightful place on the shore of Loch Nevis. The estate is beautifully kept, well wooded right down to the loch, and masses of rhododendrons everywhere. Palms grow in the gardens, and fruit, vegetables and flowers resemble those grown in the far south. The shepherd was correct. The Reddies were very kind to us three disreputable-looking tramps. We had coffee then the factor got out his jeep and took us up the hill. In short time we were back, ready for a morning departure.'

During the night the wind blew up and the boat could not come in to the pier so they were taken out, with all their clobber, in a rowing boat. They caught a train shortly after reaching Mallaig and were at Spean Bridge by early afternoon. Hours were spent trying to hire transport. There was a dance at Achnacarry that night so they went there and fixed up that returning Strathan shepherds would take them back. Yes, Billy was there, 'a fine, quiet beast so he is . . .'

Only the shepherds forgot, it seemed, so two set off to hike it, the other, his one shoe tied up in string, maybe glad to be left behind. After five miles or so they met the shepherds heading east again for the sales at Fort William, and it seemed they had looked for the party but not found them (they had dossed down in a rat-filled barn). Nine miles on, the school was reached and there was the schoolmaster with his three pupils, making a garden. 'Grand day. Come in and have a cup of tea.'

At Strathan, sure enough, they found Billy in the sheep fank, contentedly grazing. They took several of what we'd now call 'selfies' and departed, with somewhat mixed feelings about their adventures with their 'fine, quiet pony'.

THE BEN NEVIS OBSERVATORY

> Ben Nevis is monarch of mountains,
> They crowned him long ago,
> On a throne of rocks, in a robe of clouds,
> With a diadem of snow.

Byron

If you ask any of the tens of thousands of visitors to Ben Nevis what the tumbled stones once were that now lie on the summit (along with trig pillar, cairn and emergency shelter), probably only one in a hundred will know that they are the remains of the Ben Nevis Observatory which was operational in the years 1883-1904.

The establishment of the Observatory was an adventure typical of days that saw the dawn of our technical world. Robert Louis Stevenson's father, Thomas, was an engineer and lighthouse-builder, and only too practically aware of weather. He was one of the people (Lord Kelvin was another) who pushed for an observatory. He proposed a whole series of mountain stations, so that comparative studies of changes in pressure, humidity and temperature could be made. Weather forecasting as such was very new, and it is ironic that the Ben Nevis Observatory had already closed when this suddenly became so important, with the development of the aeroplane.

The Scottish Meteorological Society decided on Ben Nevis as the site for the Observatory. Big but accessible, the Ben is 'interestingly' sited in the track of Atlantic storms. Stevenson drew up plans for the building in 1879, but with no money available nothing happened.

Enter Mr Clement L. Wragge. 'The Inclement Rag', as he was to be nicknamed, was a lively gentleman of some character, and from 1881 to 1883 he was a perambulating observatory himself, climbing the Ben daily all summer, leaving sea level at 4.40 a.m., being on the summit from nine to ten and getting back to sea level at 3.30 p.m. During the ascent and return he took readings at several interme-diate stations. He was paid expenses, but did the work voluntarily.

In June 1983 a centenary weekend was organised in Fort William by the Royal Meteorological Society (the successor of the 'Scottish'), and Wragge's route was repeated. Seventy people left the Distillery on the Great Glen road at 5 a.m., a unique event in itself, and ascended by the Livingstone Stone, the Lochan, Buchan's Well and other sites, where barometers and thermometers appeared and readings were taken (in earlier times horses could be taken as far as the loch). And it was somewhere just after that that I lost my new dog Storm.

As the angle steepened, I began to work my way up through the long line of meteorological enthusiasts (who were not all fit outdoor folk). Storm, usually at heel, became detached among all the legs. When I turned to speak to him, he wasn't there! I let everyone overtake. No Storm. I hurried right up the line to the front. No Storm. I began to question people. He'd been seen running up and down obviously searching for me, then heading down the hill. Our start had been the distillery which lay beside the busy, dangerous A82. If Storm wandered on to it ... When I arrived, gasping and legs quivering, there he was sitting beside the camper-van. For a moment he looked rather embarrassed, even worried. How would I react? Had he done the right thing? My hug was instant reassurance. Full marks, too, for his behaviour. When he couldn't find me he simply went back to the start, tracking across the moorland miles. Would humans in trouble have used as much gumption?

Driving north the evening before, I'd turned down Glen Orchy for a quiet spot for the night. At one place I had to brake hard; in the middle of the road were two fox cubs who at once disentangled themselves from their schoolboy wrestling to stand staring into the blaze of light. This was not something instinct or training had told them about. They shuffled round, advanced, retreated, obviously curious, but canny. The vixen suddenly materialised and calmly walked up to the van and squeezed past, with her cubs lolloping after. I breathed again and rejoiced that, for once, a human presence hadn't caused the usual fear and flight. I watched them in my wing mirror wander up and round a bend. Exquisite creatures.

But back to the Ben. The weather cleared off the summit for this invasion – the spirit of Wragge in evidence? It was in light of his findings (and a deal of experience since) that it had been decided that midsummer was a better time to celebrate the centenary than during the more typical wildness of autumn. After all, the mean temperature during the 21 years of Observatory life proved to be just below freezing. Were Ben Nevis a few hundred feet higher, it would have a glacier flowing from its summit.

The walk was preceded by a meeting the night before at which a series of speakers ranged over different aspects of mountain weather. Their predecessors in knickerbockers and with huge mercury barometers would surely have approved. What would they have thought, though, of the three million log entries from the Nevis Observatory going on to a computer system which will allow all sorts of analytical study previously thought impossible? Meteorology has come a long way.

One speaker talked about the Cairngorm Automatic Weather Station – automatic rather ironic, as the Ben Nevis Observatory was so expensive and complicated to operate because it had to be manned. Instruments could not be left outside as they iced up. There was no electronic or microchip wizardry allowing automatic recording. To take hourly readings, day and night, non-stop, over the years meant a considerable residential staff.

I remember vividly my first experience of the Cairngorm summit weather station. I was sheltering in the lee of the cairn, in a freezing fog, when there was a click, a hum, and out of an icy drum rose a battery of instruments. I recognised an anemometer (so it was nothing 'extra-terrestrial') and realised the gizmo was weather-recording. After a few minutes it clicked and with a hum descended into the drum again. Quite uncanny. Every half-hour data were relayed to Edinburgh, and the Glasgow Weather Centre, at the press of a button, could obtain a computer read-out to assist forecasting.

At the time of the 1983 Nevis gathering there was still a functional watertank fed by a spring only a few minutes' walk from the summit. My map had the bearing to find it noted in the margin. But it was eventually vandalised. Lead from it and the Observatory was rolled down into the glen and vanished on a lorry.

Even Wragge's dogged work did not spur the government of his day to do more than promise £100 a year towards running costs. It did show the value of an observatory, however, and a public appeal to establish one was launched early in 1883. Queen Victoria chipped in £50. [1] By the autumn, the building and path had been constructed, and 17th October saw the official opening. (Wragge was not present.)

The first Superintendent was a Mr Omond. One wonders if Wragge applied and was passed over as too much of an individualist. [2] He might have found it difficult to be confined in crowded quarters, but from all we read there seemed to be a friendly and harmonious atmosphere in the Observatory. The observers were, in many cases, self-funding enthusiasts or researchers (the shortage of money for running costs was always a problem). W. T. Kilgour's book, *Twenty Years on Ben Nevis* (1905, reprint 1985).[3] shows them tobogganing and playing ping-pong – on a table carved out of the snow – when conditions allowed. They also skied and went curling on the Half-Way Lochan. Royds, who became Scott's meteorologist, trained on the Ben, and *Discovery*'s cook worked there. Bruce, one of the Observatory staff, led the two *Scotia* Antarctic expeditions; two of his party had also worked on the Ben. A young physicist, Charles Wilson, followed up his research inspired by supersaturated atmospheric conditions on the Ben to win a Nobel Prize in due course.

They had more than their fair share of snow, and after a first winter of being constantly buried by it, there was some rebuilding, including a 'conning tower' exit 30 ft up. This remained clear even when the buildings were snowed over. In 1884 something like 4,000 visitors looked in, and a local hotelier erected a 'hotel' (Temperance, no alcohol) to cater for those wanting to see the sunrise from the top of Britain. It was run by two indomitable ladies right through into the years of the First World War.

Observers did a two-month stint on top of the Ben and then changed over with a colleague based in Fort William. A sea-level observatory had been set up in the town to allow comparative studies. The summit was the more popular posting. Information was relayed by telegraph; then, later by telephone. (Tourists using this for fatuous messages would no doubt be texting today.) Government funds of £250 per annum were allowed for the town observatory, but the £100 a year for the summit station never altered, and it was forced to close in 1904. (The Met. Council in England was receiving £15,300 annually.)

To Collie and early climbers the Observatory must have had the look of an early Alpine refuge. The gully down which rubbish was tipped was named Gardyloo Gully[4] and the bucket-emptier often had to be belayed in case of a cornice collapse or possibly being blown over the edge. Angus Rankin, who was Superintendent at the time of the closure, climbed *down* Tower Ridge in 1895. The first ascent was made by the three Hopkinsons in 1892 and the first winter ascent, 1894, was by Collie, Solly and Collier. In April 1897 one of the staff witnessed the first ascent of Tower Gully by an Alpine Club group of Hastings and the two Haskett-Smiths – one in the eye for the SMC, especially when they added Gardyloo Gully itself next day.

Omond, the first Superintendent, writing in *Nature*, made the presumed first use of the term 'Green Flash' for the sunset phenomenon (could that name have been inspired by the Jules Verne story *The Green Ray* ?) Those in the Observatory almost welcomed wild weather. All too often they endured day after day of clag. (December 1893 saw only 1.1 hours of sunshine). But in really bad conditions, crawling along a fixed line to the Stevenson screen could hardly have been fun. One natural history curiosity: summit stoats kept their ermine coats throughout the year.

Clutter on the summit is nothing new. An English vicar in 1789 noted there were 30 cairns on Nevis and various names and initials in bottles, etc. Keats was one of the many early visitors. He came up in 1818, just three years before he died in his mid-twenties. 'I am heartily glad it is done – it is almost like a fly climbing up a wainscot.' As he came up the tourist path this is no doubt poetic licence. Edward Burt, who was Wade's agent and surveyor, wrote fascinating *Letters from a Gentleman in the North of Scotland* which were published after the Forty-Five. He tells of a band of officers out all day from five in the morning who came back beaten by bogs and perpendicular rocks, thankful for a break in the clouds: '… if those vapours had continued, there would have been no means left for them to find their way down, and they must have perished with cold, wet, and hunger.'

Who was first up Ben Nevis we will never know. The Commissioners for the Forfeited Estates financed an ascent by the botanist James Robertson, one of the greatest hill wanderers of all time, in 1771, and in 1774 the Welsh geologist John Williams was likewise sent up. James Dickson was another early botanist visitor, climbing up with his brother-in-law Mungo Park. Professor Forbes made climbing history by cutting steps in snow on the mountain – with a tripod.

Quite a few Coast-to-Coast or Groats End Walks take in the top of Britain. The Naylors walking John o'Groats to Land's End in 1871 referred to Nevis as *'the Ben'* which I had always thought a recent friendly abbreviation. They failed because their guide became ill. This gentleman was 'mortified to have failed, for he had been up the hill 1,200 times' (questionable: a common enough exaggeration). Most of the popular hills such as Ben Lomond, Ben Nevis, Lochnagar, Ben Macdui and the Skye summits had regular guides to assist the Victorian visitor. While the Observatory came and went, one other proposed scheme never got off the ground: a funicular to the summit.

---

1 Queen Victoria's contribution today would be the equivalent of £10,000, £1,000 having become about £193,000 in that time. The cost of the initial Observatory building (it would later be expanded and improved) was £1,238 (£198,000) and the pony path £793 (£12,700). The shilling ticket for a pedestrian to use the path would be £8 today; to ascend by pony cost three shillings (£24), later five shillings.

2 Wragge had a somewhat up and down life thereafter. He was already married (and would have eight children) with his wife, Leonora Edith Florence d'Eresby Thornton. She took readings in Fort William at the same time he was doing so on the Ben. The year after the Observatory opened he went back to Australia and was involved in similar projects, becoming Government Meteorologist for Queensland in 1887. In 1897 he saw an observatory open on mainland Australia's highest mountain, Mt. Kosciuszko (2,230m, 7,316ft). Things went awry and he moved to New Zealand, having separated from his wife and living thereafter with a Theosophist, Louise, whom he'd met in India. Leonora refused a divorce and her excessive writ for maintenance meant he never returned to Australia. He founded the Wragge Institute and Museum (with tropical gardens) in Auckland and was 'something of a character' to the end. He died in 1922, aged 70. Wragge was the first to give names to hurricanes, not infrequently the names of politicians he had fallen out with.

3 Kilgour's book is still entertaining. There is a comprehensive, well-illustrated section on the Observatory in Crocket, K & Richardson, S:

Ben Nevis (SMT 2009), the history of climbing on the mountain. Also of interest: Roy, Marjory: *The Weathermen of Ben Nevis* (Royal Met. Soc. 2004).

4 A playful use of the words shouted out of tenement windows in Edinburgh's High Street in the 18th century to give warning of the emptying of chamber pots or slops. The name was also given to the boat that used to take Edinburgh's treated sewage sludge out to be deposited in the North Sea. I enjoyed a couple of good bird-watching trips on the MV *Gardyloo* with her friendly captain, the late Ronnie Leask, a keen hill man and wild land enthusiast.

CROSSING THE CAIRNGORMS, 1892

OSLR 36, 43

Those of us who go to the hills regularly over the New Year are usually fairly philosophical about what may be granted to us in the way of success, as the weather usually stotters about between the erratic and the diabolical. Yet we still go (and are beaten up by wind and weather as like as not) for it is all part of the game, as it has always been.

More than a century ago, a quartet from the Cairngorm Club recorded a typical Hogmanay escapade which is worth retelling. Their original ploy was to walk in one day from Nethy Bridge to Braemar via Cairn Gorm and Ben MacDhui, a good stiff hike in pleasant summer conditions, never mind in the meteorological gambling season. In those days, no tarred road ran in to Loch Morlich, the Glenmore Lodge referred to is the present Youth Hostel building, and between there and Derry Lodge there was just nothing of human habitation.

They were bold lads, McConnochie, Rose, Tough and Brown. McConnochie was a great Cairngorms guru and some of his books on the area are still in print. The names

Tough and Brown are forever linked by their notable climb on Lochnagar, but they climbed in Skye and many other places too. Their account of this outing, a typically vivid piece of writing by Willie Brown, appeared in the second volume of the *Scottish Mountaineering Club Journal*.

The party left Aberdeen on the afternoon of 31st December 1891 and reached Nethy Bridge at 8.40 p.m, the journey being made by train – which would be quite a challenge today. Even by car it is a fairly devious, demanding run. They decanted into a night of exceptional darkness, aggravating drizzle and wind, the road sopping and slushy, and made for the Abernethy Hotel where they were well-spoiled by Mr Grant and went to bed with the promise of a 4.45 a.m. call.

Not surprisingly, this failed to materialise on 1st January and it was the 'late hour' of 7 a.m. before they were off. Their intended early start had been planned to fit in a useful 11 miles of walking before breakfast at Glenmore Lodge, pre-booked for eight o'clock. As it was, that meal was taken at 11.45 a.m. as the going had been fairly demanding even then. They were walking on snow from the start, and took wrong turnings at Forest Lodge and above Rynettin. Huge soft snow drifts were encountered, often forcing deviations from the track across the snow-covered heathery slopes. There was no view but luckily no wind. From Rebhoan (Ryvoan) through the Thieves' Pass, conditions improved, and shortly after eleven they spied the reeking lum of Glenmore Lodge. Over 'breakfast' they decided their original ploy was hardly practicable, and thanks to the local keeper offering accommodation in his house ('in view of the peculiar circumstances of the case') they postponed the continuation till the morrow and went for a stroll to Rothiemurchus, near Loch an Eilean, instead.

That evening they were curious to see how their host and

his family would celebrate the New Year. Brown reported: 'The entertainment opened with a dance, and concluded with a Gaelic song, which was chiefly remarkable for its extraordinary length, and its melancholy air. The singer, however, appeared to think that it erred on the side of brevity, for he apologised for not being able to remember more'.

The new day brought back the wind and the hills were blotted out in cloud. Brown noted they 'all displayed a marked disinclination to part company with bed' and they only set off at 8.45 a.m., having an hour of floundering through the snowy forest (no ski road then!), for part of the way using the furrowed track left by a herd of deer. Deep drifts made uphill work hard till the ridge path was gained. There the ground was wind-blasted hard and clear to give 'capital conditions' for walking. They dutifully noted 'Aneroid, 2,000 ft; thermometer 37 degrees'. No respectable Victorian party would have omitted this ritual if they could help it; a pocket barometer remained a useful navigational aid until it was superseded by GPS. They were soon to be grateful for their aneroid.

At 3,000 ft the wind blew the thermometer from their grasp and it smashed on the ground. By then the cloud was down too and they 'suffered considerable pain and annoyance from the small fragments of ice which the wind tore from the ground and drove in a continuous stream across the hill' and from being 'thickly coated with frozen snow'. The summit of Cairn Gorm was difficult to find in the near white-out, though the aneroid indicated its near presence. When a ferocious gust briefly tore the clouds apart they saw it just 30 yards away. They had thrown themselves face down on the snow to avoid being blown away by one gust. They decided (delightful understatement) 'by unanimous consent only to make a short stay at the summit'. One of them still persisted in noting the barometric reading while the gale raged 'with an excess of fury words are powerless to describe'. There was also unanimous consent as to the impracticability of continuing to MacDhui. Let me give a quoted, but condensed, version of the next bit just to show how little some things change.

'Readers familiar with Cairngorm will remember crags overhang Loch Avon with Coire Raibert the only opening through which a descent to the loch can be made safely had the weather been clear and the wind less violent, but in consequence of the dense mist and the drifting snow, which limited our vision to half-a-dozen yards, it was deemed more expedient to make for the valley of Strath Nethy.

'Accordingly, led by McConnochie, whose encyclo- paedic knowledge of these hills is equal to any emergency, we began to move slowly in that direction, feeling our way with the greatest care, for this portion of the hill is bounded on the one side by the crags which guard the source of the Nethy, and on the other by an immense mass of rock known as the Eagle's Cliff. When 750 ft or thereby had been descended in this cautious manner, with numerous pauses to make sure that we were not approaching the edge of some precipice, a sudden rift in the mist revealed the jagged summit of Beinn Mheadhoin, struggling faintly through a mass of sunlit and storm-tossed vapour, while all around the gloom was still impenetrable and profound. The effect was simply indescribable, and impressed itself upon us none the less forcibly because it communicated the welcome tidings that we were approaching a position of safety.

'All cause for anxiety was now removed, for the descent from the point to the Saddle (the col dividing Strath Nethy from the Avon), and thence to Loch Avon itself, though abrupt, is perfectly simple, except when the ground is ice-bound. We found snow lying to the depth of several feet, and a good deal of scrambling and floundering took place before we reached the bottom. We arrived at the loch precisely at one o'clock.'

Loch Avon was frozen over, but not safe to walk on, so they had to flounder along the shoreline, at little more than a mile an hour, to reach the Shelter Stone – in Brown's words 'exhibiting the gymnastics of pedestrianism ... scrambling over rocks, plunging into and out of snow-drifts, balancing on slippery stones, and executing involuntary glissades – these were some of the feats which our tired muscles were called upon to perform'. Ptarmigan, unafraid, greeted their arrival at this howff and they climbed in for a cheerless lunch out of the incessant wind.

At 2.45 p.m. they were on the move again, a slow and difficult toil up on to the wind-blasted plateau of Loch Etchachan. The loch was frozen but left untested as the wind bullied them on, 'at a most exhilarating pace', for Coire Etchachan and the final descent.

'As we entered Glen Derry it soon became apparent that only a small portion of that dreary glen would be traversed in daylight. Suffice to say, after much drudgery and many stumbles, we reached Derry Lodge at 6.15 p.m. and after enjoying an hour's rest and a warm cup of tea set out again, greatly refreshed, to knock off the ten miles which still lay between us and Braemar. These were accomplished without adventure, and at 9.45 p.m. (exactly 13 hours from the start) we were shaking hands at Deebank over a very mad adventure. Next day we walked to Ballater (16 miles) and returned on the Monday by train to Aberdeen.'

One thing that struck me about this expedition, as originally planned, was its sheer scale – with an almost casual 11 miles to breakfast and an equally dismissed 10 mile walk out at the end. That was 21 miles on top of a dozen miles from Glenmore to Derry over Cairngorm, with over 1,000m of ascent. Even in its modified form, it still indicates – especially under the prevailing conditions of snow-cover and weather – a walking power and stamina we could hardly match today. The writer, lawyer William Brown, summed up their crossing as 'the most interesting and enjoyable winter ascent I have made among these magnificent mountains'.

This is no isolated example. To reach the SMC's Easter Meet the same year Willie Naismith and Gilbert Thomson walked to Inveroran by Loch Tulla from Dalwhinnie, via the summit of Ben Alder and a traverse of Rannoch Moor, a 41 mile tramp. They started at 3.30 a.m., off the Inverness night train, and arrived at 8 p.m., just in time for dinner.

They were bold lads, all right, all of them, with five-foot axes, tweeds and nailed boots, no crampons (and a railway system making it all possible). Let's hope a century hence we are still enjoying 'very mad adventures'.

A CUILLIN PIONEER

1993 was the centenary of the death of Sheriff Alexander Nicolson, who is remembered in the name of Skye's highest mountain. He was the first to climb Sgurr Alasdair, but that was only one of several outstanding discoveries by this largely forgotten pioneer, whom Ben Humble in his history of Skye climbing called 'the great explorer' (B.H.Humble: *The Cuillin of Skye*, Hale 1952 is a collector's item).

The first real explorer of the Cuillin was another remark-able figure, Professor James David Forbes, 'the wonder child of his generation,' who gained his Chair of Natural Philosophy (Physics) at Edinburgh University at the age of

23, and was to pioneer the science of glaciology. For two decades after his appointment Forbes went to mountains regularly, whether Alps, Pyrenees, or Skye. He and a local man first ascended Sgurr nan Gillean (1836) by what is now called the Tourist Route. Nine years later he made the first ascent of Bruach na Frithe and drew the first accurate map of the range. Most other early travellers had been Romantics, in the wake of Scott, Turner, Horatio McCulloch, etc., heading for Loch Coruisk with its wildly inaccurate reputation of being sunless and surrounded by unscalable precipices. It needed a Skye man to explore and extol the rich reality – Alexander Nicolson.

Nicolson was born in 1827 at Husabost in north-west Skye, where his father was a tacksman under Macleod of Macleod. He proved an able student but abandoned his original vocation of the church to try and earn a living as a writer. Journalism was then left for law and he became an advocate in 1860.

Nicolson was unlucky in life. Success, fame, wealth always eluded him, and while many men could have been made bitter in these circumstances, his nature kept him content enough. Perhaps he lacked the killer instinct, the greedy self-seeking, to soar as many of his peers did. He was known as a charmer, a singer, a wit, a rhymester, a big man of open features and warm heart, 'perhaps the most popular man of his time in Edinburgh'. Fun, rather than ambition, lay behind his Skye ploys, and the love of the place, for itself, rather as a scientific objective (as with Forbes) kept him returning whenever possible. His long romance with Sligachan was to be repeated a generation later by the climbing scientist, Norman Collie. Even when Nicolson's active days were over just being there was enough. He was one of the first to climb purely for fun, and to say so.

Sligachan greeted him (as it has done a few folk since) with a thunderstorm, but he evidently revelled in this: '... among the towering black mass of the Cuillin rolled and seethed a lurid array of lead-coloured clouds, grim and threatening'. His name cropped up continually in the Bible-thick Visitors' Book at Sligachan, a treasure I browsed through by the hour as a youngster.

Many of Nicolson's doings were described in *Good Words*, a magazine edited by Dr Norman Macleod, who was Queen Victoria's chaplain, a famous preacher and influential churchman. *Good Words* was an immensely popular publication, with a circulation which would be the envy of most outdoor magazines today, its rather unfortunate title hiding plenty stories of outdoor activities. It is a pity Nicolson never produced a Skye book for he wrote good clean prose. Perhaps that innate talent for missing the boat applied again. He was no Skye ostrich though; he foresaw the vast tourist potential of the island and lived long enough to see it happen. As early as 1872 he was suggesting a bridge at Kyle might not be a bad idea. Camasunary he envisaged would have its *Grand Hôtel de Blaveinn*. Curiously, the original building there was a Victorian 'establishment for reforming drunkards'.

Thinking of books, the first, the SMC guidebook, was to come in 1907, though it was to be overshadowed by A. P. Abraham's *Rock-Climbing in Skye* of 1908. The Abraham brothers climbed all the known routes and made several notable first ascents to produce this classic. Their superb photos were all taken with whole-plate cameras. They were early motorists. Such were the changes. Nicolson had none of these aids – not even Munro's Tables.

Few briefs came Nicolson's way, and some law reporting, lecturing and general writing barely kept him going till he was appointed Sheriff-substitute of Kirkcudbright (1872) and later of Greenock (1885). Before going to Kirkcudbright he had been offered, and had turned down, the Chair of Celtic Studies at Edinburgh University, which would have appeared the perfect place for his talents: he was a notable Gaelic scholar, with a delight in Gaelic poetry and song. Plenty of the Sligachan Visitors' Book entries are in Gaelic. He retired to Edinburgh and died there in January 1893, aged just 66.

His first real mountain visit to the Cuillin was in 1865, at the age of 38, and if the weather was wild, well, he could wait, warning the impatient: 'If they are in a hurry, Skye and its clouds (and its inhabitants) are in none, and the Cuillin will unveil their majestic heads in good time and no sooner. To see them is worth a week's waiting – to see the black peaks start out like living creatures, high above the clouds which career up the cleft ridges, now hiding and now revealing their awful faces ...' For Nicolson it was all 'life and music'.

Skye saw 'few strangers except yachtsmen, bagmen and a stray geologist', yet locals (shepherds and keepers) obviously had a peripheral knowledge and were occasionally enlisted to guide visitors. When Nicolson climbed Sgurr nan Gillean in 1865, MacIntyre, the Sligachan keeper, went with him, just as MacIntyre *père* had gone with Forbes in 1836, and they went up by the Tourist Route. But the character of the man then appears: instead of descending the same way, he persuaded his companion to try a new traverse of the mountain.

So they made the first descent of the West Ridge until they came up against the late lamented gendarme and, perforce, made a 'vermicular descent' down a chimney to the screes of Coir'a' Bhasteir, a route now known as Nicolson's Chimney and still regularly used as a way up the peak. Nicolson returned to climb up the West Ridge shortly after. He was the first to comment on the super-adhesive qualities of gabbro.

111

After descending Nicolson's Chimney our explorer traversed under the Tooth and up Bruach na Frithe, a day which obviously left him well satisfied and led to many similar ventures. When Knight climbed his eponymous peak on Gillean's Pinnacle Ridge he wrote to tell Nicolson of his climb. Some years later Nicolson and Gibson were to find Knight's card in a bottle on its summit. Nicolson became a Vice-President of the Scottish Mountaineering Club and was a lifelong friend of some of its members. He didn't hesitate to wander alone if shepherd or friend was unavailable, nor did he hesitate to bivvy on the Cuillin, lying wrapped in his plaid and eating cold fare and water. He wrote lyrical descriptions of his nights out and how 'the rich gloaming still lingers tenderly in the north-west till bars of yellow light are seen in the east heralding the dawn'.

One of his outings, as unconventional and tough as any today, was largely done at night and is worth recalling. Almost incidentally it included the first ascent of that elusive and tricky Munro, Sgurr Dubh Mor. This was in September 1874. Nicolson and a friend had been visiting an artist at Loch Coruisk, so it was 4 p.m. when they set off up this unknown hill, which was bold, rather than rash, given Nicolson's unrivalled experience of the Cuillin, a steady barometer and the promise of a full moon.

They went up An Garbh Coire, between Sgurr Dubh and Gars-bheinn, a coire choked with a mass of huge boulders and giving difficult passage. Once, coming down the coire, I was glad to shelter, quite dry, in its subterranean depths during a thunderstorm – as did Nicolson on this ascent, for a less worrying shower of rain. Then, as now, route-finding was intricate and the summit was reached at sunset (7 p.m.) and the descent was started in the gloaming, again, choosing deliberately to head into unknown territory down into Coir'an

Lochain, still rarely visited and from where an ascent of Sgurr Dubh is specifically not recommended by guidebooks.

They soon ran into trouble. Halfway down a steep wall barred progress and Nicolson brought into play his secret weapon – his plaid. He was lowered down, and backed against the wall so his lighter companion could hang down to stand on his shoulders. They fought down in shadowed blackness for two-and-a-half hours, finishing with a water-spraying gully, their fingertips shredded and mightily relieved to be down safe and sound into the moonlit valley bottom. The plaid could be put away. Nicolson described this item of clothing and its usefulness: with a belt it could be made into a dress for a man, serve as bedclothes, as a bag, as a sail for a boat, a rope for rock climbing, a curtain, an awning, a carpet, a hammock – and it had one superiority, in that 'there's room in it for twa'.

Their adventure was not yet over. Nicolson tried to take a new short cut over Druim nam Ramh to Harta Coire and Glen Sligachan. It didn't 'go' – the moon disappeared again – so they had to descend and go along to the other end of Loch Coruisk for the usual crossing of Druim Hain. Blaven, which Nicolson considered the finest hill in Skye, loomed in the east. They reached the Sligachan Hotel at 3 a.m.

A year earlier (1873) Nicolson had made the ascent of the peak which would be named after him. At that time everything thereabouts was lumped together as Sgurr Sgumain, the name now used for the lower, seaward subsidiary crest. He had wandered up from Glen Brittle on a wild, wet day and had reached Lochan Coire Lagan when the driving cloud cleared briefly to reveal a monster peak overhead, 'one of the wildest objects I had ever seen'. He was back next day with Macrae, a local shepherd and able hillman.

The fine day began with an ascent of Sgurr na Banachdich – he'd recently made its first recorded ascent – from which they traversed the by no means straightforward ridge to Sgurr Dearg on what may also have been a first ascent. Bypassing the Inaccessible Pinnacle he wrote: 'it might be possible with ropes and grappling irons . . . but hardly seems worth the trouble'. What a pity he did not take the trouble, but his priority was exploration, movement, the 'leaping from rock to rock' and not any siege of a single problem. The Pilkington brothers in 1880 proved his opinion as to its feasibility. His was the first close encounter of the 'In Pinn' by a real climber. Everything that day was new.

Nicolson looked across the coire to his objective and at once spotted the single line of weakness, the Great Stone Shoot as we now know it (even though, today, it has largely shot its boulders). Right of the huge gully two other great exploratory routes were to go up: Collie's Climb in 1896 (Collie, Howell, Naismith) and Abrahams' Climb in 1907. But Nicolson was before them all, recording his accomplishment with an understatement worthy of Tom Patey: 'I have seen worse places'.

The early Seventies saw a rapid rise in ascents being made from Sligachan. Faster and faster times were recorded in the Visitors' Book and our gentle giant tartly made the following entry in 1872: 'Spent four nights here with great satisfaction. Climbed Sgurr nan Gillean . . . in what precise space of time it matters not to anyone else, especially to Brown, Jones and Robinson. Supposing I should say "one hour and fortynine and a half minutes," they might stare, but they might also say, not inaccurately, "Walker! The view from the top was not so fine as I have seen there before, being limited by atmospheric conditions to a radius of about a dozen yards".' (*Walker!* was a Victorian exclamation signifying incredulity).

Nicolson had his hard core too. He could come out with comments like: 'The loss of life is a small thing compared with the full and free exercise of our powers and the cultivation of a bold adventurous spirit; and any nation which has ceased to think so is on the fair road to decay . . .'

Nicolson travelled extensively. He once listed some of the other islands he knew and compared them with Skye: Arran – more delightful; Islay – fairest of all; Mull – beauty and grandeur, more green and woody; Jura – queenly, but lacking variety; Tiree – too flat yet many charms; Staffa and Iona – a sense of wonder; Barra – rough and rocky; Lewis – boggy; Harris – almost like Skye in mountain grandeur; Skye – Queen of them all. And who would argue with such a regal judgment, given by the man who could rightly be regarded as the Cuillins' Prince of the Peaks?

WADE AND CAULFEILD, ROAD BUILDERS TO THE NATION

If you'd seen these roads before they were made,
You'd lift up your hands and bless General Wade.

Toby Caulfeild (attrib.)

Several times recently when people have been discussing the West Highland Way I've heard 'Wade's road over the Devil's Staircase' (*sic*) mentioned, with the lines above being quoted. Wade has a lot to answer for, but, before some readers start reaching for their pens or claymores, let me indicate that the Devil's Staircase is NOT a Wade road; nor are many others which on maps have 'Wade Road' written against them.

The Devil's Staircase is a Caulfeild road – and note the spelling of Caulfeild. Even Inverness, who at least have named a street after him, manage to spell it wrongly. I note this with feeling, for in my first book I had it wrong and when this was pointed out I checked a dozen source books and found half of them were wrong too. Caulfeild was Irish – there are still Caulfeilds there. So was Wade. Caulfeild succeeded his boss Wade and would build almost three times his road mileage but somehow Wade receives all the credit.

After the abortive Jacobite Risings of 1715 and 1719 various measures were taken to prevent a recurrence. In 1725 General Wade, C-in-C North Britain, who had already made a thorough survey of the Highlands, began the construction of roads and forts and barracks (like Ruthven on Strathspey) as part of his vision of controlling the clans.

It took just three summers to link Dunkeld and Inverness more or less on the line of our notorious A9 road. About two miles north of Dalnacardoch, Wade's headquarters for the A9 job, standing off the south-bound lane, is Wade's Stone, a 7-foot monolith, dated 1729.[1]

Wade's most famous landmark is surely the beautiful bridge he built over the Tay at Aberfeldy, which was half-way along the Crieff-Dalnacardoch road he also built. Crieff was the great cattle tryst through those droving years, but the Jacobite unrest saw it shifted to Falkirk and many beasts were marched all the way to London's Smithfield.

In 1725 Wade raised the Black Watch at Aberfeldy, some 500 men of Clans Campbell, Grant, Fraser and Munro who were 'loyal' to the Crown. They formed a sort of Highland constabulary: disarming the clans, preventing cattle reiving, guiding Sassenach forces and so on. They were drafted in to build the roads. He referred to them as his 'Highwaymen' and they received extra pay, with plenty of beer and beef; there were some wild parties when any stage was completed, with beasts roasted whole.

Before Wade went south to another post (and promotion to Field-marshal) he had constructed about 240 miles of road and twenty-eight bridges, quite a feat in just six years. Between the lines I think Wade comes over as quite a decent bloke. He was still in the field in 1745 when that Rising broke out and by an ironic twist of fate it was Prince Charlie's army that was the first to cross the Corrieyairack, Wade's most spectacular creation, linking Fort Augustus with the A9 route. Rising to nearly 2,000 feet, it was challenging, if direct, and was used until Thomas Telford built the road we still use along by Loch Laggan and Roy Bridge.

The other major Wade road linked Fort William and Inverness, keeping east of the Great Glen lochs. The first shots in the 1745 Rising were fired where this road crossed the Spean at High Bridge. Wade was in England then. Cope's feeble efforts and ignominious defeat at Prestonpans led him to be court-martialled, Field-marshal Wade presiding.

Wade's bridge at Aberfeldy was designed by William Adam, the father of famous architect sons, and it was intended as a showpiece. Only Dorothy Wordsworth seems to have thought the Aberfeldy bridge ugly. Most of his bridges are simpler and functional rather than beautiful, but my own favourite, Garva Bridge on the Corrieyairack, is simple, functional *and* beautiful.

Just along from the Aberfeldy bridge a statue of Black Watch soldier commemorates the raising of the regiment, but the figure is supposed to be the likeness of one particular man. In 1740 a thousand men were mustered near Aberfeldy and marched to London where they were reviewed by Wade. The Government had secretly decided to send them abroad despite promises that they would serve only in Scotland; when this became known there were angry meetings and desertions. When the deserters were caught, three were shot, *pour encourager les autres,* and the rest drafted into regiments serving abroad. One of those shot is portrayed in the monument at Aberfeldy.

At Weem outside Aberfeldy, the hotel bears a picture of Wade like an inn sign. He was based here at one time, and it, and many of his bases, were made into stage houses, often called 'King's Houses,' which is why that name survives in several places today.

Caulfeild was Wade's able assistant and in 1732 he was made Inspector of Roads. He saw active service in the '45 and two years later became deputy to absentee Cumberland as Governor of Inverness Castle. His work on roads continued till his death in 1767 – about 700 miles in all. His main routes were in two areas. The longest began in Angus and went by Braemar and Cockbridge to Fort George with a continuation from Easter Ross through to Poolewe; so when you hear the road from Cockbridge to Tomintoul is blocked by snow, blame Caulfeild! He also developed a whole system of roads from central Scotland into Argyll, including one over Rannoch Moor, the Devil's Staircase route to Fort William, and the Rest and be Thankful road to Inveraray and Loch Fyne.

The military handed the roads over to the civil authorities in 1785 and the whole system was soon in disrepair. In 1803 Parliament set up a Commission for Highland Roads and Bridges which appointed one Thomas Telford as engineer – but that is another story. A stone on top of the Rest and Be Thankful commemorates the repairing of Caulfeild's original road. The line wends up below the current sweep of the A83, but has recently been brought back into service as a periodic diversion when landslips have closed the upper road, while it has long been a popular challenge for classic car rallies.

We began with a quote about Wade, so perhaps we can end with another, a stanza which is part of Britain's national anthem and enshrines Wade's name. It was first sung at the Drury Lane Theatre in 1745. Ironically, the tune could have Jacobite origins! The audience pleaded:

> God grant that Marshal Wade
> May by thy mighty aid
> Victory bring.
> May he sedition hush,
> And like a torrent rush
> Rebellious Scots to crush –
> God save the King.

When you pech over the Devil's Staircase on the West Highland Way you can bless Caulfeild, not Wade, and ponder on the ghost-haunted historic route you follow. Rest, and be thankful you're not a redcoat marching up that hill in full gear, and that there's still a King's House to wet the whistle.

---

1 Wade's Stone was moved with the dualling of the A9 and now stands forlorn and sunk to half its height off the southbound carriageway near layby 70. The story goes that Wade, a very tall man, reached up and left a guinea on top of the stone – which was still there a year later. Coins are sometimes still to be found on the stone, but not, alas, guineas.

Wade's Roads were as follows:

Fort William to Fort Augustus	30 miles	1725
Fort Augustus to Inverness	31 miles	1726
Inverness to Dunkeld	101 miles	1727-9
Crieff to Dalnacardoch	44 miles	1730-31
Dalwhinnie to Fort Augustus, over Corrieyairack	31 miles	1732
Cat Lodge to Ruthven Barracks	8 miles	date uncertain

DISTURBING HINDS

One bark.
The piston heads shoot up
To periscope the hill.

They kneel up,
Grudgingly,
Gout-minded,
Try a few steps.

An old bitch gives a snort.

The righteous congregation
Of successionist pride runs –
High-headed,
Panic hidden in upturned noses,
Presbyterian goosestep.

They pause on a ridge
For a last look
That leaves no doubt
About what they think of us;

Carry their caudal contempt
Out of sight.

YOUTHFUL ESCAPADES

The School

By way of introduction to this section, I feel it may be useful to provide a brief word on the unusual school about which I have often written, partly because through those years (the Sixties) I was almost continuously active with school enterprises, and because so many ventures then were well recorded.

Braehead Junior Secondary School in Buckhaven (*Buckhynd*) was opened in the building abandoned when the area's new High School was built, a necessity to take up the post-war 'bulge' in the population. When that had passed, and mining was in decline, the school was closed (1971). Perhaps knowing its life would only be about a dozen years, the school was given more room to experiment under the visionary headmaster, R. F. Mackenzie, and a dedicated staff who believed in inspiring their charges. Every Christmas for instance there was a concert which involved music, art, English and technical departments in a production that won the repeated admiration of a *Times* reviewer. At the heart of the school was the belief in the kids which led to their self-belief. When I often had visitors wanting to hear about our activities in the wilds I would send two or three boys or girls to the school's flat, to provide the visitor with coffee and to let them do the talking. To enjoy canoeing the school made the canoes, to ski we bought Glenmore Lodge's replaced stock at a nominal £1 a set, we badgered charities and trusts to be the first state school to use computers, to have a school bus, to build up camping and climbing equipment. Life was hectic but not undisciplined as sometimes thought. One didn't take the controls of a glider high over the Lomonds or do the things described here, and in *Walking the Song*, without both discipline and zeal. My ultimate riposte to outside criticism was to point out that at the end of the school's existence there was not one pupil on probation, in an area of so-called deprivation. Life was just too interesting for that. So sad that today, in this more affluent society, the deprivation is in our schools. Much of what we did would not only be missing, it would be forbidden. All the more praise then for the dedicated who labour to inspire today and the irrepressible life that finds its outlet in sport and a whole range of cultural spheres – the very areas which suffer worst from ill-conceived economic cuts. Profit ever comes from investment; Braehead demonstrated that simple equation.

TACKLING THE CUILLIN

> Risk was the salt, but he or she would be a stupid cook
> who thought the more there is the better.
>
> **Dorothy Pilley** (on her Skye climbing)

Skye is anchored in the West and we are warned that West often deserves to be spelled without the 's'. There are many stories about Skye's fickle weather. So many Cuillin Traverses are wiped out by rain, usually pushed along by wind, though (surprisingly) more Traverses fail because of ambushing heat. If it's vile, nobody sets out to try, whereas the heat catches out unprepared optimists.

I was once in the bar at Sligachan one November when there were only two locals propping up the bar, and myself sitting nearby, so I couldn't help hearing their conversation. The first man, looking at the black-night rain spattering the windows, shook his head and said 'Donald, I'm thinking it has never stopped raining since June,' to which came the considered reply after his companion took a puff at his pipe, 'Aye, just so. Which June would that be now?' There's one about a Skye lad asked by a despondent tourist if it ever stopped raining on the island, and was told that that was rather an unfair question: 'After all, I am only twelve.'

I had two attempts at traversing the Cuillin washed out. The first (1963), with three good pupils, started at the Sgurr nan Gillean end, coped with some of the main difficulties, only to be washed away after Bidein Druim nan Ramh. On the second (1964), with a former pupil and a Cambridge University student friend, we gave up after abseiling off the In Pinn. Dr Johnson of course only went to Skye once. 'A walk upon ploughed fields in England is a dance upon carpets, compared to the toilsome drudgery of wandering in Skie [Skye]'. But I would have it third time lucky.

Having recently met, quite by chance, one of the participants in our eventually successful Cuillin Traverse trip, that escapade dominated our reminiscing. Later I dug out my log book of what I wrote at the time and what follows is largely from that source. Much water has flowed over the Ridge since 1967 and the Cuillin Traverse, while still a brilliant escapade, is no longer the notable achievement of those long-ago days. It keeps its aura, however: W. H. Murray, no less, called it 'the longest and grandest day's rock-climbing in Scotland – or elsewhere'. Many do the traverse in summer these days, and there have been notable winter successes (despite the paucity of suitable conditions). The current 'record' for the Ridge is 2 hours, 59 minutes, 22 seconds (by Finlay Wild in 2013 – notes at the end). Now that is something.

Our Traverse was relatively slow but the priorities were to complete, and to enjoy the experience. The preparation mentally was as important as the technical. The Traverse was in the boys' minds for a year and they dedicated time and effort to the dream. They had climbed routes far harder than any met on the Traverse, abseiled as a matter of course, had practised moving roped wherever possible, and were fit and sure-footed. They would not have been chosen otherwise. They had relished all these things in Rum a year before, traversing Rum's Cuillin, climbing new routes, handling ropes over and over.

Another matter which was unusual was that it was very much a team effort – like our Mamores traverse, intentionally so. One or two in the group were equally capable but were happy just to act as support. They were largely unaware of all this of course; they weren't analytical or questioning, just all part of a team, of Braehead. They were taught to *think*. Forget rules on mountains. Mountains can always come up with what is not covered by rules. My constant preaching was 'Think! Think! Think!' At every moment, in every situation, there was a best procedure. Think. Find it.

For several years in a row we had camps in May/June at the head of Glen Sligachan by Loch an Athain (just over the Dubh Lochain watershed so really Strath na Creitheach). I used to compare climbing a Cuillin peak from there to a Himalayan effort. Our long bus ride from Fife to Sligachan was the equivalent of flying out to Nepal, the many tramps up and down from Sligachan to get established the equivalent of the march in to a remote base camp, and so on for an ultimate team success. The boys played all the parts: load-carrying, cooking meals, backing up for the successful outcome. Over our various visits we had had a ration of heatwaves and washouts; Skye never does weather by halves. The school newspaper once reported 'We had a super trip to Skye. We climbed every Munro in the Cairngorms.' Logical: after three days of deluge we flitted.

At our remote base we twice *saw* cuckoos, never mind hearing them, would listen to sandpipers and skylarks, golden plovers and a resident stonechat. We seldom ever saw other people (changed days).

On the whole we were more blessed than cursed with Cuillin weather. Many memories of super-heat. No other range in Scotland can keep a visitor all day among naked rocks absorbing and reflecting the sun. You grill. There are few places high up where water will be found during a heatwave. Carrying water is burdensome, climbing ropes are heavy, the sun quite merciless. In heatwaves Traverse attempts often fizzle (griddle) out.

The boys knew their history. The Ridge was first traversed by McLaren and Shadbolt in 1911, thereby ending the dreams of many famous Alpine climbers hoping to be first. T. H. Somervell of Everest fame did the first solo Traverse in 1920. In 1939 Charleson and Ford added Blaven as well, and, remarkably, in 1965 it was done in winter conditions by a very strong party: Tom Patey, Hamish McInnes, Brian Robertson and David Crabb, a two-day feat for a unique British challenge. (A note at the end collates some other statistics about Cuillin Ridge days.)

We had fun with the logistics, which felt quite Himalayan too. How many loaves of bread are two adults and eleven hungry boys going to eat in nine days? (answer, c.50). How much paraffin did we need for our cooking on primus stoves? How many tents, ropes, slings, krabs, etc., etc.? My log noted 2 stones weight (over 12kg) of sugar were carried to base. A doctor friend Leon and his lad James joined the Braehead contingent. With a support party at the start and food and water left on the ridge and all the different teams' day requirements, the campsite the day before the start looked like a grocery store that had been bombed.

We did a certain amount of training on Blaven, working out various routes up on our west side cliffs and enjoying the Blaven-Clach Ghlas traverse. A couple of memories come back. One lad, Danny, failing to get off the ground to start one climb, yelling up, 'Give me some slack. I want to take a run at it.' High on Blaven, we noticed a great to-do of gulls at the tents, and on our return, found the monolithic hunk of Cheddar, left in the burn to survive the heat, had disappeared. I'd been 'a bit gullible' someone suggested.

On our 'day-before' (yet another scorcher) I took Billy and Steve up a route on Blaven while Leon and Tom took several others over to Loch Coruisk and on up to leave water and food on the ridge for our attempt. The heat was too much for most of them so only Tom, Stuart and Eric made the col below An Stac. They hove into view at supper time yelling for tea, despite lots of drinks all day – and a swim in Loch Coruisk.

I've never quite understood why the Ridge is taken as being from Gars-bheinn to Sgurr nan Gillean, starting on the genuine last bump, ending on the last Munro but with other bumps beyond on to Sgurr na h-Uamha. Logically the Ridge is Gars-bheinn to Sgurr na h-Uamha. And that is what we would do. The Traverse is about ten miles, up and down 10,000 ft over about 38 bumps, most involving some rock-climbing, and the least giving sensational ridge-walking or scrambling. Sgurr Alasdair, the highest peak, is 3,251 ft and the ridge never drops below 2,500 ft.

If I've dwelt long on the prelims this, I hope, indicates their importance for *any* expedition. It is the leader's most persistent responsibility and worry. My log on the last night noted, 'logistics seem to be all right. Now it is up to the weather.' When I picked up a weather forecast I let out a whoop of glee: 'The whole of Britain is enjoying a heatwave and this will continue unchanged for several more days.'

The next day then, Leon, James, Stuart and Bill set off for the hard toil up Harta Corrie and Lota Corrie to the Basteir Tooth, to leave vital stove, water and foodstuffs at its foot. We hoped they would make it. We would not know until we got there – if we did. Tom, Bill, Steve and I set off for Gars-bheinn, the starting peak of the Traverse, with Hugh and Mitch the chosen 'Sherpas' who were there to be used as load carriers and so 'rest' us. Gars-bheinn is 2,934 ft but it took most of the day to reach it. We poured sweat all the way up. There were midges on top! At the highest water we stopped to cook a last proper meal. We also found a deep pool hidden in a rocky cleft, so sticky clothes were soon off for an icy dip. Torsos were white in contrast to the faces and arms burnt to mahogany in the sun. Shirts were dipped in the water before being put on – and were dry before reaching the crest.

This was at six in the evening and by eight we had levelled a platform of stones just below the top of Gars-bheinn. I think we were too excited to sleep much, except Hugh who snored away happily. The slope ran straight down to the sea with a soft, sweeping view to the Hebrides and Rum. From our eyrie, we heard the faint chug of a boat, the laughter of gulls and a cuckoo – all far, far below. Our bivouac nested among the spires of the Cuillin: peak after peak, rosy in sunset, never untouched by northern glow and later moon-washed. This overwhelming experience of beauty would alone have justified the effort. At 23.30 the alarm went off. Porridge and tea took the stiffness out of us. We stood on Gars-bheinn at midnight. Ten minutes later we were off.

Times I noted thereafter: An Caisteal – Dubhs col 02.30 (break there), Alasdair 04.00, Sgurr Dearg 07.10, Bealach na Lice 14.15 (rest till 16.10), Gillean 17.45, Uamha 19.05, so Gars-bheinn to Gillean was 17 hours, 35 minutes, to Uamha, 18 hours, 55 minutes.

The first few peaks, though long and stony, were straight scrambling and passed in a happy daze. It was just like setting out on an Alpine climb; the breathless quiet of night, the eerie half-light, the crunch of boots on stone, the serrated peaks all about us, the same feeling of unreality, the orange moon hidden in a glow of haze. Oigh Sgeir light-house winked. The stars thickened.

When it became too dark for the ridge's main difficulty just ahead we stopped for another meal. We drank all we could hold from the last natural water we were to see for 12 hours, on the flank of the Dubhs. The Sherpas settled on all six sleeping bags and went to sleep. In the first gleam of day we stole away.

The Sherpas were to have their own private escapade. The first thing we heard on return to base was that Mitch was missing, which when we heard the story, and even allowing for Mitch's talented thickness, left us wondering just how thick you can be. Nor did Hugh get off without comment from me and from the rest of the party. They both failed to 'think,' that first rule of expeditions – as they knew.

A couple of hours after leaving them we yelled across the corrie from Sgurr Alasdair to their bivvy, marked by an orange flysheet from a Vango tent. They were too sound asleep to hear. All they in fact had to do was follow a stream from there to the sea and then a cairned path over the ridge to camp, a route Hugh had already done three times. But Mitch stopped for the toilet and Hugh went on – and on – and back to camp, expecting Mitch to be in any minute. He did not arrive. So while we were on the ridge a minor fiasco was going on with the Sherpas. They all turned up in the end but it was a bit embarrassing. That is another story. Back to the Ridge.

Ahead lay the Thearlaich-Dubh Gap, a great rift across the ridge, unavoidable and a serious climbing problem. The rope came out for the climb to it, then, once fully light, one by one, we abseiled the 40 ft into the gash. The other side rears up for 80 ft to give what one of the boys described as 'a bit of a puff' – one of the few unavoidable climbs on the Traverse. The sun was streaming over mainland peaks which rose from a sea of cloud. We made the traditional detour to climb Sgurr Alasdair, the highest peak of the Cuillin (four years later another gang would be there to see Braehead's dog mascot Kitchy complete his Munros – the first dog to do so), then it was more serious with exciting situations crowding after each other, every step along rooftops hung above walls falling far and straight to the flanking corries. Knowing the twists and turns as I did we kept up a good steady rhythm. We used Collie's Ledge to access Sgurr Mhic Choinnich, one of the most exposed perches, and on to the foot of An Stac where Tom retrieved his cache of food and water.

An Stac is another airy climb, straight up several hundred feet of loose ridge, and from the top of it points the famous Inaccessible Pinnacle. Its side are sheer, so it was like scrambling along a wall with the ground way below. The rope came out again for safety. From the top we abseiled off: 40 ft of sliding down the rope, pushing out from the face of the In Pinn. (We had scrambled up the start of the In Pinn then made two pitches of it – my standard procedure. All too often you see huge run-outs made and communication becomes difficult as a result. The east ridge is not difficult, just 'A wee bitty sensational' (Tom). On the Traverse we often roped purely for protection, not for difficulty, though this slowed us down.

After abseiling off the In Pinn someone asked what we'd all be doing if back in school right then. We all laughed; with a good day's climbing behind us it was only seven in the morning. They would ask the same question several times over the course of the day. In fact one of my only girns was that they never stopped talking the whole day long.

My log noted, 'the next peaks are the killers, bumpy, graceless brutes that just have to be slowly overcome. We took good rests and a mouthful (cap-full) of water and a nibble on each top. The sun was at full power again and shady alternatives were eagerly taken. Just occasionally a wee breeze cooled our sweaty brows but, all too soon, any breeze became over-warm. We walked with the heat shimmering off our rocky world, and could well understand how people would be beaten by it. Yet the boys did it: patiently, dourly, competently, hour after hour, a lifetime of experience, with still the ready quip and leg-pull, still the unabashed confidence. We cursed the heat – and climbed on.'

Sgurr Thormaid is welcomed as you *see* progress with the change of direction. But the very complex, very upsy-downsy, traverse of Sgurr a' Ghreadaidh – Sgurr a' Mhadaidh – Bidein Druim nan Ramh is the crux of the Traverse, the hard grafting make or break hours, tricky always and always feeling everlasting. The TD Gap, In Pinn, the Tooth are lively offerings in contrast. The endlessness between them is the real contrast. On the first top of Ghreadaidh after we'd turned a trio of lesser bumps we found a marooned sheep which in panic at our arrival seemed likely to go over the edge; instead it charged past us – the day's major excitement. The ropes went on and off, often for individual pitches as on the second and third summits of Mhadaidh and tricky slabs off the Centre summit of Bidein. The boys kept making calculations of the time to reach the Basteir Tooth and were delighted to be missing a maths class right then. I made my only route-finding error for the gap down off An Caisteal so had to traverse awkward slabs with gravel on them. Wasted time. By the Bhairnich gap our last water ran out so we hurried over Bruach na Frithe ('At last!') and zoomed on to the Bealach na Lice. There was our cache which Leon, James, Stuart and Bill had toiled up to deposit. They did climb Bruach na Frithe so had a Munro for their effort.

We drank the half gallon of water straight off and romped down to the spring for more. Then followed tea, and salty beef soup, and more tea and sandwiches with tomatoes and cheese, and lashings of 'Ryvita' and jam. We ate till bursting. We paddled in the pools, threw snowballs at each other, then like seals on the rocks, we sprawled out and dreamt a happy hour away. This was the life! Maybe it was as well nobody else came along – there appeared to be three corpses lying scattered on the slabs.

Setting off again (16.10) we filled our hats with snow and relished the icy fingers of water trickling down our faces. On the col the breeze hit us like the opening of an oven door. The Basteir Tooth loomed – well translated as *the Executioner*. We took the easier option for it, conserving energy, then traversed Am Basteir, a marvellous tent-ridge in the sky, a favourite of mine.

Just Gillean now. We traversed along right, then left to the foot of a chimney up to the *gendarme*, roped for it and continued roped but moving together. We met the only other climbers that day as they were coming down the ridge. (Today the Ridge would have been crawling with people.) They watched our passing with curiosity. By this time practice had brought a fluent efficiency to the techniques, whether moving all together or belaying each other over exposed or harder pitches. There was little need to talk or dither . . . a nod and rope was coiled in, a grunt and a belay was knotted, a word and all moved off as a single unit . . . It must have looked strange, these brown-burnt youngsters moving with the rhythm of a river and smiling quiet greetings as they passed.

Smiling inwardly too, for how could these strangers guess what they had done or what would be over in another five minutes. We scrambled through a window in the ridge and were on the summit of Sgurr nan Gillean (17.45) – *the peak of the young men* – rightly so named!

All that was left was to undulate along 'the true end of the Ridge', as they deemed it, to Sgurr na h-Uamha, to stand on its summit at 19.05, just under 19 hours from Gars-bheinn. ('I think we so far forgot ourselves as to shake hands on it!'). To have done it in such conditions spoke highly of the lads' fitness and mental strength. The fact that they never stopped talking all day showed their happiness, and far from being exhausted, we dropped to the valley floor without stopping, and while I went on to reach the camp at Loch an Athain, they ran to enjoy some boisterous fun in a favoured pool.

A couple of days later we went into the Sligachan Hotel

and in a back room enjoyed fruit jelly, lemonade and cakes to celebrate. We looked at the famous 'Sligachan Book' with all the famous historical names of climbers in it, and somewhat diffidently, added ours. A climber, seeing us writing, quipped, 'So you'll be doing the Ridge?' Tom casually said, 'Aye, we done it twa days ago.' The lad gave a perfect double take. We all laughed. These are the happinesses that mountains bless us with. Thank you Tom Izatt, Bill Simpson, Steve Menmuir.

Most people take about fifteen to twenty hours to the Traverse but someone took less than three in 2013! Unsurprisingly, the Traverse, once done, became a lure for the 'super' mountain runners, those who were also competent mountaineers. I couldn't but note when Eric Beard did a run of 4:09:09 in 1963, for he was a friend. In 1984 it became more serious: Andy Hyslop, 4:04:19. Surely under four hours was possible? Des Davis and Paul Stott obliged in 1986 with 3:49:30, a good slice off. In 1990 Martin Moran clocked up 3:33:00, in 1994 Andy Hyslop nibbled that with 3:32:15 before Ed Tressider's 3:17:28 in 2007 would stand for six years until the inconceivable became believable: under 3 hours. Through 2013 Finlay Wild made 3:14:58 in June, made two more Traverses, then ran 2:59:22 in October. The person who checked these figures for me commented that that Wild's time was less than he took to just climb Sgurr nan Gillean!

With today's digital magic and good local weather forecasting the number of Cuillin Traverses has increased to being a frequent happening. In 2016 Finlay Wild and Tim Gomersal did the Winter Traverse (Gillean–Gars-bheinn) in 6:14:17. The next day Uisdean Hawthorn put in a solo in eight hours, but on 28th February 2018 he returned to complete the Winter Traverse solo in a remarkable 4 hours 57 minutes. And as a nod to the 24 hours idea: the whole Cuillin Ridge and the Red Cuillin (12 Munros & 10 tops, including Knight's Peak), over 34 miles and 23,000 ft of ascent, was done by Rob Woodall (1999) in 23 hours 28 minutes, and by Yiannis Tridimas (2000) in 21 hours 22 minutes. Is there ever an end to chasing dreams?

The Wild West of Jura

> Nous ne pouvons pas diriger le vent, mais nous pouvons y adjuster nos voiles.
>
> **French proverb**

> (We may not be able to direct the wind but we can adjust our sails.)

The wind blew gently, but enough to keep the sweat from our sun-drenched toil. Rucksacks seemed to have grown heavier and lead rather than water seemed to have seeped into our boots. The western coast of Jura is one of the roughest of Scotland's rough landscapes. Cave-ridden rock prows stand grimly against the Atlantic storms. A century ago men deserted the last dwelling that faced west. The deer and the goats alone remain to fight for a living; deer carcasses littered the hillsides of *Deer Island*, as the Norse named Jura; innumerable skeletons of goats lay among the soft, sweet-smelling droppings that carpeted the caves.

Our journey had been as arduous as through any land-scape anywhere but at last we neared our desired haven, crossed one more bog resting on impervious quartzite, headed through a gap and there was the reward. We found ourselves looking down the russet slopes of a glen to a silver-sanded bay on which the waves were chattering. Beyond a cave lay another tidy bay, the twin circles of shining water hugged by black buttresses with their deep sockets of caves and hollows.

The boys stood puzzling a minute, eyes screwed up in the magic light, ears straining for comprehension. The little splashing of the bay was clear, for there was barely wind enough to ruffle tousled hair. There was no burn of any strength. A glance showed no silver dart trailing vapour across the sky. Yet the whole world seemed dominated by a deep-set, throbbing roar – like wind waves in a forest, or a great river in spate, or V-bombers pulsing through the air. Then, one by one, through the shimmer of sun they saw the waters of Corryvreckan, and stood silent. The Inner Hebrides Island of Jura is well known for three things: its excellent eponymous malt whisky, the eye-catching, challenging peaks, the Paps of Jura – and the Gulf of Corryvreckan, this sea passage of striking myths and reality. It was this last that had us standing in awe.

We had reached Jura by sailing through one tide-race, the Dorus Mor (*Great Door*) in a small Loch Fyne fishing boat and that had been exciting enough, in as bad a sea as I have ever known in a small craft. In the tide races it had felt like riding a bucking horse or trying to float a thimble in a boiling kettle. The skipper was glad to land his teenage cargo and the teenage cargo was glad enough to be landed. [1]

Having witnessed those lesser tide races afar off – and then crashed and spun through them – there was first-hand knowledge behind the boys' silent staring. The Dorus Mor had been a murmur – and frightening – the Corryvreckan, two miles off, growled and pushed and tossed up great surges, while white, washing waves still danced at its disturbing power miles further out. There is something overwhelming in a display of natural power – Krakatau is more amazing than Hiroshima, the Victoria Falls than the Kariba Dam. The Corryvreckan, on its headlong surge westwards, is of this large impressiveness.

We streamed down to the twin bays (Bagh Gleann nam Muc), left our rucksacks above the plastic-littered tidemark, and went out to the furthest rocks opposite the tide race. Some of its vehemence had passed, but its sheer pushing, rushing bulk sweeping along made the imagination shudder. Even on our sheltered side the water swirled creamily. Shags and black guillemots sat on the undulating flow. A seal eyed us from offshore. The boys decided closer investigation would be safest from a helicopter.

This maelstrom occurs in the two mile-long gulf between Jura and Scarba. It is a mile wide, and the cause of the troubled waters can be seen in the strata on the Scarba side, where vertical runs of rock sweep down like ribs. Under the Sound, where the water rushes through at nine knots, this forms walls and hollows (soundings vary from forty to a hundred and twenty fathoms). At one place a jagged cone comes up to a mere fifteen fathoms and this creates an upsurge which crashes through the top hundred feet of speeding water to form the frightful, smashing waves and whirlpool which would be the end of a small craft.

Drunk with the sight and sound, we returned to Bagh Gleann nam Muc. Some gathered wood for the fire, some bracken for bedding, Brian and John cooked – soup, black pudding, cheese, toast, and gallons of tea. The gloaming came, the wind died away, the tide lapped high up the sands. Surely there could be few more deserted spots, and few so romantic or satisfying. Like a black shadow against the setting sun, a fishing boat came into the bay. I wonder what they thought – this utterly remote anchorage, noisy, not only with oystercatchers and ringed plovers, but the laughs and shouts of youngsters; in one bay stags munching the seaweed, in the next schoolboys roasting their sausages.

Corryvreckan comes from *Coire Bhreacain*. Legend, spinning many yarns, has given the derivation from *Breacan*, son of a Norse king. To win an island bride this hero had to anchor his boat between Jura and Scarba for three days and nights. He had three ropes made – one of wool, one of hemp, and one of virgins' hair. On the first night the wool rope failed, on the second the hemp, and in a rising tempest during the third night the last rope parted, the galley plunged into the maw and Breacan's body was washed ashore to be buried in a cave now named Uamh Bhreacain. The boys were sceptical about the third rope. There could not be that number of virgins in all Scotland. And Breacan should have used nylon No 3 as any climber could have told him.

Scepticism about the cave was fortunately lifted when the fishermen gave George directions. It lies well out on the southern arm of the double bay, past an obvious dark hollow in the hillside. It is large enough to hold a couple of double-decker buses, and the entrance is circled by walls. Fort or shrine, legend has given place to musty modernity. The boys left a note under a cairn to be sent back by the next visitor. (It was found a few weeks later by the sister of a climbing friend of mine!)

There is no bonfire quite like that built of crackling driftwood. It rose high and blazed merrily. David's wet socks scorched through and no bare flesh could come near the heat. Long after sleeping boys lay snug on top of the piles of bracken and the frost had come down, it glowed and pulsed or sent showers of sparks up among the stars. A solitary kid bleating for its mother was the only noise above the soft whimper of the waves. I lay and wondered at our being there. Many said it was mad to take a party of young teenagers to Jura in February into March, yet we ran barefoot over the grass and sand before our bothy in Glengarrisdale Bay, played 'crocker' on the sands and 'wide games' over the wild hinterland. There were no midges, just an occasional smir of drizzle, and in the whole week no human walked our way.

I let my mind wander back over the journey. We had motored from Buckhaven, in Fife, to Crinan, in our school bus. There was no sign of the boat that was to ferry us to Jura but an hour later a white dot was seen bouncing over the snarling waves towards us. We soon loaded rucksacks, paraffin, boxes of food, sleeping bags and tents on board. But there was no chance of reaching Jura that day. It was blowing far too hard. We went round and up Loch Craignish and camped for the night on a fine grassy stretch near Old Poltalloch, facing Eilean Righ, hoping to try for Jura on the morrow. 'The skipper' would do his best.

There was quite a to-do early in the morning when one tent found it had been invaded by the sea and others only just escaped an unexpectedly high tide. The skipper appeared so the crossing was on, heading out by the Dorus Mor and the light on Reisa an t-Sruith to be bowled along as huge rollers surged under us or passed by. I think the boys' yells and shouts were mostly excitement. I was wondering if maybe I should be unlacing my heavy walking boots. It was something of a relief to land at Kinuachdrachd. The skipper then set off carrying the luggage through the Corry-vreckan passage while we tramped the five miles to reach our bothy base in Glengarrisdale Bay. Fifty years on the skipper recalls 'a strong tide with the wind against it and near-vertical waves, flowing all too close to our gunwhale. Your lads were singing as if they were on a roller-coaster. I was doing anything but!'

Setting off we put up a blackcock in the woods, a snipe on the moor and a heron went flapping away like a grey blanket. We teased an interesting route over the spine of hills to descend a scabbier, wounded landscape and reach the sea – a revelational wild world for this gang of Fife coast natives. And so we came to Glengarrisdale, our base. The skipper had a fire on in the bothy and before leaving, some of the boys went out to help lay lobster pots. From the door a wide 'football pitch' of grass stretched to the fine sands. The dinghy lay high and dry while the boat bobbed beyond Maclean's Skull, one of the rocky islets. The scene glittered in sun and shadow, blue seas flecked white to a Mull of clouds and rainbows. The tents were pitched to dry out, and from the beach and glen and the brown hills around came the sounds of occupation. This was ours awhile with all the wonder of it. We slept under rafters, and my last memory was looking up through the skylight to a great show of stars.

How the days sped at Glengarrisdale! We would rise after listening to the weather forecast at seven o'clock, and only dusk would drive us indoors again, to cook a vast meal with, perhaps, pancakes and drinking chocolate after log books had been written up. The list of birds seen rose to over thirty; there were long hours at low tide among rocks and weeds looking for gunnels, butterfish, blennies, rock-ling, and thousands of tiny, transparent elvers. There were rock walls and pinnacles in plenty to enjoy rock-climbing. Our ropes were nylon and a startling 'peel' by Nabby proved their efficacy. Everyone fell off a thin wall above a tidal pool, everyone enjoyed abseiling. From the point there was a clear view to Colonsay. Driftwood was regularly collected for the bothy fire, (this was pre MBA days) and some glass floats were carried back to Fife as souvenirs.

Days were all too few. We *had to see* the Corryvreckan, so in one early greyness we set off, imprinting our Vibram boot marks on top of hinds' hoof marks along the sand, stumbling over the rounded rubble of the raised beach, on to the first headland where we met a herd of goats. These we herded onto a point in the sea where we were able to photograph the beasts. A kid slipped into a pool and yelled its head off when one of the lads helped it out. Then an adult goat, in panic, jumped – into the sea – trying to bypass us. But it was a wild Atlantic sea which came roaring up the rifts in the rocks. In a couple of minutes the beast ceased its struggle for life; that awful cessation which man refuses but which comes so easily to wild creatures (were there not half a dozen deer lying in the 'peaceful' sleep – of death – within stone's throw of the bothy?). I passed my camera and watch to Ian and scrambled down.

Knee-deep, I just reached those curving horns, but the next swelling wave caught us both and we bowled over in the foam. I held on, and between surges inched the exhausted animal onto the near-vertical rocks. With help from Charlie we got it up the rocks. Ian had used my camera to record this fiasco. I lay with the sodden creature awhile then forced it to stand, taking away my support little by little, while the humans slowly filed out of sight. We then left it alone. It began picking its way skilfully once more over the rocks and tufts of thrift.

The 'walk' up the coast was strenuous, for seldom was there easy walking on this coastline of chaotic geology: rock arches and caves galore, leering crags, stretches of raised beaches, the boulders once entwined with honeysuckle, and many of what I call 'bird cones,' the grassy cones created by centuries of birds perching on a natural viewing spot and their droppings and blowing dirt increasing the growth bit by bit. There were goats everywhere. The very names emphasised the wildness: Sgier Mhor *Big Reef*, Bagh Feith a' Chaorainn *The Rowan Bog Bay*, Bagh Uamh nam Gall *The Stranger's Cave Bay*, Bagh Uamh Mhor *Big Cave Bay*, Beinn nan Capuil *Horse Hill*, Uamh Bhreachain *Breacan's Cave*, Bagh Gleann nam Muc *Pig Glen Bay*. We travelled that coast with respect.

We were cosy enough in the bivouac above the twin bays on that northern tip of Jura. The fire smouldered. The fishing boat had vanished in the dark shadow of the hill. There was only that crying kid – nature crying out its feebleness in the dark. A goat is rescued. A goat is lost. The caves are full of their bones. Perhaps it *was* foolish to be there. It was a treacherous place, desolate and cruel. Men had long given up any desire to try and live on its inhospitable shoreline. Let those who romantically wish the drift from the Highlands to stop, go and live there. Let them grow potatoes on the old lazy beds, let them carry up the seaweed to fertilise them, carry driftwood over the rocks on their backs, let them ferry their essentials through the Corryvreckan. The vanished descendants of Glengarrisdale are happier buying their potatoes at the shop 'doon the road', enjoying TV, electricity, cars, holidays ... what we so take for granted. What if one of the boys went down with an appendix? What if one broke his back on the vicious rocks? Reality is always double-faced. There were only a few boxes of groceries, a good first-aid kit, some paraffin and stores between us and the hardest, cruellest coast imaginable in Britain.

But that was enough to let us exult in being there. I have seldom seen a gang of youngsters so happy. They were well aware of the dangers, and perhaps because of this were doubly aware of the basic blessings of life – sun, wind and water, health and strength, food, friendship and sleep. Such freedom is perhaps worth some risk; they may never taste it again.

When I woke at dawn the bay was empty, a smir hung on the hills, the kid was silent, the tide far out again. We roused ourselves. Bread wrappers flared up on the hot ashes of the fire and, breakfast over, we made a last walk out to the furthest corner of Jura to watch a wilder, wicked Corryvreckan in full display – like a lusting sea creature that would overcome the world of land.

At the end of April the skipper would take another gang of us out for days on Scarba, the dumpy island on the other side of the sound. On that trip we bivouacked below the cliffs as close as could be to the famous whirlpool. The boys, for fun, built stone and turf shelters (forever like the *planti crubs* of Shetland) and I've often wondered what an archaeologist might make of them.

Back at Glengarrisdale we were marooned for two days while gales lashed the island. We played a lot of chess! But then had to move. A Force 8 or 9 had the waves pounding ashore. There would be no boat so we went on to Plan B: over the hills to the east coast. If the worst came to the worst we could, literally, send up smoke signals. (No mobile phones in those days.) We had reconnoitred the route the day before, going up Glengarrisdale to hill-hidden lochs and seeing the way on clear, a longer route but needing to be easier as we were walking well-laden. Once over the spine to the lonely head of Glen Lealt we spotted a figure through my binoculars: the skipper, coming over to suggest we did what we were doing!

After an hour of walking up the eastern side's track we found ourselves looking down on a substantial 18th century farm house, Barnhill, famous as the remote spot chosen by George Orwell to have peace to write what would be his last book, *1984*. He was already a sick man and had to leave Jura on occasions because of his health. A curious location for a sick man to choose. And he and his young son very nearly came to grief in the Corryvreckan passage when their small boat was sunk and they were left stranded on a mere reef. Luckily they were spotted and rescued by a fisherman.

Our boat was in the Kinuachdrachd bay just a mile on but we waited for the wind to ease before embarking. I found a big eel on the rocks and the boys were knocking off limpets and feeding them to crabs. There was still a bouncy sea for the crossing. The Paps of Jura shone in a golden glow and the snowy fangs of Cruachan looked Himalayan. We were taken to Crinan. The shop opened for us and we were told just to pitch the tents on the edge of the car park. It was a cold night and the porridge soaked overnight had become a speckled cylinder of ice. By canal banks and walking and lifts we all reassembled in the Stag Hotel in Lochgilphead where the school bus picked us up at 2.30 p.m.. For Nabby, David, Brian, Charlie, John, Sid, George, Ronnie, Ian (and Hamish) one of the best school trips was over. Nobody will forget the twenty four hours spent in the company of the Corryvreckan. How much more today do we need to give children opportunities and challenges and not just courses and exams.

---

1 The skipper was David Hayes who later created Landmark at Carrbridge.

Snowed In at Glendoll

> Hail, snow an' ice that praise the Lord: I've met them
>   at their work,
> An' wished we had anither road or they another kirk.
> > **Rudyard Kipling:** *McAndrew's Hymn*

In all the years I was taking youngsters away to the hills we only twice failed to return to school on time at the end of a trip (none of those high-falutin' 'expeditions' or 'curricular experiments in physical skills'). The first, already described, was due to being marooned on Jura by storms when the boat couldn't risk the Corryvreckan, the second was when we were snowed-in at Glen Doll. Unlike most citizens, hillgoers like good bad winters. This gang was staying in the Carn Dearg Club hut in Glen Doll at the head of Glen Clova, one of the Angus glens, and had taken skis, hoping for good snow.

The snow was well down already and the frost was keen. Great to squeak up the road to the farm for eggs, Creag Mellon like a ship's bows pushing over the surging trees. We broke the ice to fetch the water from the burn and sprawled cosily before the old cast-iron stove at night.

It was an older boys' gang. They were already hillgoers, some had skied before, and the rest came tumbling after. A field down by Eggie gave a couple of training days to start – and a hilarious near-accident when one novice went shooting off down the edge of the wood just as a pheasant came belting out of it, the two on an unavoidable collision course. Both made indignant comment: 'Och, sur, it's bad enough trying to keep on ma flippers withoot a pheasant beltin atween ma legs!'

We did Ben Tirran, 2,860 ft, one day, too heathery for skis and the weather was grey and lowering. Then it began to snow, swirling down Jock's Road, not violently (you hardly noticed it) but by the time we had cooked our supper and were ready for the bed-shelf there were six inches on the doorstep. In the morning there were feet of it.

We took to the drifted forests, following up the roads through the bowed and weary greenery, then skiing down in a bliss of fine powder. Quite often the bends were too steep and tight for the beginners and we would see a figure shoot off into space and vanish. There would be a thump and a tree would unload its snow on the victim below.

I provided one spectacular fall by skiing into a tree trunk lying hidden across the road under the snow. The skis had tried to go under while I went over the top. Sore shins, one staved thumb and one broken thumb was the result. Ever tried tying boot laces with two dud thumbs? It was a good excuse for not peeling potatoes though!

After a few days of this rather wild skiing it really started to snow, and blow; the drifts piling up and up. We kept moving our bus, but in the end nothing could be kept clear. Traffic vanished in the glen. The roads were buried. We were cut off.

As we had ample food supplies this did not matter and, having skis, were uniquely mobile – and made the most of it. We skied up to the youth hostel one night, and the warden Dan Smith, hostellers and the farm kids, plus our gang, all squeezed in for a slide show. In the morning we skied down to the phone box at the hotel at Milton, and had to dig down to clear the door so we could get in.

In many places it was possible to ski over gates and fences into fields. All the sheep, cows and horses had escaped and wandered about in search of food. The deer had come down and were pinching the hay, a moorhen sat in a pine tree complaining loudly, and the dog and hares went crazy together, leaving wild tracks in the snow. It was a time when man and beast alike seemed to lay aside normal fear and enmity.

We dug out the telephone box, reported gleefully, then went on for a good traverse round the valley to marvel at the snow's casual chaos. The plough only got up to Rottal that day. On the next it came up to Milton and on to Braedownie so we eventually worked our way out, driving down canyons of snow higher than the roof.

Dundee's black slushy streets under the glare of street lights seemed a million miles from the white wonderland we had left behind, while Fife was clear enough of snow that our story was a bit suspect.

On one occasion I had this sort of situation in reverse. I was supposed to be travelling to lecture at Kinloch Rannoch but every road out of Kinghorn and Burntisland was blocked by snow. From my flat I looked down to my van with over a foot of snow on its roof. I phoned to make my apologies. 'But there's no snow in Kinloch Rannoch.' I was told.

A Night Out on Beinn A'bhuird

> The springs of enchantment lie within ourselves;
> they arise from our sense of wonder, that most
> precious of gifts.
>
> Eric Shipton

This was in December 1963. The Braehead Fife Mountaineering Club was a club open to staff, pupils, former pupils and friends of Braehead School in Fife (not to be confused with today's Braes o' Fife). Robert was a friend of mine from climbing in the Alps, and Mike a former pupil who would have made a gifted instructor, but this was before education would embrace the outdoors. I've left ideas expressed and methods followed unchanged for interest.

It was one of those weekends which started off badly yet led, in the end, to fun and adventure – all the more delightful because of the initial chaos.

We were a party of the BFMC (politely referred to as the 'BF's') and had set off from Fife on a Friday evening in Horace, once described as a 'sort of vehicle,' being in fact a home-made van with a body like a horse-box. We rattled over the Devil's Elbow to be in Braemar before midnight. There Mike and I were left while the others carried on for the Linn o'Dee, Glen Derry and the Corrour Bothy. As none of them had been there before and everything was frozen up after a wet autumn they had an eventful passage. They bedded down at four in the morning after their eight-mile hike. Our destination was the ruin of Slugain Lodge whose glen we decided to reach by a shortcut – fording the Dee. Innocents abroad in the moonlight. Waist-deep was enough so we dressed again and disentangled ourselves from the high deer-fenced fields all covered in white frost. We stomped moodily down the road for a few miles with our laces trailing. I was ill (with internal pains) and could hardly manage even a light rucksack. In 'the wee sma' oors' we lay down under some old Scots pines, determined to make a start an hour before dawn to regain the lost ground. 'We'll be glad to get off then, we'll be so cold anyway.'

It was cold, but it was nine o'clock before either of us confessed to being awake. We crossed Invercauld Bridge and set off into the Cairngorms. We collapsed at Slugain with the deer standing clear around the horizon. We felt exhausted and I was racked with cramps inside. This was our nadir. What now? Our aim had been a winter traverse of Ben Avon, Beinn a'Bhuird and over the great moss to the Coire Etchachan Memorial Hut, with the others possibly coming to meet us to climb in Coire Sputan Dearg; here we were – hardly in the hills even, feeling like death, the hills blotted out and with a mere three hours left of the short winter day.

A little later we were spanking gaily up the path towards the Sneck, Mike chattering away as of old while he raced to keep up. I swear there was nothing stronger than sugar in the tea we had brewed. Anyway, our phoenix strength drove us on rejoicing into the world of rock and snow. Ice axes were loosened for their labour. We were on top of life again.

The Cairngorms have a personality of their own; other areas crowd their beauty into small compass, here there is vastness, but a vastness almost equally packed with interest. The wildlife, the old Scots Pine forests, the heathery slopes and the great passes, corries and high plateaux are unique. They require care, for their greater elevation brings Arctic rather than Alpine conditions. Nowhere else have I so often had to fight or crawl to reach summits! They can demand the highest standards in navigation in mist. It is quite an experience to wander over their flat, featureless and invisible miles.

Near the end of the track we crossed the burn and followed up the flow coming down from the Dubh Lochan. Before the steep slope to Coire Lochain there is a smaller loch and from its end we set a canny compass course to skirt under the huge Dividing Buttress into Coire nan Clach where the guide, hopefully rather than helpfully, informed us we would find a howff under 'the second largest boulder'. We had been in deep snow since leaving the path. There was thick fog also and it was a flounder, with much barking of shins on granite all the way up to the lochan and into The Corrie of the Rocks, which was a nightmare of boulders, dozens the size of buses, covered in snow, slobbery, floury and slippery. We crawled over and round and under them while time sped by and no howff could we find. A forced bivvy loomed ahead, when with about half an hour of light left I stumbled on the built-up cave under a boulder. Either the guide places it under the wrong buttress, or it is several hundred yards out of place, or it is another howff altogether. But it was sanctuary. Periodically through the evening there were snorts and giggles and quotes about 'the second largest boulder'. When the mist cleared momentarily our calculated position was correct and we had a glimpse through the half-light to grey hills and stark crags and gullies round the boulder wilderness. We settled in for the night.

I crawled in through the narrow opening to level the floor and clear the snow which had drifted in. Mike remained outside cutting snow blocks, some of which were passed inside to serve as water supply, the rest being used to fill gaps in the walls and reduce the entrance to a small aperture. Snow takes time to melt and putting the dixie on is always the first job. I lit a candle as Mike wiggled his way in and blocked up the entrance with his ready material. Capes were spread on the floor and sleeping bags unrolled. It was cold, but with extra clothes and sitting in our bags we were cosy enough. The only thing we lacked was an air bed, the surface under us being as comfy as any pile of broken bricks. Nevertheless we slept excellently, wearing all our extra woollies (of which we carried many and little else in the clothing line, worn top and bottom they make you look like a Michelin advert but keep you very warm) inside Icelandic sleeping-bags and with a layer of newspaper and our maps insulating from ground-cold. We were about 3,300 feet up, which is higher than a great many summits.

For this trip our rucksacks weighed about twenty pounds. We had a light rope, used double for any climbing, axes, bedding, woollies, food, stove and so on. We believed in being light – from bitter experience. The rules of camping and preconceived notions should all be thrown away. Success is often the reward of dealing with the superfluous.

This includes food. Tins should be omitted completely and so can most of the utensils and containers. Our cave-dwelling cuisine was filling, appetising, and nourishing – and light. We craved liquid, so first had chicken broth (cubes) and into the half dixie of water left we poured a packet of dehydrated apples. We had bread with the broth and biscuits with the apples. Then more snow was dumped into the dixie along with a packet of 5-minute soup, dried onions and Surprise (dried) peas. A poke of salt, pepper and spices made it a tasty broth. This was followed by a macaroni-cheese dish with similar vegetables. The order in which they were eaten was not exactly conventional but then neither was the café. We cooked on a primus, still 'the best buy'. Gas is clean and easy, but it is expensive and keep running down to burn at an infuriatingly slow pace. We had one dixie and lid plus one mug, spoon, and penknife each – and lacked nothing. In winter there is always a water supply, there is no perpetual rain, the midges are absent, the peasants are away till the next summer and the beauty and fun of climbing unsurpassed. The biggest dossing difficulty in winter is condensation and only experience will deal with that. Too much warmth with too little ventilation will soon set things sweating; too much ventilation and you have an icebox. In this grotto we had more than enough air filtering through side cracks. We were cold, but not enough to leave our pits to stop up the cracks with snow. Comfort is a relative thing.

We settled down at nine o'clock. The moon filtered a tracery of light in the doorway. It was too much – perhaps the full moon was shining from a clear sky and we could be climbing on the glittering magic of night snow (another habit not in the pundit's standing routine). We broke a hole through the snow. Visibility was nil.

We lay back again and watched the candle flicker over the red granite above our heads. The cave was about tent high and about two tents in length, and the roof was twice as hard – as our craniums discovered. We lay and chatted awhile. Mike recalled the night he had first slept under the snow when at school – making use of holes which had been created on a Glenmore Lodge course: 'Second hand but first rate.' I recalled arriving on the plateau from Corrour bothy to be hit by a tremendous storm. MacDhui would be a fight. Might the lads find it too much? As if to allay my fears one of them sidled up to me and yelled to be heard, 'Is it bad enough yet that we'll have to dig in?' He said it hopefully. Last time in Braemar I heard another story. The Mountain Rescue team had gone out to find an Irish lad. He was met coming down the Glas Maol slope above the Cairnwell. Looking at the road when nearly down, he commented that the night before he had crossed that road. Why? Well, the book said to dig in if lost, and on the other side there hadn't been enough snow.

We were too comfy to bother with a last brew (which anyway might necessitate having to leave one's sleeping bag later) and slowly yawned our way into sleep. I blew the candle out and relished the brief scent of the smoking wick.

Mike pulled the stove over and lit it while still in his

sleeping bag. Tea in bed to start the day – I don't get that at home! Mike forgot to put something under the primus for insulation and when he next looked the stove had melted its way down through the snow. My boots had to be thawed out over the stove before I could force my feet inside them. Mike had kept his warm by using them as a pillow. It had been cold certainly; some prunes left overnight were encased in a cylinder of ice. Nothing unusual in that and we were soon ready for 'the white felicity of the high-towered mountains' (Sorley McLean).

Last night had given us a glimpse of a nice gully, possibly the Crocus Gully of the guide, well banked up with snow but steep below the rim of the cornice. We contoured round and up in the mist, first one then the other pressing on at top speed. The crust held and we could kick steps. The gully steepened and we began cutting. It then reared up in a shallow chute of snow-ice, crusted with the remains of an avalanche. The wind had risen too and the chips flying from the axe stung our faces as they shot about the gully. A short vertical section, a hammering-down of cornice, a wild devil's white of spindrift and we crawled out on to the summit plateau. We stood in sudden stillness while a few steps away the wind tore out of the corrie with a roar. We roped for fear of walking over cornices in the fog, but in fact the edge could always be heard if not seen – a roaring as of surf in the whiteness of the fog.

We followed the edge round to what we took to be a known position on the map and then set off navigating carefully for the cairn. We left a deep track which would ease the return. Half a mile later the cairn was suddenly beside us. We fled back along the barely discernible track, the blizzard full in our faces. An old partnership, we wasted no time. The cornice was reached and Mike baled off while

I belayed. I soon followed into the inferno and then we moved together. Soon we were sliding and romping down. Back 'home' we unroped and packed. It was only 11 a.m. The visibility cleared slightly and we could make out our steps of the search for the cave. We wondered what anyone would make of their giddy wanderings. Superimposed across their drunken course was the clear trail of a fox.

We then descended the Quoich, first on the path and then through trackless forest until it swung south to the Dee. Groups of stags stood still watching our passing. We turned off to take the line of a fault (a continuation of the Glen Tilt fault) through to Glen Derry, a remarkable steep-sided trench with a ribbon of frozen water up its length. We picked up an antler, already chewed by the hungry deer. The heather was alive with the elusive music of the tits. It was the Cairngorms as they will always be recalled. We paused before dropping on to the road down to the Linn o'Dee and Horace. We were there by 2.45 p.m. and were able to hand out tea to the others an hour later as they arrived, Robert with Alastair (Mike's brother), young Noddy and Michael. They had been on the Devil's Point and Cairn Toul the day before and learned much of step-cutting, glissading and compass work. By 8 p.m. Robert had dropped us at our homes along the mining coast of Fife. Mike would be at work at seven o'clock while for the lads, it was school on Monday as usual – but with more than usual tales to tell.

Along The Lines

Over the years railway lines have led me to varied experiences, both at home and abroad, from an annual trip on some heritage 'steam' routes to world classics like Spain's

Talgo or South Africa's Blue Train. No memories are sharper than those of a lifetime ago on our Highland lines.

Back in the Sixties one school party had a snug Hogmanay camp in the forest in Glen Carron; a handy spot for hills like Fuar Tholl, Sgorr Ruadh, Beinn Liath Mhor to the north-west, and Moruisg and the pair of Sgurr a'Chaorachain and Sgurr Choinnich to the south-east. The camp was blessed with deep snow, even at valley level. We needed to travel home by train at the end, and to save over five miles of hiking to Achnashellach station, decided to use the wee halt below Glencarron Lodge. We then decided to make sure of the train by sleeping overnight in the small waiting room (folding tents hard as boards after a week in the woods would have been some chore in the morning dark.) We had a crowded night but were perfectly snug in this alternative bothy. Come the morning we were ready in plenty of time. I then noticed that the signal light had gone out, so one boy was sent to climb up and bring down the lantern which we then filled from our primus stoves, replaced on high, and set the signal to red. The train duly stopped and we started to pile in when the driver yelled at us to turn the effin' signal to green! Later he informed us that the station had been closed for some years, but a train driver will always stop for a red light. There is nothing there at all now. That Glencarron halt, like Achnashellach station, was made as a private facility serving the lodge and its sporting fraternity.

Some of that Glencarron party were also involved in a search operation for a student benighted on that eastern pair of Munros. The small Glenuaig lodge at the head of the glen, we were told, once belonged to a British lady who had become a Muslim and had even made the Haj pilgrimage to Mecca – a bold venture for a woman, especially in the nineteenth century.

Our school parties often used trains on Rannoch Moor and one welcome port of call was the station at Gorton (long gone) where a Mr Murray would provide hot cocoa and regale the kids with stories of the Moor in winter when he had to physically de-ice the points and sometimes, on coming in, *stood* (rather than hung) his coat behind the door. There was a conning tower giving wide views over the Moor, good for spotting deer. Further up the line was a one-time linesman's cottage, Rowantree Cottage, which was no longer used and became a bothy we used several times. We were once based there, and camping as well, during a botanical search for the rare Rannoch rush (*Scheuchzeria palustris*) and only when a student joined us off a train from Glasgow at the weekend did we hear that President Kennedy had been shot several days earlier. He had to produce a newspaper before we believed him. We must have been some of the last people in the world to have heard the news!

One time we ran out of bread while at Rowantree Cottage so one fourteen year old boy was dispatched with a rucksack on the morning train south to get off at Tyndrum, buy the bread and return by the afternoon train. He was back at Tyndrum Upper, mission accomplished, with hours to wait when a massive diesel engine pulling a long train of alumina tanks for the Fort William smelter pulled in. The driver asked what the lad was doing and then said 'Och, that's too long to wait. Climb up' – so he travelled over the Moor in the engine cabin. At the bothy we heard the rumble of this mighty engine slowing, then stopping, so tumbled out to see why. A small figure climbed down the cab's ladder to drop onto the track, gave the driver a wave, got a toot in return, and off the train rattled. Wonder if that could happen today? An edict later went forth that all railway assets (such as buildings) were to be sold or demolished; so sturdy Rowantree Cottage was reduced to a pile of bricks.

One of Mr Murray's stories concerned the 'Ghost Train' that regularly went up to Fort William very early – not a passenger train, and crossing the Moor it was legitimate for the guard (remember when we had guards?) to have a snooze. So after leaving Bridge of Orchy one guard did so. Then at Corrour Station, the summit, the train made a jolting start which detached the guard's van. The van began to run backwards, and was soon belting along. Rannoch Station, alerted, saw it descend from the snow shed and over the viaduct. Procedure demanded a runaway should be sent into a siding to crash into the buffers, but realising the guard might be on board, they let the runaway through – as did Gorton, as did Bridge of Orchy. Soon after Bridge of Orchy the line rises steeply so the van slowed, stopped, and ran back to come to a halt at the Bridge of Orchy platform. The stopping woke the guard who checked the time and then wondered why on earth they were still at Bridge of Orchy, and then, what had happened to his train?

Something crazier occurred at Achnashellach in those distant nineteenth-century days. A mixed goods/passenger train was travelling Inverness to Kyle and when the driver reached the halt at Achnashellach he noticed he had lost his carriages. So what did he do? He went into reverse and hurried up the line to look for them! (He was duly sacked for the resulting unscheduled meeting. Luckily nobody was seriously hurt in the crash).

When Braehead parties went to the Alps it was by train, Kirkcaldy to London, change stations, down to Folkestone or Dover for a Channel ferry train to Paris, change stations again, and so on through to Martigny or Sion or wherever. The journey always went smoothly, but today, would anyone allow only an hour between a possible King's Cross timetabled arrival and a departure time from Victoria? Our Martigny base was a campsite in an orchard next to the railway and you could almost set your watch by knowing the times of passing trains. A former pupil recently recalled the best of that site was our having permission to pick and eat as many plums as we liked from the trees. We pigged on plums.

In the Seventies I used to run winter mountaineering courses at Gerry's private and idiosyncratic hostel not far from where we had camped in the woods a decade earlier. The hostel was an old linesman's home alongside the railway. On one occasion a bright spark threw his rucksack from his train to save having to carry it all the way from Achnashellach station. Unfortunately he forgot there was a bottle of wine in it. More than once the woodshed at Gerry's would have a train-hit deer hanging up to mature the meat; people encountering this on a dark night tended to return with rather white faces.

I often met clients at Achnashellach station. For economy its lighting was put on to an automatic system to light up for ten minutes before a train was due and go out ten minutes after the arrival time. This was theoretically not a bad idea but as the trains never arrived on time the lights always went out before the train trundled in. This duly happened when I was there to meet a lad from London. He appeared to have missed the train; there was no-one on the platform. I was about to leave when I heard a thrashing among the rhododendrons at the end of the platform and, on looking, found my client lying on his back, weighed down by his rucksack, arms and legs waving like a demented upside-down tortoise. He had made the erroneous assumption that platforms are always longer than trains and had happily stepped out the door into the blackness.

As a teenager I once set off to cycle from Crail in the East Neuk of Fife to a schoolboys' camp at Blair Atholl, but a ferocious wind blowing from the west made progress almost impossible. Tired of fighting the wind I stopped at Markinch with the intention of taking a train to Perth and cycling on from there. Having deposited my bike and kit in the guard's van (remember the days of guards and guard vans?), I promptly fell asleep and missed Thornton Junction where I should have changed to the Kirkcaldy-Perth train. I woke up in Kirkcaldy. I stood on the platform in cycling garb feeling foolish while wondering just where my bike might be. Happily, however, it had been unloaded at Perth, though once I finally arrived there I walked what felt like miles of platforms before I found it.

In the late 1940s our mother, my two brothers and I cycled all over Scotland, for nobody had cars then. On one occasion we arrived at outlandish Carbisdale Castle youth hostel with one bike beyond fixing, even with the good tools and spares we carried when heading into the far north-west. Carbisdale Castle was a huge Scottish Baronial mansion built by the Duchess of Sutherland in the nineteenth century; during World War Two it was pressed into service as the home of the exiled King of Norway, Haakon VII. Not many youth hostels have a hall with its walls hung with paintings and classic marble statues along its length. When ultimately its upkeep proved ruinous, the SYHA sold the castle, in 2011.

Next day we had quite a thrill crossing the railway bridge's attached footbridge over the Kyle of Sutherland to reach Invershin Station and on to Inverness, the guard's van crowded with our four steeds. They were still all steam trains in those days.

I've another steam train memory. All along the Highland Line there were small workmen's huts, weather-proof and usually with a small cast-iron stove and some coal. At that time, in the 1950s, I was living in Paisley; there was always fierce competition on Friday nights for hitching up Loch Lomond's A82 and on one such night when transport completely failed I tramped on and on till somewhere near Ardlui I called a halt. I found one of these wee huts and spread my blanket in it. Hours late I woke in horror for the whole world was shaking and roaring and bursting into fire. Armageddon? No; just a train passing and choosing that spot to empty its fire box.

A last Moor memory. When our Braehead gang of teachers and pupils canoed across Rannoch Moor from the A82 Glen Coe road eastwards we, perforce, had to lug our canoes up to Rannoch Station at the end in order to return by train to our Bridge of Orchy base. The stationmaster was a bit nonplussed at being presented with canoes ('Never had them before!') and after flicking unsuccessfully through papers trying to find out if he should charge by length or by weight he decided to charge by weight – he knew about rates by weight. So the awkward canoes had to be carried into the scales one by one – except we ensured it was the lightest canoe that was carried in seven times. As the canoes were of various colours he was either blind, or turning a blind eye. I suspect the latter. Why make anything harder?

NO CHOICE

There are thin red lines in fat little books that show
  us where to go,
And summits call in summer time and summits call
  in snow.
There's no cure for potent ills, there's no cure for
  climbing hills
For we would have it so.

With choices made when all is said, there was no
  choice at all;
There's nothing we could do, no arguing with the
  thrall.
We saw the route, we saw the hill, the way so many
  go
So fell for it; that's all.

FURTHER AFIELD

Misguided Sometimes

Through all my years climbing in the Alps (mostly 1960-80) I very seldom had any connection with local guides (there were no UK guides then!) and on almost every occasion I found something, some practice and procedure, some outlook, which was questionable. Weaned on Victorian literature I found this both disappointing and worrying.

My introduction to the Alps was traditional enough, a spell at Arolla, a mainly student party, happy to find their feet in this new world. I'd come to it rather later than I might have, for all my Alpine reading had been of the exploits of those beyond emulation. *Gervasutti's Climbs* was only dispiriting, the allure eventually came from Janet Adam Smith's *Mountain Holidays*. She made it sound *fun*. I never did question where continentals began to learn the ropes. Arolla was an explosion of experiences. I didn't want to go home when everybody else had to.

From every climb or summit our eyes had been drawn to the startling image of the Matterhorn, the mountain of Whymper and Tyndale, an allure I could not resist. I hurried round to Zermatt and frantically searched the campsite for some British climbers. There were none. Up then to the Hörnli Hut. Maybe someone there planning for that dream image. No. Day faded, then I was approached by an *aspirant* guide (I'll call him Otto) who offered his services for next to nothing, no doubt looking for another entry in his *führerbuch*. I agreed. No sooner on the bed-shelf than an English party came in. Never mind, I liked the idea of partnering someone with a famous guide's family name on the most iconic mountain in the Alps.

We set off at 04.00, Otto setting a good pace that had us well ahead of everyone by the Solvay Hut. I amused him by naming all the features of the route, later by refusing to use any fixed ropes. We seldom roped, conversation a periodic, 'OK Brown?' and the pace then increased. A biting wind discouraged any summit lingering. Otto was delighted. 'Next year, we do the Zmutt, yes? No charge.' We were back at the hut in four and a half hours, greeted with concern, 'Why had we given up?' The answer caused quite a stir, the old guardian dancing about and taking us into the guides' room. A wrinkled figure out of Whymper scowled at me, 'That is no way to treat the Matterhorn,' then shot out a hand, 'Congratulations'. I was nonplussed. After all, it was just a decaying Curved Ridge writ large.

Otto suggested we did it again at the end of the season when less cluttered with people. 'Up and down in three hours!' Perish the thought! However we exchanged addresses, photographed each other and, best, he knocked even more off his modest bill. That night I caught a train at Sion, homeward bound and happy enough. The following year, another good season nearing its end, out of curiosity I rang Otto to see if he would do a cheapie deal on some taxing objective, something to challenge and where I'd learn more. I'd not the slightest interest in the Matterhorn again.[1]

To my query however Otto apologised, he wasn't free,

he had been contracted by the Hörnli refuge for the Matterhorn that year. My heart sank. How could someone with a
life in mountains ahead sign on for a season of hauling tourists up *that* route? My bitten apple of the Alps turned sour
in my mouth. How could he? Never mind, with companions I managed to get myself up the Dent Blanche, Monte
Rosa and other 4,000ers quite happily enough. I'd never be
involved with a guide again I'd decided. But somehow I did,
twice, with questionable experiences both times.

I was camping at Zermatt in 1970 with my brother and his
wife, climbing friends and former pupils. Two newcomers
went off for the Matterhorn (you do, don't you?) while Jim
and I went up to the 'home hut' for me, as a member of the
Monte Rosa section of the Swiss Alpine Club. I've no note
or memory of why we were to go with a Ludwig Imboden,
a St Niklaus guide, but presume Jim was financier and
wanted me along. Should be instructive for a big snow day
traversing Liskamm, Castor and Pollux.

We set out at 2.00 a.m. and certainly Ludwig's skills
were welcome on the Grenz Glacier. 'Walk as on eggs.' We
were on the Lisjoch at 6.15 a.m. (book time five and a half
hours) where we had the only real pause of the day and
were on the summit an hour under book time from there:
good front-pointing up to a waving sweep of snow ridge.
'Piz Palu plus' I wrote later. We walked 'on sun and air' to
the West Top – a Leslie Stephen first – halving book time.
Castor was soon climbed (10.00 a.m.). I recorded 'N Ridge,
a wicked wind, Ludwig a bit shouty and loses English under
pressure'. The crest was narrow; at one stage my ice axe
went right through its wafer. Breakable crust made a sweat
to the Zwillingsjoch and the surprise of Pollux being rock,
not snow. Jim found the rocks a bit 'puzzling' and declared
Ludwig a worse slave-driver than I normally was. The

top rocks were turned on ice, chips flying off in the wind like shards of glass. 11.50 a.m.; 9h 50 - four hours under book time from the hut – but with only half the day's miles covered. No waiting allowed. 'Look at the panorama' – and we were off after two minutes.

'Descend to a Madonna clasping plastic flowers and a fixed wire down a gully to a long rambling ridge. Jim tiring. Ludwig yelling "Relax!" Hardly encouraging. Eventually I insisted on a pause before trailing over below the Schwarztor; a breeze moderated our hot hell onwards, the snow slushy, the glare punishing. Ludwig kept Jim on a short rope which was frequently not long enough for safe-guarding crossing crevasses. Strange how lacking in safety measures they are, relying on strength instead. On the long slog below the Breithorn crevasses were welcome: they gave us the only times to catch our breaths again…'Finally down to the mess of ski things.' Ludwig really skeltered so we landed at the foot of the slope gasping like stranded cod. I blasted him! Safety had no call for such continuous speed and he was ruining the enjoyment of his party. I went first then, in what I thought of as a guide's pace – steady above all. Not slow – any fit Brit broke book times – and now teaching I suppose (which is what I did). Ludwig had only been a professional for a couple of years and was still in his mid-twenties so the enthusiasm no doubt will be tempered with experience.'

We were given no breaks until at the Trokkener station, 13 hours to the minute since leaving the Monte Rosa hut. (Book time 18-19 hours). I was not pleased noticing Ludwig boasting gleefully to others about our time. Look good in his *führerbuch* no doubt. Not in ours. Why not stop at the first drinks spot and relax a bit? His 'Quicker the better, get it over' was Otto over again: misguided by guides. Jim would have enjoyed the day much more had we moved a bit slower, had some proper breaks and more food and water. Instead he will recall being hurried and bullied and ending dehydrated and weary. But a potentially far more dangerous example of this sort of guides' attitude I'd encountered a few years before.

An Alpine meet of a British club was being held at Fafleralp at the head of the Lötschental and I thought it would be fun to join them after my companions returned home. Find someone to climb with. We finished our season by joining the meet at Fafleralp, said hello, then Bob and I went off to traverse the Oberland. Day one took us over the Lötschenlücke to the Koncordiahütte where we met a young Australian doctor, John, who had weeks ahead free and shared our financial constraints. He'd join me at Fafleralp. We continued over the Grunhornlücke to the Finsteraarhornhütte then by the Oberaarhorn to the Grimsel. What I recall of that was how we traversed a pass, climbed a peak, made the exit to Grimsel, caught a bus to Gletsch, train to Brig, train to Goppenstein, bus to Blatten and walked up to Fafleralp all in the day – an impossible equivalent say, of doing the Cairngorm Four, walking to Braemar and ending the day in Inveraray.

My friends departed, the weather broke for several days, and John and I (camping) were well integrated socially with the club (mostly in the hotel) where plans were made and remade. The club had its contracted guide and an *aspirant* helper. I'd early misgivings when, eventually ensconced in the Bietschhornhütte, the next day's plans were to traverse the Bietschhorn, with a party of eleven. The guidebook described it as 'expressly the most difficult of the big peaks in the Bernese Alps ... the climbing is tiring and fairly difficult,' the rock often bad, our SWS Ridge 'on the whole, rotten;, delicate. AD –, two short pitches of III'. (In our conditions, harder.)

The composition of the party worried me with its wide range of ages and alpine experience – or lack of it. I was prepared to look after newcomer John (and had a Reverend third also on the rope), but only another experienced couple would form a rope independently. The *aspirant* guide had two clients and the guide, Edi, as I'll call him, had the only lady (well experienced) and William who, frankly, should not have been there but, as club president, was dutifully participating. An unfit, flabby businessman, he was out of his depth from the start. My log noted, 'William, dear soul, finding it way beyond him' – and that was before the climb itself.

The route was mostly rock, sensationally narrow in places, snow preventing any traversing below difficulties, and just went on and on. My pair improved all day, John having quite an introduction to alpine work. High up there was a notorious Red Tower which, done direct, led to the 'thinnest ridge ever'. Eleven duly signed the summit book but it took an hour for everyone to arrive. William was exhausted. He had peeled several times and had, basically, been hauled up by Edi. Even before the start of the ridge he should have been made to return – and he should have known this too and so should the meet leader. This 'not wanting to let the side down' can have such consequences all too often. Edi himself wrote later, 'How could I have turned such a fine man back when he came ... full of good will to do the climb?'

We descended the North Ridge. I wrote, 'much snowier, sloppy stuff – with seemingly endless *gendarmes* which had to be abseiled off or climbed down. Only one tricky abseil as holds ran out before reaching snows... North Top, and turn off down the ridge towards the Klein Nesthorn. Easier, so moving together. William very tired indeed. Eventually contour down left onto a tongue of rock running onto the steep slope above the *bergschrund*. Dark by then ...' (My log described a fantasy sunset, the lights of Lötschental like fallen constellations, the Plough arcing round through the hours of dark). 'Abseil off, interesting, 260 ft, with ropes all joined, from an ice bollard. Schrund a 20 ft wall with only bridge here and huge depths elsewhere. I'd noticed it from the Schafberg at dawn when Edi was studying the route off. William was all in but able to think and obey. Pile clothes on him.'

It was here John and I received the lowered William and I noticed the seat had been worn out of his trousers with all his helpless slithering down. I thought he had on red underpants (how twee!) but, catching him, found the red was blood. I don't think I've ever been so coldly angry. John was appalled and, as a doctor, concerned. This situation should never have been allowed to develop.

Crossing the glacier we were eventually completely supporting William. 'Down and across, up a bit, and an icy slope down to moraine gap glaciers. The *aspirant* had gone on with his two partners. Edi cut steps up to a wee icy tarn. By then Dr John and I had decided enough was enough: William mustn't go on, any further effort could be very serious. Edi thought so too – and was all for giving him a boost from an injection so as to continue. John vetoed that – the worst medical idea – so William was made comfortable and we left Edi and John with William and the rest of us descended by moonlight to the hut, arriving just before 4.00 a.m., 26 hours since leaving. At 5.10 a.m. the two fittest of us scampered down to Blatten to call out the helicopter. (This was 1967 remember.) We'd a last irony, seeing the helicopter rise over the Schafberg then fly up to the Fafleralp hotel while we made our weary walk back up (no road to Fafleralp then) and, on arriving, finding Edi and John relaxing over breakfast on the terrace.'

Edi owned a mountain hotel so a year or two later we stayed with him there before our traverse of the Balmhorn-Altels. There was much chat and generous (guilty?) hospitality, sampling the local wines in Edi's cellar. The next day I felt 'grotty' on the hill but curiously, improved with height gained. Not a drinker, it took me a while to work out the reason why.

Of the Bietschhorn I wrote in my log, 'This was bad. William's abilities were known early so no reason to drag him over the peak, bullying him till we followed a blood trail from his hands, etc. then going on to the last gasp, reducing the man to that state ... I'd say Edi was 65 per cent responsible, William, who should have known better than to tackle such a *grande course*, 20 per cent, and the meet organiser, 15 per cent (a good organiser, competent climber, but too kindly: the steel must come through the velvet at such times).' I still shake my head at the memory.

---

1 Well, not with a guide, and that following year we did traverse the Matterhorn. We met Otto on top, were greeted warmly, and told the weather was fine for our descent of the Italian ridge. So of course the weather broke, we had a big thunderstorm and snow fell all the way down, a 17 hour day, an introductory Alpine epic. At a famous chimney we were held up because an Italian guide was climbing up the slot. Our ice axes were singing so we were quite happy to join him in hauling up his client, hand over hand, like a cork from a bottle, the guide's, 'Presto! Presto!' being replied to with a bleated, 'Momento, momento' from below. What on earth were they doing, there? Then? Guides, oh, guides!

THE VALLEY OF A THOUSAND HILLS

What shall our children's children do on the high places?
1 Kings 23:38

We are working up a stream that tumbles and gurgles down the steep dusty slope, a gang of kids, as mischievous as any such, but our 'hunting' is real enough. We are looking for snakes, poking with our sharpened sticks under boulders and among the brittle bushes. We are great hunters of course; we are death to any snake we find.

We are in the Valley of a Thousand Hills, our ringleader the local chief's son, my blood brother. I still bear the scar on my left wrist where we mingled our blood together. I wonder if he remembers? How did his life work out in that spectacular landscape, carved out by timeless times between the Drakensberg to the west and the Indian Ocean on the east?

I can remember our pestilential gang of boys being chased from a *kraal* by one irate grannie who told us, in no uncertain terms, to f. off. We went racing off, laughing of course. Her words stuck in my mind, my only remaining Zulu vocabulary, and sixty years on I was able to try them out on a visitor from South Africa. Suddenly turning to him I shouted out the words and burst out laughing at his startled face. I have long forgotten my best friend's name but remember the words of a grannie's ire.

The Valley of a Thousand Hills was not a name to slip from memory, besides I have been back. Alan Paton in his heartbreak story *Cry, the Beloved Country* opens with a description which has always remained in my memory of the world I briefly knew: 'There is a lovely road that runs from Ixopo into the hills. These hills are grass-covered and rolling, and they are lovely beyond any singing of it.' The Valley of a Thousand Hills was not just rolling but a superb jumble of knobbly hills, of *bergs* and *kloofs*, of the patchwork greens of steep fields and clustered villages, 'strung like emeralds on the copper thread of the yellow-brown waters of the river' (Bulpin), with 'falls and rapids scalloping into the landscape, a masterpiece of natural sculpture'. The Valley of a Thousand Hills' resonant name, the originator unknown, only came into use after the Boer War, decades after the pioneers pushed on up-country to eventually create the road from Durban to Pietermaritzburg. Pioneer farmers carved out Hillcrest and Botha's Hill, the places where we lived, on the edge of the mighty valley. So peaceful then, there was a previous black history as bloody as our own, though I don't think any Scots clans were terrifying cannibals, not even the Campbells. I was astonished to read recently of two adventurers in 1893 canoeing the whole length of the valley, a seven day epic.

We boys were, all boys are, natural savages at that age. Think *Lord of the Flies*. I can recall racing through the long grass and bushes at the back of the hotel to chase the wild careerings of the hens that had just had their head chopped off and 'hadn't the sense to know they were dead'. The stands of aromatic eucalyptus, an early import from Australia, dropped their fruits, a bit like those of an oak, so when the seed part fell out, little spiky cups remained. These we could fit on the ends of our fingers to turn our hands into the claws of lions and do our own imaginative hunting and fighting. I would lead a Zulu *impi* as readily as defend Rorke's Drift, or fend off attacks on a Boer inspanned camp, a natural savage. But the hard learning about race and creed, the inheritance of Adam, was soon to come. This was in 1942. I was eight years old.

Sadly we (parents, young brother) were to leave, but would do so precipitately following what happened to me. My 'best friend' and I were alone together playing with my Hornby train set. This wended among the furniture in the *rondavel* we occupied among the gum trees in the grounds of the hotel (a *rondavel* was an up-market imitative version of a native round thatched house). The hotel owner came in and, seeing us, angrily kicked my friend round the room and out the door with loud curses. How dare a black boy enter a white *baas*' hotel? I never saw my pal again, which is why I wonder how he fared, for his life would scream through the horror years of *apartheid*. Why do children – everywhere – always find they are born to inherit worlds of cursing?

Return to Kilimanjaro

> Kilimanjaro, Meru, Mount Kenya. Only the manic will slog to the top of these ex-volcanos, but some of the world's best walking can be had on their slopes.
>
> *Fifty Best Walks in the World 2018*

My two years of National Service in the RAF I look back on as the longest paid holiday of my life. Sort of. Both the year in Egypt and the year in Kenya still merited service medals, the former arriving fifty years on![1] Kenya was one long joy. As a lowly telephonist with easy working hours, a camp swimming pool, good *muckers*, Nairobi on the doorstep and all of East Africa beyond, how could it be other? We had many civilian friends and on free days were never in camp. We ranged the Ngong hills where I made two oil paintings and came interestingly close to a lion; we had the extravagance of game parks on another doorstep. In Nairobi we met theatrical types; years later in London I decided I must see *The Mousetrap*, then in its '25th whatever year,' and as soon as it began, realised it was the play I'd seen in Nairobi: I knew 'whodunnit'. We had the free run of various family homes and, as enthusiastic Christians, all manner of social occasions, from baking to feed the hundreds of Crusaders from the Prince of Wales and Duke of York schools, to taking time off to become a secretary/gofer for the team during a Billy Graham-style campaign. Yet there were airmen who never left camp and were bored or homesick.[2]

As a Scot I often attended the Church of Scotland's St. Andrew's church. The minister was the Rev. David Steel – father of Sir David Steel who became first Presiding Officer in Scotland's newly devolved Parliament. One day services were cancelled as a lion lay sprawled at the church entrance. On another we received startled looks from the elders lined up in the porch to give out hymn books. I had a large briefcase which went everywhere and had been nicknamed 'the Baby'. As we entered one of our gang turned to ask me all too audibly, 'Did you remember to put the Baby in the boot?'

Despite being in a country overflowing with good things, the camp food was so bad that eventually a strike was organised and the mess balcony painted with 'We want food fit to eat'. Our gang simply ate in town whenever possible, the posh Norfolk Hotel, which still exists, our favourite, even though it was supposedly for officers only. One of our 'civilian attachés' was a high-up civil servant, with a remit over all airfields, including our RAF Eastleigh outside

Nairobi. He used to collect us in his car and we'd exit in the boot while the gate guards would spring to attention and salute. Being a Classicist, his Ford Consul was called 'Fabius'; we travelled in it (not in the boot!) to the Mountains of the Moon. We also had a holiday in Mombasa, travelling down by the 'Lunatic Line' as it was first called.[3] There were some outstanding curry houses in Nairobi and we had an arrangement with one whereby we would hand over any game shot and in return be given a full meal, with all the trimmings, for four people.

I've a thousand memories like these. There were grimmer times. One of our gang was an RAF photographer and we would see Kikuyu villages where the cattle had been hamstrung and the people gruesomely butchered by the Mau Mau. Mt Kenya was out of bounds because of the State of Emergency at the time, which was a real sadness to one whose heroes were Shipton and Tilman.[4] We did see Thomson's Falls, named after Joseph Thomson, the Scottish explorer who was the first European to travel from the coast up through dangerous Masai county to Lake Victoria and come back alive. He was special – and the antithesis of butcher H. M. Stanley – and today is mentioned honourably in Masai school textbooks, while tourists are taken on 'Thomson treks'. He won through by befriending not shooting; a very unusual Victorian.

If Mount Kenya filled the view looking north to the equator, looking south there loomed the huge bulk of Kilimanjaro, at 5,895 m (19,340 ft) the highest summit in all Africa, often appearing with a dome of rosy summit snows rising from morning mist or later heat haze. This was an allure not to be denied.

I organised a group of us to climb Kili as a farewell treat before I returned to the UK. We arranged leave accordingly.

The RAF then decided to repatriate me early. Even an offer of signing on for another year wouldn't change their decision. Home I went, and was duly demobbed well ahead of time. Kili had escaped me. To rub salt in the wound, not long home, I received a telegram (you paid by the word): 'SURVIVORS FABIUS CONQUERED KILI'.

If you look at a map of the Kenya-Tanzania border you'll note it runs straight in from the coast then makes an odd sidestep to enfold Kilimanjaro into Tanzania, where logically it should have been in Kenya. Apparently this was at the behest of Kaiser Wilhelm (Germany had Tanganyika) who complained to grannie, Queen Victoria, that the British had all the good African mountains and couldn't poor old Willie please just have one. Victoria obliged. We were good at drawing lines on maps in those days. I'll come back to Kili – eventually.

In 1971 I took a sabbatical, and with a companion, Alistair, trekked, climbed and travelled in Andes and Africa as well as Norway, Corsica, Atlas and the Alps. The African section would be 'Cape to Cairo' we hoped. We did make it 'Cape to Kenya' which still had a ring to it. The journey was a tough one at times, few white wanderers were heading through recently-independent, often touchy Black Africa in 1971, especially with South Africa stamps in their passports. Apartheid (apart-hate!) was tightening its grip at the time. One typical experience: driving a borrowed Mini in the hills inland from Cape Town we saw a VW Beetle leave the road and end upside down. Some lads had been injured. There was some blood. We had noticed a hospital not long before, so flagged down cars to see if someone could help. Talk about Jesus' parable. Seeing who the injured were, the reply often came, 'I'm not taking effin' *kaffirs* to bleed all over my car.' ... 'Anyway, the hospital is only for Whites.' But our South African stay could also help at borders; we had stories, experiences to tell, could empathise. We rather enjoyed the provocations on our road ahead. Zambia alone gave an unfriendly border: we had all our gear scattered and scrutinised (how do you explain ice axes?) and we were tricked out of our Zambian money. Most times people were welcoming and friendly, poverty a happier house than wealth.

We climbed Table Mountain, went up into the Drakensberg Mountains into vile weather which had the Tugela Falls in riotous spate, but we still made Mont aux Sources 3,299 m (10,822 ft) which took us into Lesotho; we visited my childhood sites in Natal, and joined family in Pretoria; made sorties into the Chimanimani Mountains and climbed Sapitwa 3,002 m (9,847 ft) in the splendidly wild, seldom-visited Mulanje Mountains; ticked off the Victoria Falls and the astounding ruins of Great Zimbabwe; sailed up Lake Malawi (Nyasa) and, with difficulty, through Tanzania to Dar es Salaam before inland again for the intended high point, Kilimanjaro, Kilimanjaro at last.

Africa seemed such an endless world: one could drive a hundred miles and the landscape or skyscape remained the same, with the friendly familiar smell of the earth and the Pentecostal voices of people, so many people, people who smiled and sang.

My log noted that in South Africa it had been almost impossible to talk to any 'Black' (simply speaking to a petrol pump attendant would see the person clam up, afraid) but in Malawi 'the other extreme. A completely Africanised land, shabby, ticking-over, disorganised, happy-go-lucky – and frustrating'. Bus travel, once discovered and booked, was invariably slow, and jam-packed with a hundred noisy passengers, ran hours late and often broke down. We also had rather a lot of luggage. I recall at the Zambia-Tanzania border a crowd of kids diving for our pile and had the comical sight of each kitbag being carried on the heads of two *totos*, looking like leggy caterpillars. We could hardly get away from the friendly Tanzanian immigration and customs. Tea and chat. But no bus came. Hours passed. It rained. The Rest House was closed. In the end we had to overnight in a filthy hotel with a dead rat sizzling at the entrance. And I was having the runs and headaches. On one bus run we were held up by a solitary man digging a big hole in the road and he was not very keen to fill it in to let us past, so a crowd from the bus did so, the whole episode treated with merriment. Roads could be in a dreadful state, some of the drivers were maniacs, there were near-accidents and on one harder-than-normal bump we had the spectacle of our baggage flying off the roof. It always seemed to rain hard at the wrong moments. Sometimes we managed to obtain lifts which could be even more hair-raising. Often we stood for hours getting nowhere, packing was always a sweaty slavery, clothes became disgusting and if washed didn't dry in the heat and humidity. We were 'on the road' from November 1971 through to the end of January 1972.

The one curious break was our travelling up the 560 km (350 miles) of Lake Malawi (Nyasa) in the good ship *Ilala*, a steamer built in Jarrow in 1948 and carried overland in parts through Mozambique to Lake Nyasa and then reassembled by the Nyasa Railway Company. She replaced one of the same name which made the same extraordinary journey in 1875. There was still very much a feeling of the *African Queen* about her – and even about reaching her.

The train managed to make the 140 mile journey from Malawi's capital Blantyre to Chipoka at the south end of the lake last sixteen hours. The train started elsewhere we were told, and would reach people waiting at Blantyre for 5 a.m. At 6.30 a.m. the train passed through Blantyre without stopping, its three carriages packed, leaving 800 folk stranded. Our second-class carriage we saw did have room. We quickly hired a car, threw in our two kitbags, two cases, two rucksacks, and grip, and set off for Balaka Station 70 miles up the line to intercept the train; there we waited for two hours before fighting in to our seats in the 'reserved' 2nd. After a two-hour wait we headed off on 'a quite incredibly horrible trip … More fun at Chipoka, 8 p.m., for boat tickets and then *ferried* to the *Ilala* which was berthed at the pier!' First class was full but travelling cooped-up in the bowels packed with 500 others with no facilities for three days was a test too far to contemplate. We weren't provisioned at all! After several hours of bargaining, and paying the full 1st class fare, we could have camp beds at night in the 1st class saloon.

We were roused at 5 a.m. so tables could be laid. I had a real bath and was on deck chatting to the Belgian captain as the big sun turned the lake to fire among the heralding of unknown birds. We saw clouds of lake flies looking like smoke over the water and were told that when the swarms hit shore, the locals went crazy over them, catching myriads and turning them into something like gnatburgers, a nutritious addition to their constant diet of fish. We sunned on deck, with iced drinks from the bar and talked politics and school and people in common with the handful of passengers: eight adults and two children. At any stop, dugouts would swarm around the ship and hands would reach out from the lowest deck to buy mangos and dried fish (food was not provided other than in 1st class). We had breakfast, lunch, teas and coffees, dinner etc. On Christmas Day, the saloon was festooned with bunting, with a tree, a Christmas cake, and crackers and wine for dinner – turkey of course.

Startling contrasts, those three *Ilala* days. Passing wooded islands and shoreline at one point, Alistair spoke what I was thinking, 'Could be Loch Lomond.'[5]

We were crowded into a boat to land, had to sweat with our gear up to reach a road and fight for a bus seat to Karonga itself, the actual town. The bus departure place at Karonga was a sea of mud, and estimates for onward travel varied from 'tomorrow' to 'March'. Nothing was open. A lift took us to a Rest House but no transport ever appeared. We made bully beef and mash. My log commented 'Thundery within and without' and by morning I had the runs. They were not to be 'shits that pass in the night' and were no doubt the beginning of my ultimate woes. I suffered while others kept on lookout for anything on wheels. This time it was a lorry which did take us over the hills, a last glimpse of the lake far below, and a Rest House at Chitipa, once more on the high tablelands with kinder conditions, and near the border with Tanzania. An Italian and an Irish couple had been stranded there for days.

I was in a bad way. My temperature was 102°F at one stage yet we somehow pushed on. Iringa gave a three hour wait, the only food bananas – and cokes. Hours in buses gave numb bums and bruised kneecaps. Pleasant hills lay south of Morogoro and we ran into elephants while going through the Mikumi National Park. I'd somewhat recovered by the time we reached Dar es Salaam. *Haven of Peace* it was, with the civilised Agip Hotel (remember Supercortemaggiore?). We'd hardly recovered, eaten, repacked and collapsed into bed (air conditioning!) when the city exploded in a cacophony of blaring car horns, ship's sirens, church bells, and fireworks. 1972 had arrived! Now things would get better.

When we left Dar I was feeling fine but Alistair was sickening. We had to proceed; the next train wasn't for another three days. Away from the sticky heat, life felt better and the train certainly was. I reported for dinner (there was good food and friendly service), but A.L. stayed horizontal and next morning was feeling sick and had turned rather yellow. He wouldn't even look at Kilimanjaro as it came into view. At Moshi, with its Germanic station, close to the border with Kenya, we found our heavy baggage wasn't on the train. We headed to the Livingstone Hotel and got A.L. into bed. I'd read Scott's *Bride of Lammermoor* right through on the train, and now had a chance to write a few letters and a long memo to John Cook, our Chairman of the Scottish Mountain Leadership Training Board of which I was a member, about the recent Cairngorm tragedy when several children died on the plateau in a blizzard; incongruous, sad matters to be thinking about in the torrid heat and African bustle.

We were now joined by Bob Wilson and Bill Wade,[6] friends from climbing in Alps and Atlas who were 'signed up' with us for the Kilimanjaro ascent. Next day, in a hired Fiat, we headed to Arusha, open country and much cultivated, aiming for the Ngurdoto crater (precipitous rim and ash cone within) and Momella Lodge where we overnighted in a *rondavel* with a bark roof. The mountain Meru dominated the view. Meru was a three-day climb, but at least we enjoyed walking up the forest below it. There were giraffe and elephants but it was the birds I kept adding to my list: rollers, a hammerkop, Kori bustard, pratincole. After another couple of hours a ranger drove up and collared us; we were not supposed to be on foot or alone in the Park. We did however have the best ever view of Kilimanjaro, free of its usual frown of cloud. We nearly didn't make the drive back to Arusha as a violent storm flooded the landscape and dust turned to mud. 'Interesting driving.'

Our lost luggage had caught up with us, and with A.L. restored to health there was a mighty sorting-out day. A tin of cocoa had burst open in one kitbag. We took a taxi to the bus station and a bumpy bus ride to Marangu, start point for our ascent of Kilimanjaro. The small hotel was, for us, very touristy, reflecting the lure of the highest, whether Ben Nevis, Mont Blanc or Kili. The gardens gave me happy birding: green pigeon, black-headed weaver, wood owl, spotted eagle owl, red-backed mannikin, sunbird ... At last my eighteen-year wait for Kilimanjaro was being rewarded. We had a local guide and helper, always just called Anderson, his real name being unpronounceable, with a few porters to carry gear.

To begin with we went up a big road through the *shambas*, then a rougher Land Rover track to pass a plaque to German Hans Meyer and Austrian Ludwig Purtscheller, who made the first ascent of the mountain in 1889 (in 1848 the Royal Geographical Society had ridiculed the missionary Johannes Rebmann's claim of having seen a snowy mountain).[7] We were then into the jungle with strange giant heaths and other exotics. We were nearly up through it when we reached the Mandara Hut at 2,700 m (9,000 ft). Once it was called the Bismarck Hut. Bob, lagging, was caught in a deluge. Others arrived and tents sprang up. Our hut group was eleven. 'Much rain overnight' I recorded.

Setting off by 6 a.m. after tea and porridge we had a magical view of stars, some now 'below our level' so to speak. Both Mawenzi and Kibo were white-washed with snow. Going slowly, Pole! Pole! (Anderson's refrain slowly), we reached the Horombo Hut (once Peter's hut) at 10.10 a.m., now at 3,720 m (12,000 ft). Next day was more directly up with a valley of giant groundsels on our right. After a 'last water' pause we undulated along under a bluff with odd glimpses of Kibo's summit snows, like cream poured over ginger cake. We gained the wide saddle, a desert plain really, between Kibo and rugged Mawenzi. We had been carrying basic climbing gear ever since South Africa, mainly with Mount Kenya in mind, but with Mawenzi plastered any hope of climbing on it disappeared (so much for carrying up ropes etc). Some descent and then a long gradual haul up led to the Kibo Hut (4,703 m, 15,200 ft). The scale, both of and from the mountain is astonishing; after all the summit is about five times higher than Ben Nevis, but Kili gives new meaning to the word horizons. They curve, seen way beyond the oceanic scale of plains, plains that fade away to seeming infinity. The immediate landscape views are fairly grim. Barren. Mawenzi hedgehog-spiky. We're above where things grow happily, above where humans have ever lived.

Both A.L. and I were thoroughly acclimatised and full of beans, Bill and Bob came in slowly and a bit white, the altitude telling. I recorded, 'Glad just to feel fine'. I rigged a space sheet to melt water and retired for an afternoon nap. Snow fell.

I rose with a splitting headache and my guts in rebellion, so took some pills and seemed OK at supper. Only three other people joined us at the table in the tiny hut, sited in what I called 'a black midden of a spot'. At midnight I reeled out of the hut, staggering all over the place before emptying 'both fore and aft' as someone put it. There was absolutely no chance of being able to go up when our guide, helper and friend Anderson called us from sleep at 1 a.m. I lit the tilly lamp and primus and collapsed back to bed. Everyone was off by 2 a.m. 'Just isn't fair' I girned to my log. At 8 a.m. I yielded up my sleeping bag to our porters who set off to grab bed space for us down at the Horombo Hut. I had to stop and rest every few hundred yards across the Saddle, more often for the rise. Pole! Pole! and how! It was forcing strength out of weakness, toothpaste from an empty tube. At one stage I lay there looking up to circling vultures. I was convinced they were on a gastronomic tour of inspection. I've never had to struggle on a descent like that before. I wasn't long in when Alistair arrived (3.30 p.m.) and the others a bit later. Both the fit A.L. and Bill (who looked shattered) made Uhuru, the true, more distant summit round the snow-filled caldera of the one-time volcano, Bob stopping at Gilman's Point, as the majority seem to do – the altitude winning. I was doubly peeved as I was so well acclimatised.

That was more or less the end of our African safari. Bill was heading to Uganda, Bob was flying home, and Alistair and I were content to relax a bit. The travelling had been tough. I did not regain full strength for six months; this the only such illness in my life. In Nairobi I found I had lost a stone-and-a-half in weight. My state also ruled out any idea of climbing Mount Kenya, for the others as well, as I was the only experienced climber in the party. In Nairobi we stopped with John King, an old climbing friend, and enjoyed some social life with other members of the Mountain Club of Kenya. A.L. showed the Club slides of our Andes days. I was able to visit many sites remembered from eighteen years before: we dined in the Norfolk Hotel and the New Stanley; went up to Kikuyu to the Alliance High School which still bore the imprint of Laurie Campbell, its charismatic headmaster and our host in RAF days (see *Walking the Song* for an extraordinary connection with him); visited Thomson Falls; and best of all, had a day at

Lake Nakuru to prove that one can envisage, or meet, a million, in this case of flamingos. Nature in numbers is numbingly awesome.

Belongings were packed in a tea chest to go by sea as we struggled to make the 44 lb flight baggage allowance. They'd catch up later. A last look round the amazing Bird Room in the museum, a farewell to the paradise flycatchers in John's garden, a run out through the clouds of blue-flowering jacaranda trees to Embakasi Airport, and it was a Jumbo home to the UK. On a shelf as I write is a tattered garland of everlastings, flowers woven by Anderson, a garland given to each of us as we left Kilimanjaro, the name remembered as he sang rather than spoke it, 'Kilima N'jaro'. The memories are bitter-sweet. Mostly sweet. Even if it was *Kwaheri*, for ever, to Kilimanjaro.

---

1 My Kenya General Service Medal was simply handed over on leaving the country; the one for my previous year in Egypt's Canal Zone came later, a lifetime later, through the post. The medal came then for the same reason that other medals for other places (most notably for the Arctic Convoys) were meanly refused recognition as combat zones by successive UK governments. 'Only about ninety fatalities in the Canal Zone?' Hardly tallied with hundreds of gravestones though.

2 With hindsight the Fifties seem to have been a period of Christian religious revival, both at home and in the 'Colonies'. For me, there had been the Scripture Union at school and Varsity and Public School Camps in the holidays, and then, within the RAF, always groups of evangelical enthusiasts who also linked up with like-minded 'civilians'. 'Crusaders' were a sort of Sunday School for teenagers, in Nairobi, entirely drawn from the posh schools mentioned, the white sons of the Kenya elite, already facing the new realities of demands for African independence, with its extremist element of Mau Mau. Posters proclaiming 'God has the Answer' were plastered all over the city. The 'team' were from South Africa, with leader/preacher Ken Terhoven, a sidekick Roger Voke, a large choir, catchy theme tune, all very Billy Graham campaigning in character, and completely non-racial. Would things were so simple today.

3 In 1895 a railway began to be constructed from Mombasa on the coast up to Lake Victoria, a distance of six hundred miles. This would traverse unmapped and scarcely explored country, going through deserts and vast plains, coping with the Great Rift Valley and a hundred miles of bog in Uganda. Much of the way there were attacks from hostile tribes, while bridge construction and line-laying was held up for months by man-eating lions. This was speculation gone wild: a lunatic railway. The magnificent, tragic, entertaining saga is told (in 550 pages!) by Charles Miller in *The Lunatic Express, an Entertainment in Imperialism* (1971). J. H. Patterson, *The Man-Eaters of Tsavo* (1907 & reprints) is a hair-raising account of one problem, mainly facing the Indian workforce brought in as labour, who also endured nasties like tsetse flies and malaria.

4 Mt. Kenya, 5,199 m, 17,058 ft, rises at the equator and was first climbed in 1899 by Oxford geographer (Sir) Halford Mackinder, a feat at the time, though he was accompanied by six Europeans, including two French Alpine guides, sixty-six Swahili, two Masai guides and ninety-six Kikuyu, two of whom were killed by hostile tribes. They ran into atrocious weather, extreme terrain, porter strikes, thefts, and a first attempt that ended in an unplanned bivouac. Finally Mackinder and the two guides made the summit, Batian, by a route (not the *voie normale*) now graded IV. The second ascent, over the lower twin top, Nelion, was made by Shipton and Wyn Harris in 1929, before Shipton and Tilman made the audacious traverse of the mountain over Batian and Nelion in the following year. Shipton and Tilman were both rather bored, prosaic coffee-planters who met up in 1929. They climbed Kilimanjaro and Mawenzi. After their Mt Kenya doings, they became more than happy to become perpetual explorers of mountains the world over. I must just mention a delightful book, recently reprinted, by Felice Benuzzi, *No Picnic on Mount Kenya* (1952). Benuzzi and two friends, Italian prisoners of war, successfully broke out of a British POW camp to make a bold attempt on the mountain – and then had to break *into* the camp on their return.

5 The *Ilala*, after a recent refit, still plies Lake Malawi, much more upmarket, on an erratic weekly schedule but no longer going up to the north end of the lake.

6 Bill was a professor of Constitutional Law at Cambridge University and had been one of a party involved in creating the new constitution for independent Uganda. Bill went on to Kampala after Kilimanjaro to stay with the Attorney-General and family – at a very stressful

moment. When Idi Amin had grabbed power in January 1971 one of the things he did was to take brides from different tribes to try to curry favour. He then thought it might be gainful to have an Indian wife as well, and his eye fell on the Attorney-General's daughter. She was promptly packed off out of the country. Amin's response, a few months after Bill's visit (August 1972), was to dispossess and expel all Indians, an economic idiocy. What happened to the Attorney-General is not known; he was one of thousands of Amin's 'disappearers'. Amin himself would flee the country he ruined in 1979.

7 The first missionary to set up in East Africa, near Mombasa in 1844, was Johann Krapf. He had a naïve vision of establishing Christian centres all across the continent, and in 1846 was joined by Johannes Rebmann. The pair alternated exploratory journeys inland and in 1845 Rebmann clearly saw Kilimanjaro, only to have his report scorned by the armchair geographers at home, the RGS being particularly nasty about this 'Baron Münchausen'. (In 1849 it was Krapf, in a brief spell in the rains, who was able to see and describe Mount Kenya, Africa's second highest mountain.) The first attempt to climb Kili was by a German, mapping in the area, who got up to about 14,000 ft. The first person to reach the snows was Charles New, an English Methodist missionary, in 1871. He returned, but his party was despoiled and he died while returning to the coast.

THE RISHI GANGA

> We need the dispossession of travel to balance
> the accumulations of everyday life.
>
> **Eric Shipton**

Nanda Devi is one of the world's most spectacular mountains – India's highest at 7,817 m – and is reached by one of the most remarkable approach walks, if 'walk' can be used for the eight or nine days of first gaining, then fighting up the Rishi Ganga gorge. There is nothing like it. I've met some of the climbers who have been on peaks like Kalanka and Changabang and it is not the climbs but the walking-in that drew comments and superlatives.

Nanda Devi sits in a basin of flowering meadows which, rightly, was called the Sanctuary, for it is enclosed by a gigantic rampart of peaks with no easy access gaps in their encircling. Only the two rivers, draining north and south from the central hub of Nanda Devi join to force their way out through the Rishi Ganga Gorge. Nanda Devi has an Eastern Summit which attaches to this mighty rim so the peak itself cannot be circled at Sanctuary level. And, above all, near and from afar, soars Nanda Devi, a peak of sculpted beauty when seen from a distance, an overpowering presence when near her – her, for she is worshipped as a goddess. No mountain presented such allure to early explorers and no mountain had such defences.

W. W. Graham, in 1883, managed to reach the Gorge by a complex bit of exploring but forcing a way up it proved impossible. In 1905 Longstaff gained a col on the eastern rim of the South Sanctuary (named the Longstaff Col) but saw no way to descend into the basin.[1] In 1907 he forced a route into the lower gorge and climbed Trisul but made little progress beyond where Graham had been. In 1932 Hugh Ruttledge prospected towards a col on the South Rim (today's Sunderdhunga Col) but thought it impossible as a route in. The only way had to be up the Rishi Ganga, and that had become a dream, a challenge and, ultimately, a success for Shipton and Tilman, in 1934. In 1936 Tilman would stand on the summit of Nanda Devi (Shipton was on Everest) which remained the highest-climbed peak till 1950.

A group of us first thought of the traverse to Nanda Devi from Nanda Devi East, that peak which attaches the mountain to the rim of the Sanctuary. This would be a plum new route. Alas, the Japanese did it[2] and our party amicably divided into those still intent on Nanda Devi, by its repeated route, and those who would like to be based in the more unknown Northern Sanctuary where there were many fine unclimbed peaks on offer. Eric Roberts and his party chose the former and climbed Nanda Devi and our party had an equally successful time. But peaks are just peaks. The walk in was extraordinary and it is this I'll record. We made a wise choice; the original plan was far beyond our capabilities.

I kept a day-to-day log but also wrote many air letters in miniscule hand which were sent home whenever possible and it is these I will quote. I was lucky in reaching Delhi just as the family we would stay with were heading off to Kashmir[3] – so I went with them to live on a houseboat and be the tourist (at useful altitude). Charles, Donald, Christine and I then made an acclimatising trip to Smythe's Valley of the Flowers, in the monsoon; but then the flowers came with the rain. We made a novel exit of our own over an unknown pass to Badrinath. On the way in we met a splendid, big black-bearded Sikh, who stopped to chat. When Charles said he was from Sheffield the response was, 'Oh, Sheffield. I'm a Bradford man myself.' After our visit to the holy town of Badrinath we all gathered at Joshimath, via the Mussoorie Express from Delhi and a bus to Rishikesh. (Without today's roads Shipton and Tilman had ten days of trekking to reach this point.) Our medic was last to arrive as he had been fighting the customs over the medical kit. It was only allowed in after being listed in triplicate and had to be checked out again at the end, they said. (It wasn't; and we'd made sure most of it went to the people at Lata, for whom it would be treasure.) We had arrived relatively trouble-free – believing the Seven Ps, that 'prior planning and preparation prevents piss poor performance' – and also praying for no ambushing disasters to come.

Every expedition faces horrific logistical work. We brought some food from the UK, bought most expensive items in Delhi, shopped in Rishikesh (and watched a kitbag of food fly off the roof of the bus to roll down the hillside into the Ganges) and finally, in Joshimath, purchased sacks of *ata, dal,* etc.. We met five Australians there with their LO (Liaison Officer) who were also heading for the Sanctuary and they, our seven, two locals and all the gear made quite a load on a lorry which took us to the starting no-place. Carl Linnaeus wrote in his diary (1732) '... as soon as I came onto the mountains it was as if I received new life and a heavy burden had been taken from me'. Just the feeling at the start of a Himalayan sortie . What follows comes from the letters home.

9ᵀᴴ SEPTEMBER

We are now immune to hair-raising roads and only shut our eyes occasionally. We were dumped on the verge of the road in the middle of nowhere it felt, above the Dhauliganga. (Lata village, our first landmark, is half-an-hour above the road.) We camped, a tarpaulin over our pile of gear, and tents or brollies sheltering us from the rain. It rains about half the time but is a vertical, well-behaved precipitation, not at all Scottish. The Aussie LO is a pleasant climber and not a military shop steward. The day went in sorting out porters. They dribble in from a departing Japanese trip but there aren't enough, so we will need goats as well. They carry porter food, so this avoids the porters for porters Catch 22 situation.

14ᵀᴴ SEPTEMBER

There were no vital hold-ups. The porter food was repacked in 6-18 kg panniers for the goats. 'Goat-man' is quite a character. We all wended up the hillside in haphazard fashion, through Lata where our men come from, and up, up. I was glad when a porter caught me up at our Bhalta camp site. It would have been annoying to overshoot. Loads arrived over many hours and we grew impatient waiting for that day's

food box – only to find it was there already! I stoked a wood
fire and we cooked a meat, veg and spiced macaroni dish.
Chapattis with cheese and/or jam and good coffee saw dusk
slip into stars. The porters' fires wink among the trees. Goat
bells tinkle. It hardly rained all day but Sher Singh was firm:
'Monsoon finish two days'.

We were astir by 5.30 a.m. and soon left the glade to
the crows and smoke. The climb was steeply upwards *all
day*. 'Very vertical mud' someone called it. Huge pines
were draped in Spanish moss: a vertical Mila Dorcha! The
irksome rain returned for much of the day – and night. Lata
Kharak was an exposed ridge and sordid in the extreme. My
tent was in one of the last loads to arrive (I'll carry it myself
in future – hours crouching under a brolly tend to pall.)
While I was rigging a shelter to cook under, all the tent sites
had been taken, so mine was perched on a platform built of
kitbags. A goat is slaughtered – to propitiate the Goddess of
Weather we hope. Rain fell all night.

It rained for the seven hours of march the following day
too: a double stage. At the end of the day it took some time,
inside sleeping bag, inside tent, to warm up and dry out a
bit. We suffer because of wanting to be *in* the Sanctuary
for the maximum good weather period. Days matter. (They
mattered more to Shipton and Tilman who had limited
time in the Sanctuary – if they reached it – from the limited
amount of food they and three Sherpas could carry there.
In June they were floundering up to their waists in snow at
this stage and were having to find a practical route as well.)

We climbed, endlessly, to a pass with a stone arch at
4,252 metres, then kept up and down at that level on a path
which felt as if only glued to the cliffs by mud. Some of the
porters were in bare feet or old gym shoes. Maybe it is as
well we didn't see the drop below: 1,650 metres to the gorge

of the Rishi Ganga. It was long thought impenetrable as a big 'curtain' of cliff added to its defences. Our long haul up was to gain the height needed to outflank these outer defences.

Dharansi, at 4,145 metres was passed, an open site the porters were keen *not* to use under monsoon conditions. They have neither tents nor sleeping bags and survive under tarpaulins in remarkably cheerful fashion. A col beyond was 4,237 metres and on a bit, we suddenly plunged over 700 metres down a slope to forest level and camped at Dibrugheta, 3,499 metres. A roaring torrent from Dunagiri was crossed by a bridge consisting of a solitary log. The goats filed across quite cheerfully! Having cooked the night before I retreated to tent comforts; an eerie site with smoky fires and voices muffled among the dripping trees. Nobody seemed very cheery and supper was tired-looking pasta and corned beef floating in a gravy of rainwater. Only Charles, Ian and I could be bothered making chapattis and coffee.

Everybody dried or singed clothes over fires in the morning and it was eleven o'clock before we set off. The path contoured up and down and in and out – good horizontal progress for a change – till we came back to the Rishi Ganga itself and crossed it by a doddery bridge to camp on the other side (Deodi, 3,292 m). Tents and clothes hung from the birch trees. The porters sang. They also slaughtered another goat. The victim's belly is slit and a hand rips out the heart which sits beating on a plate thereafter. Frank, who is a surgeon, was full of admiration. A porter came and daubed my brow with red powder. We had 'teuchy' goat for supper.

Did the sacrificial goat maybe work? Or Sher Singh's weather sense? The monsoon rains appear to be over, just as predicted. We can expect cold, clear days now until winter comes. Today's route was a real yo-yo: up, down, up, down,

300 metres each time. A valley came in from the south, from Trisul, climbed by Tom Longstaff in 1907, the first-ever 7,000 metre peak to be scaled. Longstaff may have looked into the Sanctuary but the Rishi Gorge defeated him reaching it. After the monsoon in 1934 Shipton and Tilman returned to explore the southern section of the Sanctuary and would look up to Longstaff's Col from below. They found what would be the line to climb Nanda Devi and escaped by the nightmare Sunderdhunga pass on the south rim, abseiling off ice bollards among avalanches, heading they scarce knew where.

We had another up, down, to where the Ramani River comes in from the north. The mighty side of Changabang (the peak recently climbed by Bonington *et al*) lies that way. The gorge becomes sheer now and camp is a small level area held between cliff and torrent. My door is on the edge of a straight drop to the river (mustn't sleepwalk) and the noise colossal, the precipices amplifying the sound.

I'm finishing off this airletter as we have a postie. The Aussie LO has been ill and Frank is worried enough to suggest he makes a rapid exit to lower altitude in case of pulmonary oedema.[4] Goat-man takes his beasts back from here. One animal got on the cliff and knocked a stone down on a porter's head. Sher Singh grinned. 'Only head. Duralam Singh thick skull. OK.' – but he'll go out too just in case. The porter carrying the First Aid Box is suffering from a strained back! Donald, Stephen and I went on to get photos down to the camp. The track is suddenly very exposed as it teeters up the overhang above the gorge – a mere dent in 600 metre crags. Rhodies and birch make welcome handholds but some bits are really scary. The fun is about to begin. It feels as if we are regrouping and preparing for action – sending the wounded out and writing last letters while we can.

All the sites are rapidly being fouled. The porters rip down wood to burn, ground is churned to mud, hygiene minimal and litter everywhere. (The Sanctuary is now closed to allow it to recover both from human despoilation and from the ravagings of the goats. This spot had, for generations, been as far as man and goats had managed, but the locals found another way in and threatened to graze the Sanctuary to death.)

17TH SEPTEMBER: IN THE SANCTUARY

The last letter went off from the Ramani camp. We thought we had had impressive walking by then, and so we had, but the next two days just overwhelmed us. 'Mind-blowing' truly describes it. I have never been so scared for so long at a time, ever. It left us exhausted from mind to toes! Our admiration for Shipton and Tilman reached new summits. They broke through here the year I was born. It was all unknown country to them and they often thought they were about to fail but always found a tenuous continuation. They often had to ferry loads so repeated dangers constantly. Shipton's *Nanda Devi* tells in modest fashion what was one of the great feats of exploration.

Our day began early (fires flickering into life at 5 a.m. with a 7 a.m. departure). We began with a brutal 600 metre grass slope which shrank the river below to near-silence. From a spur we had a fabulous view of Nanda Devi, framed in the vee cleft of the Rishi Ganga, the summit imprinting a plume across the bluest of bluest sky and the new snows reaching far down into the shadows. We wended on with a continued supply of awkward wee places to deal with (the thin track was just marked out by passing feet), on slopes that were never less than frighteningly steep. We wound in and out and up, higher and higher, till we came to a nasty gully with a drop of 1,000 metres to the river, with muddy slabs beyond. The remains of a piton and rope hinted at the dangers but the porters with our ropes had romped ahead! One of the Aussie porters lost his load of *ata* (flour). It went tumbling down, visually and audibly, all too like a human falling. The porters are amazing. Awkward boxes or sacks are simply carried on backs and held with ropes. They have a sort of emergency ripcord so a tug can shed the load. I think the porter did that here to save himself tumbling off.

The famous Tilman Slabs followed but they were decently tamed by fixed ropes. The last reach of slabs had none and was quite an effort, with the equivalent of two Ben Nevis north faces under one's heels. Technically the going is easy enough but when every step over long hours has to be safe, it became a bit of a strain. Hard to describe as there is nothing comparable. The opposite side of the gorge is simply sheer cliff for thousands of feet, choughs minute specks on it and big waterfalls just tiny spouts. A few tent-spaces dug out on the slope indicated Bujgara campsite but we walked on past its spectacular setting. The bluff beyond was edged by track only as wide as our feet, impressed into the steepest vegetated slope I've seen. It rose and fell from the path in staggering scale, sliddery Ochils grass at a 70° angle.

Ahead loomed more prows and rocky bluffs, one, the 'Pisgah' of Shipton-Tilman, so called as from it you could view the Promised Land. We lost about 300 metres to round one spur and at once doubled back to toil 300 metres up, traverse under the next wall, go down a rake, scramble up to the next – then, far from the route keeping low, we turn up again on wet slabs, vegetation, a gully bed and haul out to the crest of the final barrier. You might have heard my yell of relief and glee from Pisgah top. I felt as if I could reach out a hand and touch Nanda Devi. The peak was no longer away ahead, a remote framed beauty but now filled our world: a stark, bold, intimidating mass of black and white. New snow was down to the moraines just above the level where I stood. Just 200 metres ahead a pillar of smoke rose in the still air. This was the Tilchaunani camp. I was soon clasping the most wonderful mug of tea in the world. The tents were pitched on slabby platforms cut into and built out of the steep hillside: split-level living. Eight porters had simply dumped their loads and shot back to Ramani for a second carry the next day. Water was scarce and a porter made a spout from a rhubarb leaf to catch the trickle. I had one pee exit in the middle of the night. The world was breathy-cold and there was an extravagance of stars. Nanda Devi, so ice-white by day, was a black blank, but recognisable shape, against the silver sheen of stars.

The exit from Tilchaunani was by fixed ropes over another band of slabs. We were able to look away past the mountain into the northern half of the Sanctuary – right to the peaks of the Eastern Rim (one of which Shipton-Tilman climbed as well as making several cols on the rim). This, the Uttari Rishi, is now our home till winter comes. Being on the south side of the Rishi Ganga Gorge meant we had first to cross to the other side, but below was impassable gorge so we'd have to go on to first cross the river draining the Southern Sanctuary, then the northern torrent.

Donald and I were off first and even with fixed ropes we trod like Agag. There was a huge gully to cross, the first of many ins and outs. We rested on a spur after a boulder bit and had a neck-craning view up to Nanda Devi, then, at last, at last, a long, descending traverse. We just about died when two turkey-sized Himalayan snowcocks went squealing off from our feet with the suddenness of grouse but the noise of pigs. We found the skulls (with horns) of two *burral*. Down in the gorge there were snow pigeons and a pale gentian stared between the grasping birch.

The Aussies had chosen a quicker line from camp (crafty Pommies!) so already had a pulley system in place across the gorge of the first river. The whole drainage of the Southern Sanctuary roared through a cliff-girt gap half the width of a country road. A good long-jumper had made it onto a big boulder from which a high step onto the cliff on the other side was possible. They had just rigged up a pulley system from cliff to cliff and it was soon busy as what felt like dozens of people and dozens of loads were hauled across. The pegs all held! As up to four loads of 56lbs plus, crossed at a time, they had been well tested. Hard work but fun.

It was only after I'd done my share of work at the crossing and was wending on up onto the ridge between the two rivers that it suddenly struck me that we were technically *on* Nanda Devi. Quite an emotional realisation! We went on along rotten crags to where the valley opened out with the second river. A high bank would have to do to anchor a rope across to the other side (our turn to rig the crossing). Porters began to arrive but, naturally, the ropes were at the rear this time.

Impatient Donald went on to cross on the glacier snout upstream. Peter arrived next and it was all pretty shambolic with three sahibs yelling at each other, the roar of the river and the milling mob of porters who mostly refused to cross as camp was only going to be 300 metres away on the other side. As the money was already across it spoke loudest. The ropes sagged and had to be held aloft overhead at both ends by several people. It always seemed to go slack when an unpopular local lad was halfway over! No sahib was dipped in the water!

I withdrew to prepare supper at the temporary site while

others ferried loads and haggled over paying-off most of the lads. Stephen and Frank opted to go round by the glacier snout rather than risk a wetting but they left rather late and had an unscheduled and uncomfortable bivvy when frosty darkness caught them.

Next day some of the good porters roll up with loads doubled from Tilch. More will come later. We brew with them again. Righ Singh is a real character in a tartan tammy. He has been up Trisul, the Devistan peaks and to Camp II on Changabang with Chris Bonington. Sher Singh is his brother. These two, Donald and I carry hefty loads and go off to recce for our permanent base camp. The Aussies are to be camped at the Shipton-Tilman base by a tarn beyond the white, granite-covered snout of the Changabang Gal (glacier) but it is a bleak spot and we settled for a flowery, grassy slope before their glacier where there is a spring of delicious water and an abundance of dead wood for the luxury of fires.

The others went back to the first river crossing to help with the last loads and ensure everything is over both rivers today if possible and up here tomorrow. We should manage with the porters available. Sher Singh spots porters descending from Tilch. We could hardly see them, even with binoculars. Without 'Braggart' Singh, the ineffective, blustering 'head porter,' yesterday's shambles was avoided. Most cheerfully splashed through the river with just minimal rope aid, treating it as a big joke if one sat down in the foam. Six of us, seven porters (everyone – except Frank – cooking) took a 56 lb load up to the Base Camp. Our choice seemed to meet with approval. We had a cheery night round a fire with a tin of UK ham and spicy rice, while Righ Singh showed off his chapatti-making ability. Pity we couldn't just go on and on with just such admirable company. There is a pow-wow going on now about our date of exit and which porters are to come. To make doubly sure a letter in English can be taken to the Lata school-teacher to translate and read to them. The Rishi Ganga under snow is not anyone's idea of a place to be caught in (Shipton and Tilman made their exit in torrential monsoon rains).

I scribble away to get these air letters off with the departing porters. Our only loss on the crossings was a karabiner falling into the river. Our chosen Base Camp is 4,500 metres, yet we are able to load-carry and romp about unaffected by altitude and we sleep like babies. Much as we enjoy the gregarious porters (and ourselves) the best is about to start: the bliss of solitude, in one of the world's most inaccessible and beautiful places. We all have our small individual tents, plus a couple of high level ones, we can plan, change partners, do as we like – quite the antithesis of an 'expedition'. Shipton and Tilman would approve! We are overwhelmed by Nanda Devi, a marble-white sculpture rising to a summit far above our Sanctuary base, the whole sweep along to the East Summit falling in a *3,000 metre*, multi-pleated curtain of snow and ice. Shipton called it 'a wall perhaps unequalled anywhere in the world'. Unimaginably grand. Outside my tent is a spread of bright pink alpine bistort.

Everyone has now retreated to tents. Candles glow and odd conversations are muted by the river. I wouldn't be anywhere else in the world. I'm falling asleep as I write so must stop. Goodness knows when or how the next letter will reach you.

The 'next' letter went out with the Australian group in early October. (They were turned back just 30 metres from the summit of Changabang.) On the 11th we were all in camp, stuffing ourselves with jam chapattis and wondering about one last summit before the exit date we'd agreed, when we heard voices. In our Sanctuary? In trotted Goman Singh (another of Sher Singh's brothers) and four porters, several days early, but urging us to get out pronto as winter was coming sooner than thought. This was a bombshell. A hateful idea. In a stroke, from our lonely paradise, to return to life as we'd almost forgotten it, with its frantic din and pressures. To suddenly have to face the brutal Rishi Ganga on the morrow. Doubling up stages. Hurry. Hurry. Sher Singh, Righ Singh and the others rolled in before dusk. They brought a *real* treat: a bag of fresh apples and newly lifted potatoes. They also brought mail which scattered us to our tents.

So that was that, the ending all too like an execution. The exit was to be as dramatic as the entry and the prospect concentrated the mind thoroughly. A Japanese expedition doing Nanda Devi had stripped off many of the fixed ropes and there wasn't time to fix new security. We all had heavy packs. The porters were carrying 60 lbs or more, having scrounged gear we no longer needed but useful to them. Sometimes we had to face inwards and teeter down and along a path mere inches wide with, often enough, a 1,000 metres of nothing much below.

Donald threw a stone and began counting. It had not bounced before going out of sight. We stayed at Bujgara on platforms hacked out of the slope, 'a swallow's nest under the eaves of Nanda Devi,' only 150m lower than base camp and biting cold. Tents froze and when unrolled at Deodi, next day, were still frozen. Righ Singh became chapatti king. The porters' idea of tea was to fill the kettle with water, milk-powder, tea and vast amounts of sugar and slap it on the fire. When it boiled over it was ready. The Tilman Slabs were still roped, mercifully. By Ramani we had lost sight of Nanda Devi but relished the glory of autumn colours among the woods. We overnighted at Deodi with some relief to have the main difficulties behind. The thought of it under snow...

It rained and brought the snowline down the slopes just above. The local weather lore was uncanny. Dibrugheta was an exquisite camp site, with a stately tree-girt meadow and a view to ragged winter peaks. (Shipton called it 'one of the most lovely spots it has been my good fortune to behold') We had delicious rice flavoured with spices which came from wee paper pokes hidden in Righ Singh's waistband. The rice was thrown into the pressure cooker and deemed ready when grains began crawling out the safety valve. I hid behind a tree while it was cooked.

I woke at 3 a.m. Cold and clear. The porters were still round the fire, laughing, talking, clearing throats. They don't seem to need sleep! At my 5 a.m. alarm call I crawled out to find our world muffled up in snow. We double-marched to make Lata: up and downs, and long traverses, snow slippery (or frozen in shadowy corners). We unpacked our ice-axes; the porters might have a stick, some only wore plimsolls, food was short, shelter they had none. We had to get out. Going through the arch on the final ridge was a great releasing of pressure. 'All downhill now!' – quite literally so; we'd taken two days on the uphill.

We relished a merry party in Sher Singh's brother's house. We gave away everything we could as presents and paid the stalwart men to whom we owed so much. In a day or two it would be whisky and sodas before dinner in Delhi, the magnolia blossom on the veranda magnificent, and servants spoiling us, then on to the Taj Mahal and other marvels, to metamorphose into tourist mode, Nanda Devi and the Rishi Ganga fading into dreams (sometimes nightmares), becoming, for us, part and parcel of the legends and history.

The year before our visit a strange, sad legend was added

to the mountain which we had almost worshipped all those weeks.

Many years ago, an American climber, Willi Unsoeld, later to be one of the climbers to make the first traverse of Everest, saw Nanda Devi and was so captivated by its beauty that he vowed to return and, if he ever had a daughter, she would be named after the peak. Well, he had a daughter, a vivacious blonde, who grew into a competent climber in her own right. Thus both Willi and Nanda Devi Unsoeld journeyed up the Rishi Ganga in 1976 as part of an American expedition to try the mountain by a new and difficult route – the prow that faces down the gorge. Nanda Devi fascinated the porters by her name, her beauty and her personality. They simply adored her. Three climbers made the summit and others were on the prow not far below the summit, including Willi and Nanda Devi. They were in their tent when she complained of feeling ill, but it was no ordinary tummy trouble and a few hours later she died – on the mountain after which she had been named. She is still there, and the locals believe she was 'called home,' being some human incarnation of the goddess-mountain, Nanda Devi.

---

1 Shipton and Tilman looked at this possible pass in 1934, then in 1936 Tilman, Houston and Pasang crossed it following the successful ascent of Nanda Devi, the summit pair being Tilman (usually a sufferer from altitude sickness) and Odell, the older, British members of a happy Anglo-American expedition. That expedition is described in Tilman's *The Ascent of Nanda Devi*, 1937 (also in the compendium H. W. Tilman, *The Seven Mountain-Travel Books*) while Shipton recorded the 1934 expedition in *Nanda Devi*, 1936 (also in E. E. Shipton, *The Six Mountain-Travel Books*).

2 Nanda Devi was first climbed in 1936. A Polish team climbed Nanda Devi East in 1939, the French doing likewise in 1951 (and failing to make the traverse to the Main Summit). The Indians made the second official ascent of the main peak in 1964. In 1975 the East Peak was

again climbed, and the traverse again failed, though the Main Summit was done by the 1936 route. In 1976 the Japanese made that challenging East Summit-Main Summit traverse, a year which also saw the first new route to the summit created by the American team. A party of three succeeded and then came the tragedy described at the end of my account. We were there the following year. To preserve its very special nature, the Sanctuary was closed in 1982 and few expeditions have wandered up the Rishi Ganga since.

3 When planning our trip, we decided we must have someone who was a medic in the party and I wrote off to sound out some contacts. By an odd slip, one of my plea letters went in the wrong envelope but the recipient, Frank, said he would jump at the chance of joining us. So he was roped in and it was his friends, the Greaves, who were our marvellous hosts in Delhi.

4 By pure chance we met the Liaison Officer in Delhi after the expedition. He was fully fit again and shook us warmly by the hand and, with a twinkle in his eye said, 'I hope you achieved all your hearts' desires.' He knew. We were only in the Sanctuary on a trekking permit and not licenced to climb mountains. Several peaks, one very important (it had repulsed the Bonington gang), were climbed which gave us a problem. If a climbing party paid through the nose, had the expense of an LO, and headed for a virgin peak only to find a sardine tin on top, they would not be best pleased. So I was delegated to write something to prevent this eventuality ever happening. I wrote a well-researched survey of the Sanctuary but concentrated on pointing out the fine peaks and routes waiting to be done and, almost in parenthesis, mentioning the summits already climbed, including ours. This was published in the authoritative *Mountain* magazine. A few weeks later a letter arrived from India, from the Indian Mountaineering Federation, and my heart sank. Had we been found out? Would we be banned from the Indian Himalaya for life? No: it was a courteous letter to ask if they might reprint 'this very useful article' in their journal.

The following was written in Egypt's Canal Zone during my RAF National Service days in 1953, and, from their very simplicity, the words revive in me something of a euphoric week spent in Jerusalem, at a period of peace, at eighteen years old, rediscovering the world of exotic, far places and living life to the full. This was just how it was.

A DREAM OF JERUSALEM

O, for the shock of the Arab world
With the sting of the sand in the air,
For the dusty road and the camel path
And the play of the sun in the hair.

O, for the smell of the sweet-meat stalls,
The busy shops in The Chain,
The chatter of a thousand tongues –
Like Pentecost again!

O, for the nights on the rooftops there
With the stories running wild
Or the sight of the city at dawn
And the smile of a passing child,

For the tramp of the Legion men at dusk
And their wild cry from the wall
And the last farewell on the Bethany road
Where the cypress stand so tall.

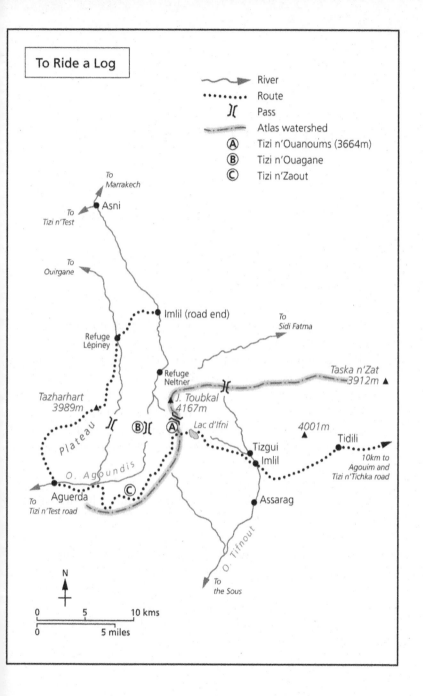

To Ride a Log

River
Route
Pass
Atlas watershed
Ⓐ Tizi n'Ouanoums (3664m)
Ⓑ Tizi n'Ouagane
Ⓒ Tizi n'Zaout

To Marrakech
To Tizi n'Test
Asni
To Ourigane
Imlil (road end)
Refuge Lépiney
To Sidi Fatma
Refuge Neltner
Taska n'Zat 3912m ▲
Tazharhart 3989m
J. Toubkal 4167m
Plateau
Ⓑ Ⓐ
Lac d'Ifni
4001m ▲
Tidili
O. Agoundis
Tizgui Imlil
10km to Agouim and Tizi n'Tichka road
Ⓒ
Aguerda
To Tizi n'Test road
Assarag
O. Tifnout
N
To the Sous

0   5   10 kms
0   5 miles

THE ATLAS ALLURE

The Mountains

*I am not an empire-builder. I am not a missionary. I am
not truly a scientist. I merely want to return to Africa to
continue my wanderings.*

So wrote the unusual Victorian traveller, the geologist Joseph
Thomson, whose curiosity was to lure him to explore the
Atlas Mountains in a way nobody had done before. I am
often asked why I keep returning to those mountains and
my reply would be the same as his. One falls for a place,
as one does for a person, with no logical reason; it just
happens. After spending a first three-month winter visit in
1965 I decided to repeat the experience the following year –
and somehow, heading there became a habit.

In the Atlas I found a people and a culture I could admire,
a simplicity of life, still rooted in family, culturally rich, the
very antithesis of our cramped, rat-race, broken culture of
the West. *To Ride a Log* was the second year's greatest joy
rather than the hard climbs we had made, the 'going-on,' the
wandering amid grand scenery, meeting hospitable, friendly
people, diving into their simplicities. You encounter much
the same people and experiences in all parts of the world
where there are harsh mountains and deserts; I just found

the Atlas at the right moment, as it were, for me. I know it was good because many of my friends also kept returning again and again.

We might stand on top of some distant mountain and see another alluring summit (like Lalla Ariba) on the horizon. Someone would suggest, 'Let's climb it!' so the following season we would engage mules to carry our gear and, as often as not, wend through green and blossomed valleys to reach and climb the goal – and view another. Like Joseph Thomson we were fascinated by everything and everyone, not truly scientists, but revelling in the flora and fauna, the often startling geology, till we absorbed the Berber world into our beings and *had* to return, *had* to continue the wanderings.

TO RIDE A LOG

> Travelling hopefully is within the reach of almost everyone, while to arrive needs a little more judgement, determination, skill, and perhaps some luck.
>
> H. W. Tilman

MAP, P.203

During our first Atlas winter in 1965 four of us set off on the ploy of crossing the range north to south, starting at the Neltner (Toubkal) Hut on the familiar north side then, from the *tizi* (col-pass) at the head of that glen, the Tizi n'Ouanoums (3,664 m), down to the *Lac d'Ifni* (2,312 m), the only *lac* in the barren massif and a remarkable contrasting sight as a result. From there we would follow the Oued Tifnout on out from the *lac* due south; the Tifnout later becomes the Oued Sous which turns west once on the plains to eventually reach the sea at Agadir.

The crossing went well, the *lac* bivouac a delight but, on waking, the sky showed all the signs of a storm coming in, and we knew what that could mean. Rather than continue into the unknown we packed up and fled for 'home', back over the Tizi n'Ouanoums. After the stony flood plain, that route entailed 4,440 feet of slog up an ever-narrowing gully. Crampons by the sun-blasted *lac* looked odd, but in that icy tube of gully they were our Mercury's wings. Nearing the top one of the party gave an icicle the size of a rugger forward's thigh a whack only to have it topple and shoot off down the fall line. Yells of 'Below!' Quiet, in the falling snow, then 'Missed!' The storm was in full force by the *tizi* and in the maelstrom we nearly missed the hut (3,207 m). One of the weary party fell asleep at supper and gently lowered his face into his hot, very hot soup. Only amusing later.

The complete crossing went on the bucket list for the following year but, having crossed the *tizi* to the *lac*, I would do almost anything to avoid that interminable ascent or descent. Quite illogically we decided to go for the N-S crossing while away west of Toubkal, climbing at the Lépiney Hut, and then set off in the opposite direction to first relish the weird world of the Tazharhart Plateau: a 'désert de pierres, plat, nu, vide, si haut perché qu'on n'aperçoit rien sous le ciel'. We gained this by a mere 900 metre gully up through the cliffs, hard labour with heavy packs, then headed off across the stony void. Many exhausted butterflies (Bath Whites and a few Painted Ladies) were flopping about and others had sunk into the snow, sad corpses in their little pits.

We had already spent quite a bit of time marking these butterflies for Bristol University and some would turn up in the grounds at Clifton. They make an astonishing migration from West Africa, over the Sahara, over the Atlas, passing the Bay of Biscay to end up in the West Country. Marking entailed a colour-coded dot of paint on a thorax. We did wonder what the local shepherd boys reported home when they saw us rushing around like madmen with our huge nets.

From the far end of the plateau we undulated over various rises to reach Adrar Makouz, 3,067 m, the most westerly 3000-er of the Toubkal massif, before beginning to descend into the depths of the Agoundis valley whose headstreams drain the western Toubkal massif. Young lads in tattered cloaks were grazing flocks of sheep and goats, controlling them with well-aimed stones, their piping voices haunting the hot haze of afternoon. We ached with weariness and stopped at a stream to brew and cool our feet, still 600 metres above Aguerda, the village we wanted to reach, hoping for accommodation rather than bivouacking (we did not carry tents). Once there we were taken into a cool room for welcome glasses of mint tea. We could hear whisperings and rustlings in the next room but no woman would appear in the guest room. A big *tagine* (stew) was carried through and we broke freshly baked bread to dip in the dish and convey the food to our mouths. Clive kept saying 'Bloody good stoof' so often that the locals copied him and no doubt the next European to reach Aguerda will be greeted with 'Bloody good stoof'. Next, a *couscous* was carried in and mercifully we were given spoons rather than coping with fingers. More tea and walnuts rounded off this feast. We were then left to settle for the night.

The room was an effective night storage heater and we lay gasping and sweating on our airbeds. I felt something crawl across my face. I wrote in my log, 'Bugs ... crawling, scuttling into every fold of flesh or clothing. Attacked, they exploded *pop*, leaving a smudge of blood (ours) and a smell which hangs horribly in memory. Scores scuttled into cracks in the walls when I shone a torch on them and there were long, hairy ones which fell on to us from the ceiling. The place was heaving and they waded through the DDT powder we fought them with. Only the cold towards dawn stopped the assault. In the early light we could see the squashed remains and the smell lingered. We'd not had nightmares.' Our bites were real and irritated for weeks. (This was to be the only such experience in fifty years of Atlas wanderings.)

We hired a mule for our ambitious journeying eastwards, too complicated to describe. For much of it we followed up a long valley but then took various side gorges and high *tizis*, the mule astonishing us with what it could cope with. On steep descents the load seemed ready to topple over its head and the lad desperately hung onto the mule's tail. We were going against the lie of the land so had endless ups and downs. The Tizi n'Zaout zigzags were so tight that the mule had to zig, then zag after only a couple of steps between. There were thirty zigzags. At another place we walked along a *seguia* (water channel) which I reckon ran for eleven kilometres to feed water round to irrigate the barren southern side of the mountains.

'The mule was freed of its load and turned to graze on the stiff yellow tussocks. We set up the gaz stove while the muleteer kindled a small fire. He produced the delectable tea and chapatti bread while we stewed apples, made chicken drinks and boiled eggs. Sweaty feet were cooled in the river and dried in the sun. The mule rolled on its back, snorting and waving its legs in the air.'

Our two objectives of a north-south crossing and re-visiting the Lac d'Ifni (to continue the exit south from there) now meant going on into the highest peaks, towards the Tizi n'Ouagane (3,750 m) beyond which lay the Neltner Hut and Toubkal, instead of following any immediate drainage which would have taken us to the Oued Tifnout – but below the *lac*. We had dismissed the mule lad who had become worried about coming so far from his known world. A shepherd watched us stop to make a proper meal: soup, corned beef and veg. We could have rolled over and slept there and then. The shepherd took the empty tin as treasure trove. He refused any food. He kept shouting, determined, however unintelligent we appeared, to get his message through. Waving at the water and then the sky rather suggested rain. The last thing we wanted was a storm with the chance of blizzards on high and flash floods and washed-out tracks below.

Eventually we came on our wanted side gully, to face another 600 metres of rough slog. A pinnacle on the col never seemed to draw nearer. The rocks were vividly tinted, one immense wall above would have given weeks of rock climbing, and it was only a flanking crag. 'As our energy ebbed, the tide of day also slipped away; the valley vanished darkly behind us and the ragged gendarmes above our heads seemed to grope up like hands to set the twinkling stars in their places. At last, the col, over 3,350 m (11,000 ft) up, with the last shimmer of dusk seeping away ... The sky had cleared again and the moon blazed the ragged rim of peaks with light. Jbel Toubkal (4,167 m) swept down and down in junior summits to the Lac d'Ifni which lay like a clouded mirror still thousands of metres below. Duvets and crampons were donned.

'We descended, steeper snow than expected, for about 600 metres before we found a stream. With crampons squealing on the iced rocks we scrambled over for long, welcome drinks. Another half hour and we were able to take off crampons, make an awkward scramble into a nook overhung by a huge boulder, the stream alongside. We cried 'Enough' with one voice. Before long we sat in bed, mugs in hand, looking out on the moon-washed desert landscape, the night breathlessly cold and magical. Here surely was Obadiah's 'nest among the stars'. Roughing it? It is civilization that is roughing it. Fools, we may have rushed in; but angels are so boring.

When Toubkal's summit was caught in dawn's 'noose of light' we wended on down another 600 metres to the valley of boulders, river hidden below, to reach the ink-blue Lac d'Ifni. We set up the stove in expectation of a second breakfast – which soon arrived: three small trout for which we swopped half a box of matches. Rolled in oatmeal and cooked in butter they were delicious. One of the fishermen then started beating the ground with his pole and came over to show us his trophy, a large adder. He said transport was possible down the Tifnout-Sous from Assarag, our intended exit. That would save days of walking out. To escape the *lac* a tenuous path wiggled over 100 metre sheer cliffs to gain the natural dam of red rocks which held this well-secreted stretch of water, one maybe three times the size of the Green Lochan in the Pass of Ryvoan, and often as colourful.

We picked up a *seguia*, the finest ever seen, stone-lined, a metre-and-a-half deep and the same across. Walnut trees began though we were still over 1,800 metres up and the landscape became two-tone thanks to the magic of water: above the *seguia* was starkly barren, below was green and prosperous, 'the water of life' made plain. The *seguia* ran for many miles, now and then through a village, sometimes cascading down to a lower level of lush, green terraces, fitting together like Matisse cut-outs. The chunky red boxes of the villages in that verdant setting rather mimicked a landscape by Cézanne. We were greeted and 'guided' constantly and constantly asked for aspirin. To conserve our stock we handed out Ovaltine tablets, which we indicated were also a renowned aphrodisiac. The women went unveiled and wore brightly coloured garments and greeted us with smiles by their washing troughs or when passing with bony cows. This rich world glowed too with a frothy pink mist of almond blossom. It was beautiful beyond the singing of it.

Assarag, four and a half hours we'd been told, but we took most of that just to reach the Tisgui confluence, the big stream draining much of the world east of Toubkal – a temptation in the sweltering heat to go up it and return 'home' to the cooler, snowy north side of the Atlas. No. We had to complete a real crossing. The only N-S crossing I knew of was by Robin Fedden and party who wrote telling how they crossed from the Neltner Hut *tizi* down direct to the *lac* and on for Assarag. They arrived at 6.30 p.m. but 'out' transport always departs early in the day. We hoped so.

We toiled up to the village of Tisgui hoping to purchase eggs and maybe eat before going on in the evening coolness and were at once invited into a house, kicking off our dusty boots and collapsing on the cushions in the cool guest room. The ceiling was painted like a medieval castle at home. Our host spoke a bit of French.

A tray appeared with bread, butter and fresh hard-boiled eggs. It was salty bread, curling and hot from the ashes – baked since our arrival while we sipped a coffee. We tore off pieces of bread and dipped them in the butter, also fresh, for nothing could keep long in that stupefying weather. We then sat back for mint tea and with the greatest difficulty refused invitations to stay the night.

We were told Assarag only had one bus a week, leaving *at night*. We had to get out my log book to find out what day it was. The bus left that very night! Did we make a dash for it? Our host was emphatically against this. 'Non! Non! Assarag – fini. Allez d'Imlil à Tidili.' We found Imlil was the next village on, where our Tifnout became Sous, but of Tidili we found no trace. The conversation became repetitive.

We must go to Tidili.

'Une piste à Tidili?'

'Oui.'

'Est-ce qu'il est possible d'y aller en voiture?'

'Oui.'

'A Assarag?'

'Non! Non! Assarag fini. A Tidili.'

Our gracious host came to the edge of the village to set us on our way. The last two hours before dusk were always cool and enjoyable for walking. We would walk in companionable silence, savouring the delicious solitude. There was another big village across the valley with a *kasbah* and a succession of threshing floors. After half an hour we turned a corner. There was the expected Imlil and, beyond, a wide red ribbon of road with a lorry standing on it!

The lorry had a huge log on the back and we dreaded the thought that it might go off even as we watched. No-one appeared for a while and Roger suggested we bivvy under it to make sure. 'They might not see us and drive off,' Clive cautioned. We decided it had to be going somewhere useful – no doubt to Assarag. The driver came eventually and agreed to give us a lift, departing at first light. We would have to sit up on the log!

'Allez-vous à Assarag?'

'Non. Tidili.'

We groaned. 'Où est Tidili?'

He pointed eastwards. I began reading names off the maps, one or two received nods but there was no Tidili.

Tidili however was in the direction of the major Tizi n'Tichka road over the Atlas from Ouarzazate to Marrakesh and we could walk to it from wherever Tidili was. But why go east? It would mean struggling up to 2,438 metres at least to escape this valley and there were others, and hills between, all along the wall of the Atlas. We gave up. We would take the adventure. We slept out on a threshing floor. The night was cold with a huge ripe moon which faded the lesser stars but left the constellations swinging the night hours through.

Behind the driver's house was a monstrous machine, bulging with wheels and long arms, used for dragging the trunks of walnut down to Imlil. Walls, ravines, terraces, were nothing to its determined progression and were simply rebuilt afterwards. Our transport had ten wheels, on three axles, each axle with a drive. Some of the wheels were cruelly ripped and cratered, but at least one of every pair seemed bearable – we hoped. A thick log was chained on the back with a smaller one loose alongside. Everything was built with massive strength: the metal cab, front fender, winch and heavily protected lights; twenty feet of gargantuan machinery powered by a Perkins engine.

Our morning departure was leisurely; crowbars, jacks and so on were heaved aboard, then baskets of food, then the co-driver appeared and after him, a third person for the cab armed with a rifle.

'Riding shotgun.' Clive suggested.

I managed to sit on our rucksacks between the log and

the cab while Roger and Clive straddled the log. I had qualms at the first bend but survived the journey without being squeezed into the cab by the log. The smaller log shot off at that first bend so I hammered on the cab's roof. We all trotted back to collect the log and heaved it up again, this time wedging it in place. The pace was slow, but at least required no physical effort on our part. Mentally it left us exhausted and exhilarated.

For several hours we groaned eastwards, up-valley. The road was simply scoured out and in places, as we passed, the edge crumbled beneath us to slither away suggestively out of sight. At some of the bends we had to reverse for a second attempt, the co-driver leaping out to place a wedge under the rear wheels before they reached the edge, or to yell before the stern of the battleship ran back into the bank.

The countryside was bleak but there were villages where the windows had eyes that followed our passing. Some villages were perched on outcrops, some hidden in the side valleys which sent us into sweeping detours. Eventually we stopped outside a house. We were invited in: carved beams, good carpets and silver teapot. Drivers do well obviously. In a corner on a stand there was a Victorian monstrosity of artificial fruits and flowers under a glass dome.

Everyone seemed to be armed with rifles and bearing curved daggers. Our host made mint tea and the lorry driver brought out bread and sardines from a basket. Several tins were emptied into a dish and the bread broken and distributed. We dipped it into the common dish as usual. Sardines never tasted as good at home. A transistor radio blared. We produced Kendal mint cake which was broken and passed around. The drivers thawed, or simply were awake now, for it was still only ten o'clock, and began to ask questions – and satisfy our curiosity.

The timber went on from mysterious Tidili to Marrakesh and thence all over the world. Our driver lived in Marrakesh but for several years had been working for this French timber company who were extracting walnut trees from the south of the Toubkal massif. Each day he took a load from Imlil to Tidili, returned, loaded, and then the next day repeated the process. His name was Bourgemâa ben Amou, a charming person, independent, friendly and kind. He posed with his lorry and we took the photographs which we later posted to Marrakesh.

We climbed aboard again and drove on up to the watershed, over 2,400,m, with magnificent views in every direction: northwards, the scruffy scree slopes of Jbel Iferouane, 4,001 m, filled the near view; west we looked back to the country we had walked through, a landscape of troubled reds and purples below gathering storm clouds; east we looked down to a great valley and further mountains, and south to scrub-studded slopes which continued to the distant lifeless volcano of Jbel Siroua.

We dipped to splash through a stream and the branches of a tree nearly decapitated the pair on the log. The landscape became devoid of soil, being bare red sandstone over which we juddered our way. For a mile or two there were road gangs out; they ranged from young children in flimsy rags to toothless crones in accumulated *djellabas*. One or two workers had limbs missing, some had swollen goitres and others eyes glazed with trachoma. Many bore ancient-looking weapons and there was great yelling and shouting as we passed.

The going was downhill now, a gradual descent in spirals and sweeps over every surface imaginable, through the odd village and finally on to a big plain. It was all very reminiscent of a Western movie. We clattered into the last outpost in a cloud of dust. It could have been down Mexico way with the swarthy, armed figures and adobe-style buildings.

'Tidili.'

'It's real then.' Roger whispered.

Bourgemâa pointed east to the next range; the pass through it led to the Tizi n'Tichka road, a day's tramp he reckoned. We were profuse in our thanks. I got Bourgemâa aside and asked him if I could offer payment at all. He would have none of it but the gesture was correct for he invited us to 'come along in' and perhaps someone would take us on the next stage.

We went into the biggest house and stumbled up a dark stairway. Soon a dozen of us were sitting or squatting around a table eating another *tagine*. There was the usual fresh bread to dip in the gravy. A laver went round and then we shared out the rest of our Kendal mint cake. French, Italian, English Scots, Arab and Berber were grouped together in the Tidili Transport Café. Bourgemâa tipped off his load and roared off for Imlil in a cloud of dust.

We were invited onto an even larger lorry which took two big logs and with a giant of a driver to match, we set off over a desert plain to a distant sneck in the hills. On our left lay Taska n'Zat (summits up to 3,900 m) stretching ridge after ridge ahead, rimmed still with snow but the southern slopes dizzy in the heat shimmer. Once into the pass we were up to about 1,850 m again, the road swinging in constant bends, demanding endless fast handling of the heavy wheel. The guard slept. We hung on, unimpressed now by the impressive, drugged with a day of thrills, punch-drunk with heady shocks. The whole sky had clouded over and the heat was weighted with threat. The old shepherd had warned us: he was only a couple of days out.

We came out to the blessed main road in the late after-noon, jumped down, shook hands all round, and watched the huge lorry grind off for the 2,260 m (7,000 ft) pass of the Tizi n'Tichka and Marrakesh. We followed in a bus an hour later, a bit of an anti-climax, but feeling smug too. It rained all the way over the Atlas, and the streets of Marrakesh were awash.

This was an early journey, 1966, but gave me the taste of what would become a life-long enticement: travelling on day after day, every day an opening of experiences, of meeting kindly people, of finding a forgotten ancestral simplicity. Journeying in the Atlas allowed one to become free of the complicated and overbearing demands we allow in life. Life becomes very simple and in the simplicity (which is not poverty) lies a great oceanic satisfaction. Travelling is a sure way out of life's discontent.

THE GLITTERING SUMMIT

In April 1970 a party of us went up to the Neltner (Toubkal) Hut in the Atlas Mountains to enjoy some winter climbing. The only other people present were a Moroccan businessman and his two teenage boys who were there to ski – real skiing, mountain skiing, heading up on skis to some summit or *tizi* and then relishing the downhill runs.

Jbel Toubkal (4,167 m) on skis is a classic and, given the right conditions, allows a run down of over 1,800 metres from summit to Sidi Chamharouch (2,130 m). I only managed that once and it was nearly the end of me. We broke the descent at the *refuge* (3,050 m) to brew and pick up our heavy rucksacks (as it was our last day) then headed off down-valley. At some point I ran my ski tips deep into a bank of drift and was pitched forward with my face in the snow – and unable to free it with the weight of the rucksack (c.30 kg) on my head. My 'friends' thought this 'arse in the air' pose hilarious and took photographs while I was waving desperately for help as I was being asphyxiated! But that's deviating.

One early morning of the April 1970 visit, I left my companions to sleep and set off alone to crampon up the firm snow of the *voie normale* Ikhibi *sud*, a hanging valley, and reached the summit as the early morning light was setting the peaks on fire. Before long the sun's heat would turn the snow into porridge, hence my early start. A subsidiary Top of Toubkal, Tibheirine (3,857 m), a kilometre to the north-east, was catching that dazzle of sun in an unusual fashion. Its summit glittered like fire. Weird. So I went to investigate.

The summit cairn of Tibheirine had been replaced by an aero engine and the glitter came from thousands and thousands of rounds of ammunition strewn on the slopes. The scene reeked of oil so the crash could not have been very long before. For the plane to hit the very tip of Tibheirine was unlucky: a few feet in any direction and nothing would have happened. On a later visit, the peaks clear of snow, we found the wheels down one side of the mountain and wreckage everywhere. I was fascinated and picked up several small working parts, but when I found I was cramponing among shattered boxes of high explosive I thought maybe I'd be safer elsewhere. I tiptoed to the snow and, adopting a convenient piece of fuselage as a toboggan, shot off down the Ikhibit *nord* corrie which reaches the valley slightly below hut level. With Toubkal's growing popularity this northern corrie would become our favoured way up the mountain. As I was going down to

Imlil and not coming back up to the hut that year, I decided not to carry the additional weight of my trophies and gave them to the two delighted Moroccan boys. And that was that I thought.

In a journal appearing in the winter following I read of a British party intending to go up to the Neltner *refuge* but being turned back at the Imlil roadend because the authorities were searching for a crashed aircraft. This was suspected of flying arms to Biafra, a now largely forgotten West African conflict but big news then. So that was what I had found!

The next spring I again headed up to the Neltner and, by coincidence, there was the father and the two boys whom I'd met the year before. So what happened once I'd left? The next day they were ordered to go down, as police and military personnel swarmed all over the place. They chose to say they knew nothing about any crashed aircraft, all too aware of the hassle they might have faced. Under a watchful eye the boys stuffed sleeping bags and belongings into their rucksacks, at the foot of which nestled the bits and pieces I'd given them, and set off to ski about half way down to Sidi Chamharouch, under that day's snow conditions. They met endless groups of soldiers hurrying up the track.

I was home again after the discovery before it dawned on me that I might well have come on some of the crew. I had also brought down a packet of biros and a pair of new jeans still in their wrappers and the boys were all for going up to see what they could find. Maybe it is as well the military arrived. There had been a crew of six. And years later, we encountered them.

They had been buried by the recovery party half way up the corrie, on a gravelly ridge slope, and now their bones were beginning to surface. The doctor in our party examined them and gave a laconic 'Ah yes, impact fractures.'

HAPPINESS IS A *HAMMAM*

In Britain a *hammam* was often more likely to be known as a Turkish Bath, which to me always conjured up images from the days of Harun al-Rashid or Suleiman the Magnificent or the overcooked paintings of the Orientalists or even the reality of pillared, marble halls erected for superior Victorians. On several visits to Turkey I never met such establishments. *Hammam* is an Arab word and how very much the institution was, and is, treasured in deserty lands. We discovered their benison on our first visit to Morocco in 1965.

A *hammam* is simply a public steam baths, a historic system through centuries before showers and bathrooms were ever thought of and to which everyone, rich or poor, young or old, men and women would resort. They are now being installed in the more up-market hotels and *riads* but in a rather sanitised and lifeless fashion whereas, for the ordinary citizen, they are still a cheery, social occasion, besides being an extremely efficient way of getting really clean. A friend once commented, 'I've never been so clean – and never before cooked'. The initiate would agree, no doubt, and be somewhat overawed by proceedings.

Certain periods of the day will be allocated by any *hammam* for the use of men or women, if it is not able to run two systems at the same time. Most will have an entrance lobby where one pays (before or after) and may be able to hire towels, shampoos, etc. Most people go prepared, taking their own essentials, women especially, for they make a real social occasion of a *hammam* visit. After all, it is the one place where they can gather completely man-free! Interestingly women are much less restrained than men and are more likely to go naked or in some skimpy covering, whereas men's etiquette today demands the wearing of pants and men will change or wash within their covering while facing a wall. Genitals must not be seen. (Wasn't always so. In 1965 everyone went naked, which had me wondering about reaction to our gang of very pale, uncircumcised *Roumi*. Perhaps there's been some edict from the Ayatollahs.) More recently I was surprised to see an uncircumcised boy of 7 or 8 years standing in the steam being vigorously 'done' but was told by his father this was a special cleansing because that afternoon his circumcision ceremony would be taking place. (He had somehow missed soon after birth when the ceremony normally occurs.) There can be a religious element in going to the *hammam*, particularly if attached to a mosque, and particularly on a Thursday evening in preparation for the main Friday Prayers. Women make their visits into a much more cheery occasion. Every sort of soaps, unguents, shampoos, essential oils or whatever is taken along with a range of scourers, a mat to sit on and some refreshments. It is *the* place for gossip, as well as time for being thoroughly scrubbed and massaged, often by professionals. Hair is often removed from all intimate parts, which may surprise a tourist visitor – and have her offered the same service. (No offence at a refusal!) Toddlers may be taken in. The whole atmosphere is of hours of hilarity in the steamy gloom. Medina shops, especially those near a *hammam*, will offer a wide range of items for sale to take to the *hammam*, like the *kiis*, a rough flannel glove, glutinous-looking soap ('like engine grease'), rough-surfaced ceramic scrubbers, pumice stones and much more. Getting clean is serious business!

Having left clothes in the changing room, which may

double as the cooling-off room, one passes into one, two, or even three ever-hotter rooms to settle eventually in the hottest which will be filled with steam, creating an almost ghostly scene with muffled echoes of conversations. Hottest is very hot. One sweats mightily, which is the intention. There are taps or tanks with boiling hot or cold water available and one fills a couple of buckets as fancy dictates. There are professional 'torturers,' as a friend called them, who give personal scrubbing, massage, limb manipulation, kneeling for kneading one's back and such like. I've always funked this extra, feeling I'd probably disintegrate under the treatment, but braver friends declare it as very therapeutic. Nor have I ever managed more than an hour being slowly poached. Once satisfied, and, indeed, wonderfully clean, one reverses the procedures, passing from cooler to cooler rooms and finally sitting in the changing room in relaxed stupor. In Taroudant, where we go frequently, we are served refreshing coffee with pepper in it. That's it then, the *hammam*.

Today more and more houses will be built with proper bathrooms, toilets and probably a shower so the *hammam* will only be used on special occasions. Having said that, the *Rough Guide to Morocco* notes there are something like 250 *hammams* in Fes. Over the years I saw our mountain base (my 'second home') install a battery-operated TV and then a shower heated from big gas bottles, till now, everything is electric. The more primitive *hammams* will still exist in poorer city areas or remote rural locations (I'll mention one shortly). A curiosity that puzzled me for years was seeing, in remote hamlets, a tall, dome-shaped structure made of woven reeds with a small entrance at ground level. This proved not to be some sort of animal or bird pen but a one-person *hammam* for village women. The structure would be covered to be proofed and the person involved would occupy it to enjoy a primitive form of steam bath.

Some of the *hammams* that gradually appeared in the houses where our guides or muleteers lived were not much bigger than what I've just described, being mere cubbyholes, sometimes of ingenious construction, only for single occupancy – but still welcomed after days or weeks trekking and climbing, with only cold mountain streams otherwise available. Most have gone, for every home in the Atlas has been rebuilt in my lifetime, with definite improvements in that department.

One primitive experience I recall clearly was at Imilchil, 'the Lhasa of Morocco,' our only three day stop-over on our ninety six day end-to-end traverse of the Atlas. (The stop was to catch the big weekly *souk* for stocking-up on food and fodder and to see our mules reshod.) The loo was simply a cubicle with the usual hole in the floor (a French contribution to civilisation?). Placed over this was a square duckboard on which I perched to slosh about the hot water that came in basins. With a shirt stuffed in the ventilation hole and water draining away so easily, it was more similitude than classic *hammam*. In the circumstances, the result was far more satisfying than my one experience in an immaculate posh hotel's 'spa' – which I'm sure cost me more than all the rest of my life's *hammams* combined.

In 1990 a *hammam* provided an unforgettable end to an already memorable trip to climb Jbel Siroua (Sirwa) 3,305 m, the isolated mountain that acts as a sort of fulcrum between High and Middle Atlas. We were three, plus Ahmed, the proprietor of the delightful Auberge Souktana in Taliouine (Tali-ween), who organised the practicalities and had us all transported to the start. After climbing the summit, a spike in the wrecked plug of a volcano, we had several exciting days exploring, 'just heading south,' through a maze of gorges and pinnacles, to find the cliff-face village of Tisgui and eventually hit the great south road. On that last day it had rained and rained, which ensured we ended drenched with sweat and lower parts covered in mud (*glaury* is the good Scots word). Before Ahmed set off to hitch home to collect a vehicle to retrieve us the next morning, he had ascertained that there was a *hammam* in a nearby hamlet. Ah!

We set off for the *hammam* in late afternoon, the route proving complex, and the village a mere group of poor houses beneath the bulk of a decaying *kasbah*. Civilities completed, we were led to the *hammam* and left to ourselves. This proved to be a subterranean site and a gloomy passage led to the *hammam*. Our clothes were left in a small cell of a room and a rickety door took us into the solitary basic steam room, nothing more than another cell. Minimalist *hammam*ing! There was 'barely' room to move but the heat was terrific, and the week's grime was soon being sweated out of us. The only light was one candle and the gloomy, steam scene could have graced something from Danté's *Inferno*. But what bliss!

Once cooled off (throwing about buckets of cold water) and dressed in clean garments, we made our exit to find it was pitch dark and of course nobody had a torch. The way had been complex enough in daylight; under the stars, even desert stars, it was 'a considerable challenge' – a euphemistic comment later. Through fields with prickly pear hedges, spiny argan trees, collapsing rock banks and ditches dry or ambushingly wet, it took over half an hour to find the tents. 'You know what I could do with right now?' asked a sweaty companion. 'A visit to a *hammam*.'

This mixed-blessing *hammam* visit reminded me of one made by explorer Joseph Thomson and party in 1888.

Living in a Marrakech house, these infidels were not slow in trying dangerous social adventures. Disguised, they went to visit an 'ordinary' family, they brazenly attended a vast, important court ceremony, they had dancing girls smuggled in one night – and also decided to sample a *hammam*, definitely off-limits for non-believers. (They had already been attacked and nearly lynched by fanatics in Marrakech. Their cheek was extraordinary.)

Being told a visit by Christians would not be possible received the reaction, 'that of course was the more reason for going; for what else did we travel for but to do things and see things that other people had not done and seen?' There was a Marrakech tradition then that, after the 9 p.m. call to prayer, family parties could pre-book the sole use of a *hammam,* so they sent 'their most intelligent and fluent liar of a servant' to fix a visit. They went in disguise, surrounded by all their concerned servants and helpers, not least their Jewish interpreter, David Assor, 'who, to the fear of detection, added all the imaginary horrors of a thorough washing, an operation of which he had no practical experience in his lifetime'.

There was consternation on entering as they met the last of the users coming out, with lanterns, and had to hide in a dark cellar till the coast was clear. They found the vaulted cooling-changing room seedy in the extreme and quickly pushed on through a hot room into the hottest. Apart from only being lit by candlelight the room was standard. 'Our cook turned out to be skilled and he kneaded and rubbed, pushed and pulled, sat upon us, and rolled and tumbled us about with all the style of a *hammam* hand, a professional slap to mark the end of any particular operation.' Poor Assor was thoroughly 'done'. They were to make a hasty exit when they found 'a most horrible open sewer' in a corner of the changing room. Thomson decided the *hammam* was 'something to be seen *once* in one's life'. Today, with the country's growing affluence, a visit *once* to a *hammam* is much more likely to lead to pleasing repetitions. I can vouch for that.

A last *hammam* anecdote. Mousa's café in Taroudant is a favourite place for our groups' relaxing and dining after Atlas explorations, sitting under the brollies and watching the world go by on the main square. This was the Café Argana and, when alone, I often took a basic upstairs room for the fun of being in the heart of that busy world. Mousa (which means Moses) was the long-time waiter and a great character, full of teasing fun yet firm when need be. When a raging lunatic came among the tables with abusive language it was Mousa who put an arm round his shoulders and quietly led him away. In contrast, an orphaned boy with Down's syndrome was always greeted with a kiss and allowed to beg among the sitters, and the deaf and dumb shoeshine was always welcomed. At the end of the day there was always a hand-out of food for the homeless. This, of course, is a side of Islam we don't see on TV. Mousa spoiled us thoroughly.

On one evening everyone within hearing range was being embarrassed by the loud complaints of an American tourist. Nothing pleased him and even Mousa began to look disconsolate. At the end of his unappreciated meal the man shouted for his bill and Mousa, who chanced to be looking at me, gave the ghost of a smile and quoted an outrageous price. My eyebrows no doubt shot up and I received a wink – to which I gave a happy thumbs up.

There was a *hammam* just round the corner from Mousa's, one which our gangs used regularly whenever we descended from the heights of the Atlas to the heat of the Sous. The hours varied for men's and women's use, the former early and late, the latter through the day till after dusk. To ensure no visitor confusion, a board on a string hung at the entrance with the appropriate side showing HOMMES or FEMMES. The peace of Mousa's on this occasion was being destroyed by the crass, self-centred arrogance of a British trekking party, about a dozen folk, mostly men. Day was starting to cool and shadows lengthen and good aromas were coming from the kitchen via the hole-in-the-wall servery. In the eyes of the locals the group were offensive both in behaviour and dress (undress), but the people were too polite to say anything. Eventually the group's leader began to get his noisy party organised: the girls to explore the *souks*, the men to head for the *hammam* (they'd brought towels, etc) and supper at their smart hotel would be at eight o'clock. At the word *hammam* I had a brainwave.

I called two *gamins* and explained what I wanted. They walked off round the corner with exaggerated nonchalance but with big grins on their faces. When they reported to me next day they just exploded with laughter, doubling over to slap their knees. (What joyous mirth!) My injunction as to keeping quiet had obviously been disregarded. There were knowing smiles from the café regulars and Mousa gave me a great hug. The imps had simply flipped the sign for FEMMES to read HOMMES. You can imagine the result: part of Taroudant folklore now.

LALLA ARIBA!

> He who does not travel does not know the value of men
> **Ibn Battuta**

And then we looked down on the tent, the camel hair *kaima* of the nomads, a solitary dark shape among the tawny, heaped geometrics of the rock strata. The terrain looked like one of those schoolboy landscape models built up in contour layers before the covering plaster was applied. Beating sun and scouring wind left this a naked world. A corduroy of strata stretched away as far as the eye could see. We were on our second day out, crossing this barren bastion of the southern Atlas Mountains. Our water was finished and we were relying on the accuracy of a boy's description at the start as to where there was a well. The tent implied water. On seeing it I let out a thankful yell of 'Lalla Ariba!'

Lalla Ariba marked the highest point in the area, not much more than a ripple among the bellyfolds of these plateau lands which were cut through here and there by canyons like the Todra Gorge. Nicola, Lorraine and I had started from Marrakesh, in a rickety bus that had us queasy and hardly appreciating the magnificent Tizi n'Tichka road, then we headed east along the Kasba Road to the Todra, whence a juddering commercial Land Rover taxi had ground up the road from the throat of the gorge to its distant infancy where we started out from the Tizi Tirhirhaouzine, about 1,800,m. Ah well, 'better to walk than to curse the road,' as they say in Zambia. The only lorries we met on the way were heavily laden with big big bags of charcoal. There were crag martins flying about the gorge like demented bees and many of the 'everywhere' black wheatears (Morocco has at least seven wheatear species).

Our trek would end walking down the Todra Gorge to the narrowest gut to reach the start of public services, where we'd reward ourselves with a night in the Hotel Yasmina, in front of which a stream gushed out of the pebbly gorge floor and which was overhung by a 300-metre cliff. We would take out bedding onto the hotel roof for coolness but not to see any sweep of stars overhead, rather the black loom of rock overhang. A stone kicked off the cliff edge would have fallen outside the hostelry. No wonder this is a prime rock-climbing area when you can drive to the gorge, camp or stay in cheap hostels, and step out straight onto great warm walls and buttresses of reliable limestone. But it was the start of our wandering we remember most: Lalla Ariba and the hospitality of Berber nomads, the reality beyond the reach of wheels.

The altitude of our starting spot made sure we didn't go racing off. Any sudden exertion had us puffing. We followed the watershed (ironic name when there was no water to shed) for such often gave easier lines to follow than flanks which could be broken by crags and seamed by gullies. Our rucksacks were extra heavy for we had to carry water (large bottes of Sidi Harazem or Sidi Ali). We walked till the sun set the sky on fire, quickly cleared a bivvy spot and settled in before dark (fighting to keep weight down, we didn't even carry torches). The dark of course gave us starlight, the stars a diamond dazzle, weighty with wonder, the piercing marvel of desert skies. I counted several satellites on their flights and wondered what isolated tribes, untouched by so-called civilisation, would make of these sudden intruders in their known heavens. (Counting satellites was a much more efficient means of inducing sleep than counting sheep: I never managed beyond seven.)

We made several brews and then ate the apple flakes we had soaked on arrival. Into the pot went the main course, a tin of haggis with potato powder and a few fresh vegetables. We then made a cuppa soup (that order of eating required no washing of the pan between uses). On haggis: our regular Berber helpers had a taste for it as we took out tins every year for trail food which was safe for Moslems to eat. On meeting up at any year's start we were often asked.

'Any haggis this year, Hameesh?' (This sortie was unusual in that we did not have mules doing the donkey work; there weren't any.)

Soon abed, Nicola commented on the incredible *quiet* of our nowhere bivouac. A listening landscape. No gentle munching by mules. No gentle wind in trees. No distant barking of dog or sad call of jackal. Just before dawn I noticed the Plough was standing on its handle and the moon hung faint on the horizon. Sunrises are such rarer treats than sunsets. We were up at the yawn of dawn, one cold enough that I'd taken the stove into my sleeping bag and we sat up in them to have breakfast in bed. You cannot hurry muesli. We managed some hardening *hobs* (bread) with *La Vache qui Rit* cheeses and drank plenty of liquid.

After a couple of hours going, and warm in the glare of sun we had more brews and peeled off our thermals. We were in a world of sweeping simplicities but with plenty complexities in the detail. Huge views under huge skies. We crossed a Tizi n'Ousri to gain our mountain objective, flanking up the east face, following crags round and finally a ridge to the summit that was crossed by the many wee walls of strata. 'Sort of Torridon stripped bare,' Lorraine suggested.

Lalla Ariba is 3,148 m and we found a stone man and shrines on top. The ground was littered with sheep's horns, probably indicative of sacrifices to honour whoever Ms Ariba was. *Lalla* is a female honorific like *Sidi* for a man, and in place names, Sidi or Lalla will commemorate some revered person or saint, often, in gentler land-scapes, with a small domed building (*kouba*) marking the site. Many were places of pilgrimage. I never did learn who or when there was a Lalla Ariba. The name so caught our fancy that it became one of those in-phrases of our Atlas parties when faced with special moments. A sudden view, an unexpected surprise, and we'd call out 'Lalla Ariba!'. I still do it.

I have known an occasional Berber in our parties refuse to summit a peak knowing that it was a revered site for some *sidi*, this almost-worship of such being anathema to the more serious religionists. In 1871 when foreigners (Joseph Hooker and John Ball) made the first ascent of a 3,000 metre Atlas mountain by a foreigner (Jbel Gourza) there was some doubt over the name for they called it something else. But what put it beyond doubt for me was their describing derelict buildings on the summit. I knew these and had been told Gourza was a sacred summit where, until recent times, a cow was taken up and sacrificed each year. Mountain tops the world over can have religious connotations. On the second last day of the twentieth century I climbed Adrar Mkorn near Tafraoute in the Anti Atlas, a hill climaxing happily in a short climb. I wondered if Mkorn had any local religious significance for, if the summit was a mere rock-wide perch, at the foot of this final difficulty the ground was littered with *thousands* of empty sardine tins, heaped thigh deep and spilling down the slope. The pilgrim picnic spot after the climb I could only speculate.

The view from Lalla Ariba was so sweeping we became aware of the actual curvature of the earth in the far horizon. We could see Jbel Ayachi in the extreme north-east end of the range, a peak dominating the Trek es Sultan (the Sultan's Road) which runs from the ancient capital Fes to the south, to the Sahara, to Timbuktu. Ighil M'Goun was end-on, hiding its miles of undulating crest, which tops 4,000 metres (over 13,000 ft), the only place where this altitude is reached outside the Toubkal massif. (Toubkal, highest in all North Africa, is 4167 metres, 13,670 feet). Lalla Ariba was strictly the summit shrine, the map gave the hill's name as Amalou n'Ousri.

We took a tortuous route down to a valley falling away from the Tizi n'Ousri. *Azibs* (animal shelters) were built in under a cliff but were not in use though the ground was deep in dry droppings of sheep and goats. We followed another barren undulating valley till, over one rise, there was a view to the *kaima*. That called for the first yell of 'Lalla Ariba!' followed by 'Water'.

As we neared the tent a tall, craggy figure came out to meet us. We exchanged the traditional flow of greetings as we shook hands, then placed them on our hearts (I tend to do that at home!). Lorraine later said the man's hand was hard as ram's horn and Nicola said he could get a bandit part in any spaghetti Western – something I've often thought meeting people in wild areas, only to encounter gentle, kind hospitality. We were invited to enter the camel-hair tent. These tents are made by combining long, narrow lengths of woven material. By the Isli *lac* I once watched a girl working on the loom for these. The width was only about two metres but the thick warp threads stretched a good eight metres. The lengths are then sewn together for the required tent's width. The weave is loose, keeping the tent light in weight and airy in the normal heat. On the rare occasion of rain the wool swells to make the tent watertight. The main central part is held up on two transverse spars, perched on poles which are guyed out, and on each side the material runs out and down to ground level where it is pegged out, creating two sloping-roofed, curtained-off 'rooms' on either side of the central area, into which we stepped. At a word, a woman, darkly robed, her face with tribal markings, and rough jewellery on neck and wrists, appeared from one of these ends. She added her welcome. In some Moslem societies she would have stayed hidden, but Berber women have much more freedom and are never veiled for instance. She

232

happily shook our hands, each time lifting her hand to kiss her fingers. Berber women find any contact with women from other lands both fascinating and hilarious.

Lorraine and Nicola were old Atlas hands so were at home in these situations. But the learning curve could provide surprises. We were once seeking cheap digs – in Tangier, I think it was – when our helpful tout, advocating a particular *auberge*, enthused that the girls could get 'a room and a man'. The pair looked a bit startled till it was explained the promise was for *arum* (bread) and *aman* (water), i.e. sustenance.

Our host's wife in the *kaima* brought in a *kanoun* (brazier) and retreated into the hidden end again. Mohammed used a small bellows to stir the charcoal into life and set about making the everlasting *atay* (mint tea), the regular lubricant for Moroccans from Agadir to Zagora. This is a complex ceremony with washing of the green tea (from China), breaking of an extravagant amount of sugar from a big cone and stuffing the pot with it at the right stage in proceedings. Here it was some dried substitute aromatic herb, as mint grows only in well-watered places. The tea is poured out and back (in the traditional bulbous teapot, a British introduction!) until it meets the host's approval. It is then poured from a height so the tea froths up in the small glasses used – mimicking the sound of water falling, the dream of desert imaginations. I can still recall the time when, as an honoured guest, I was asked to prepare the mint tea. Would I forget some step, mix up the order of doing things, make a hash of the quantities and produce a woeful beverage? Fortunately it was greeted with a '*mzyen*' (good). The *kaima* tea was very good, '*mzyen behoof*'. Why don't we step aside at times and follow such graciousness, so relaxing, instead of our infernal hurry, hurry? There is one nice feature: however short or prolonged a visit, when a third cup of tea is consumed it is time to leave. Now that is something we could copy!

We had no language in common beyond our knowing standard greetings and some essential food-organising words yet enjoyed every minute of our unexpected break, explaining, through a few place names on the map, where we were heading, by mime having the position of the well explained (you don't camp at the well in case of polluting it) and all our family details (amazement at Lorraine and Nicola being unmarried). Mohammed had two sons elsewhere and the youngest, ten year old Aziz, was out with the herd (what on earth did the animals find to eat?). There were two young girls who had remained hidden, too shy to appear, but he called them to come and say hello. They retreated behind the curtain and, thereafter, we could hear their smothered giggles. He explained how the family followed a circuit each year, the route depending on the water sources which depended in turn on the winter snowfall. Winter saw them head for the oases near Boumalne du Dadès. Mohammed was powerful-looking yet graceful, with a deeply lined face that could have been hacked out of gabbro, a firm nose, a few days' stubble – and eyes that twinkled. He wore a sort of turban and a striped *djellaba* the colour of the tent. His sandals, with the soles made from motor tyres, stood at the entrance. A few carpets covered the ground inside, one with tassels at the corners which he showed could be tied up together to hold clothes etc. when carried on a camel. We were looking at minimalist living, contented with needs, not wants, and with Nature's 'primal sanities' (Whitman). We had kicked off our boots on entering (as one does) and he was amazed at these and thought them so heavy. He said the crude bellows, painted red and patterned with brass studs, came from Boumalne's *souk*.

We had relished our glass of *atay* when the curtain was drawn aside and his wife, Ayicha, laid on the low table – the only furnishing – a plate of hot-from-the-griddle flat bread and a dip of what he called *jbin* which seemed a mix of oil and what looked and smelled like cheese powder. We squatted round on cushions made from left over *kelim* pieces (carpet-making is big business in the mountains and along the south side of the Atlas). He broke the bread (you never *cut* bread; it was the staff of life) and distributed it round the table with a command to eat. After a 'Bismillah' (*thanks be to Allah*) we were happy to oblige but felt a bit embarrassed knowing how little they would have in the way of supplies. But hospitality in the mountains and desert is a sacred Berber obligation. And we knew that to offer any monetary payment would be regarded as an insult. We took care to leave something of the food as not to would imply we had been given too little (what was left at any gathering would probably be all the women and children would have to eat). Over the 'afters' mint tea we produced a slab of our then everlastingly popular Kendal Mint Cake and shared this with our hosts and they clearly liked it. We managed to get them to keep the rest of the packet. Then there was the third glass of tea. Time to go.

We booted up in the sudden smiting of sun outside while Mohammed slipped on his sandals. Ayicha came to the door to see us off. Lorraine and Nicola received kisses on both cheeks. Lots of smiles and laughter. Up on a ridge, like the Fiddler on the Roof, a boy was perched playing some form of stringed instrument. He was given a yell, 'Aziz'. He scampered down and, in turn, took our fingers to kiss them in greetings. The instrument he had been playing was created from a rusty old oil can, the strings from heaven knows what. He was shy but after being instructed to take us to the well, grinned and bounced off with enviable energy, his shrill singing giving the echoes life. Song and laughter is a good gauge of a people's contentment level.

The well was topped with a crude iron structure and when he wound the handle we saw the 'rope' was simply a peeled length of inner tube from a tyre, and the bucket a U-shaped portion of tube threaded through by the rope. We filled our Sidi Harazem/Sidi Ali bottles again. That water would have to last a couple of days till we might reach a name on the map which implied houses and therefore water.

We watched the boy's figure shrink back into the distance till all we had was a dot and an echo, the *kaima* lost among the crags. I thought of Baden-Powell's words, 'The really rich man is the man who has fewest wants'. We had here encountered just such a richness of being, one that showed up the moral poverty of the West, and gave us much to think about. Here were people living in peace; no war, no crime, no poverty, no unemployment, no social fears and yet many would call them primitive. Long may they escape the contamination of so-called Civilisation.

We hefted our rucksacks and headed off; headed on.

HELL ON EARTH

> Gandhi, on being asked his view on Western Civilisation, replied 'I think it would be a good idea.'

Only once in my life have I led a group which was a disaster. Most groups in the Atlas were of friends or mountaineering clubs, or special interest groups (botanists, ornithologists), many who returned again and again. When approached by an American company to run Atlas treks for their clients I saw no reason not to. They would pay well, for a change, and could be interesting. Having studied their brochures I worked out a programme, one set at their top grade, where people coming should have ice axes and crampons – and know how to use them.

The first year with Americans was interesting. The group was mostly middle aged, and apart from one very fit young man, hardly up to the standard expected. Nevertheless they did their best, even the lad with one leg an inch shorter than the other and the 55-year-old lady who gave me a great hug following her 'experience of a lifetime' on Toubkal. I've a vivid picture of my rope to her blowing out in an arc from the blizzard as we neared the top where we exchanged grins (hers of thrill, mine hiding a deal of concern!). The fit lad, David, and I met up the following spring in Granada and climbed Spain's highest summit, Mulhacén, on skis. The next year I was told there were just six clients; did I want to cancel? If only . . .

The six were two couples, a single woman and a single man. I met them at the airport and we went to our Marrakech hotels, the singles and I in our usual modest Foucauld but the couples to the La Mamounia, one of the world's most renowned and expensive hotels. They were disappointed not to have the Churchill Suite; an Arab prince had priority. We met for a tasty Moroccan meal in a restaurant with fine Moroccan décor, a treat which was unappreciated. Instead we had a big argument when they declared that 'no way' were their wives ever to carry more than 20 lbs on their backs. So what if we faced going over snowy passes carrying every-thing needed? 'We don't go.' 'But that's what you signed up to do ...'. Our day in Marrakech was hardly as programmed but we did see H.M. Hassan II and the President of Senegal pass, standing in an open car, obviously unaware of the inconvenience this caused to the visitors.

When we went up to Imlil as a first base for Jbel Toubkal, Morocco's highest peak (4,167 m), we set off on a walk (so I could judge capabilities), the two wives dressed almost undressed, and arguing blue murder when told this was not acceptable. 'We're paying, damn it, the locals will have to learn.' We sat on the terrace of a Berber friend's house looking over iris-edged green fields to the snowy peaks, a fabulous view, which Max, the solitary man, praised and the others hardly noticed, being more worried about any possible consequences of drinking the mint tea provided. The wives then quit and retreated to stay at the posh hotel down in Asni saying their men could do Toubkal. The non-stop-complaining single female did likewise. When ice axes and crampons were produced for checking I noticed all the gear was new. Except for Max, they had no winter experience at all.

Fortunately, I thought, the weather was changing so I suggested we do other things first and come back for Toubkal, but this led to more arguments along the lines that the programme said Toubkal so Toubkal was demanded. So we trogged up to the Neltner Hut and sat out the three-day blizzard. I was alright, I had *War and Peace* (seemed appropriate); they were bored to distraction. The toilet facilities were frozen so they eventually had to brave the blasts, go out, and lower their trousers in the spindrift – about the only thing I ever had to smile about. At the end of the trip they simply gave away the unused, expensive ice axes and crampons as they couldn't be bothered packing them.

I did feel extremely sorry for Max who was a mountainy type with his heart set on Toubkal. The following year he visited the UK and we had a splendid day traversing Ben Nevis and he planned to join me the following spring for Toubkal, but never did; he had a heart attack and the Ben was the last of his ticking-off country summits. He was an osteopath and more than once I overheard the others snootily referring to him as 'the bone man,' they being brain and heart surgeons, whose main conversation topics seemed to be the Dow Jones and medical litigation, on which they wanted daily communications 'back home,' difficult in pre-satellite days.

Once off the Atlas they demanded to go to Fes, a two-day drive away at the other end of the country – and not on the programme. I was more or less told 'We're paying, so you'll do what we want.' In the end I shrugged and arranged the sortie, one I was happy enough to do anyway for we drove through spring-bright countryside, visited the Cascades d'Ouzoud, one of the world's most beautiful waterfalls, and descended from the mighty cedar forests of the Middle Atlas to reach the exotic World Heritage site of Fes – where we had two nights in the super-superior Palais Jamaï Hotel. *That* seemingly was the objective. Couldn't they boast of that when home: Mamounia, *and* Palais Jamaï! But why sign up for a winter mountain trek? Any travel agent could have fixed up the hotels (they'd obviously never heard of the best of all, the Gazelle d'Or at Taroudant; but it was much more selective about its customers). Fes is one of the most exotic cities anywhere and I said I'd be happy to show them around. No. They just spent the day by the hotel pool.

That night there were strawberries on the rather disappointing menu, which brought out the boasting again: 'Say, we can tell folks back home we had strawberries in March.'

I couldn't resist the temptation and pointed out how the fields would be irrigated and the likely hazards from their manuring (they were taking pills for every risk conceivable). 'No! No strawberries!' When they left the table I called the waiter over and ordered a big, big plate of delicious strawberries.

They still wanted the second part of the programme: crossing the Atlas to see gorges, kasbahs, and the edge of the desert, so we set off for that. I was joined by a Scottish Mountaineering Club friend, Barclay Fraser, who would share a cultural campervan drive home across Spain afterwards, so I had an independent witness to the misery of these born-again Christians. The Tizi n'Tichka summit had a triumphal arch and every village was decorated by carpets hung on display: the King had passed the day before. When we turned up at our Kelaa des Mgouna hotel we found the royal progress had commandeered all the hotels along a hundred mile sweep of the south. A Thompson's tour group of 30 was in trouble, but being known, we were surreptitiously given two attic rooms, one for the men, one for the women. Far from being grateful, that raised the storm of storms and one of the men came out with 'Say, this King, who does he think he is?'

On the return run, to give the driver a break on the tortuous descent from the Tizi n'Tichka, we stopped at a café-restaurant perched over a scenic gorge. 'Coffee time,' I suggested, and driver, Boneman, Barclay and I trooped in. The two couples and the female stayed in the bus. 'Not coming?' No, their mugs were in the baggage on the roof. 'But it's a restaurant. They've got everything needed.' No, they might just catch something . . ..

The last night's Folk Evening with the best food of the trip and even a *fantasia* from galloping tribesmen in flowing robes and firing off ancient guns was of no interest – except that they told me they had booked a five star hotel in Casablanca for a night rather than leave Marrakech at six o'clock in the morning. Would I arrange a bus then for this change?

Two weeks of this group had me distraught. It took two months to get over the experience, with feelings akin to those of a bereavement. At the airport old Max put an arm round my shoulder and apologised on behalf of America! It would be many years before I would accept any group from across the Atlantic, and that was through contacts who assured me this gang of oldies were great fun. They went together on a trek every year and were perfectly happy 'roughing it'. So they were. They were beaming cheerfully at the airport and one laughed, 'OK Hamish. We all believe the world is round and none of us voted for Bush.'

The last straw with that group from hell was receiving a copy of the pages of complaints they'd made to the company who then demanded what I had to say about them? The first complaint was that 'all I did was talk about Morocco,' then that 'I'd fed them dog food, a thing called haggis'. 'They often had only picnics instead of decent meals in the middle of the day' ... I didn't read more; it would not have done my blood pressure any good, and what I had to say was pretty pointed. They, the company, had sent a completely unsuitable group, resulting in a miserable time for all and no doubt I'd be fully justified in suing them for compensation but, anyway, I wanted nothing more to do with their clients. I'd *my* reputation to think of.

Things don't seem to change. Kipling, writing of Americans a century ago, commented about 'The dead weight of material things passionately worked up into gods, that only bore their worshippers more, and worse, and longer.' There are many delightful Americans of course. I've some good friends across the Atlantic – now. But for years after this group, when I returned to Imlil, Berber friends there would grin at me and ask, 'Any Americans this year, Hameesh?'

REMEMBERED MOMENTS

The following are simply three very different moments, incidents, experiences, which have never been forgotten. Morocco is never far from mind and odd moments often happen at home too. One example – when I laughed aloud on reading a postcard left in a book for sale in a Peebles charity shop. It is dated 14th October 1955, an early date for a tourist visitor (Independence came in 1956). The picture is a typical view of Marrakech's Koutoubia minaret:

Dear Cathryn, The postal service from Morocco is very poor. The temperature is 35° night and day. The smell of donkeys and horses is overpowering. Wish I had brought ear plugs – the noise from the street is so great I can't sleep. Food very spicy – the meatballs have given me diarrhoea. Having a nice time. Love, Mum.

1. THIRD TIME LUCKY?

For our 1966 winter in the Atlas Mountains our expedition bought a fairly unreliable grey and cream-coloured Bedford van for £65 and drove out to Morocco (and back), crossing from Gibraltar to Ceuta in the *Virgen de Africa*. The vehicle wasn't in its first flush of youth but nevertheless took us not only up and down to our mountain base at Imlil but over the Tizi n'Tichka and down to Zagora and the desert.

On one of our descents to Marrakech to re-provision and enjoy a touch of city indulgence, we were stopped by a policeman at the roundabout before the city gate. He pointed out that we only had one headlight. We explained it had been shaken off by some dreadful road on our driving across Spain (its loss wasn't ever noticed). Besides, we never drove at night – daytime driving was quite nerve-wracking enough. But he was not impressed: we had to get another headlight.

The chance of finding a Bedford headlight in Marrakech seemed slight, but years on, I often wondered. Anything seemed to be discoverable in Morocco's souks, or could be made one way or another. When, on one visit, my own campervan's accelerator hinge broke (rusted through!) the garage simply made a replacement. When a road-hog Italian removed a wing mirror, a garage reconstructed one that did for the rest of the van's life. During this 1966 visit the musical member of the party, back in Tangier, decided to buy a squeeze-box if possible. 'Was it possible?' he asked a likely lad, who at once replied 'Of course. New or second-hand?'

We forgot about the headlamp. At least till the next descent on the fleshpots when we ran into the same policeman at the roundabout. He said he could fine us on the spot and only because we were visitors to his country was he not doing so there and then. We promised we would have it replaced. And didn't.

Finally our three months in the Atlas were over, and we faced the long drive back to the UK in our overloaded ark. I was not doing any driving as I'd just broken a big toe – while birdwatching (I was following a rare brambling when a terrace collapsed). My balloon-like toe was being protected in a duvet boot so I couldn't drive. (Just being a passenger was so boring that in the end I jumped ship, so to speak, in Rabat, spent days marvelling in the Prado

in Madrid and took the famous Talgo express train to the
French border. The Louvre in Paris followed.)

Approaching Marrakech we were suddenly in a panic: if,
by an outside chance, the same policeman was on duty we
could well be fined, and we doubted if we could raise the
necessary between us. This could be complicated. Wonder
what a Marrakech police cell would be like? Cheery lot we
were. And it was the same policeman. A fair cop.

As we neared, the policeman turned and looked up at
a passing stork, flying with a twig for its nest among the
El Badi Palace ruins in the city, and studiously followed
its flight, his back still to us, until we had swung past and
away. A very diplomatic policeman: and with hindsight,
how very Moroccan. Back in the UK the van was sold for
£70 – still minus one headlamp.

2. A Cannibal Adder

The Anfergal meadows owed their verdure to a stream which
only flowed for a few hundred yards, not far below the Tamda
lac. The earliest nineteenth-century travellers like Charles
de Foucauld and Joseph Thomson, when crossing the Tizi
n'Telouet, heard of the lake but were told it lay, rather improb-
ably, on top of a mountain. The lake shrinks and grows from
year to year and what looked like the exit stream actually gushes
out of the hillside at a higher level than the Tamda water (we
found no genuine outflow). So this stream may or may not be
the origin of Anfergal's brief resurgence. We camped there on
several occasions despite its reputation for adders. Our closest
encounter with an Anfergal adder was when one of our botanists was filling his water bottle in the stream and an adder
promptly dived into its mouth and became stuck.

On the way up to the Tamda I came on the curious sight of one adder busy eating another. I could only conclude that our muleteers, going on ahead, had seen an adder and killed it (they always, often needlessly, killed any snake encountered). However it had died, another adder then found the victim, and not wanting to miss a free lunch, started eating it. This was no easy job as the 'neck' had been shattered (muleteer's stick?) so there was an initial double thickness to be taken in. This was possible by the great expansion built into snake jaws – then it was just a matter of sucking in the rest. A very odd sight: one adder with another disappearing into its jaws. I took a photograph and hurried off.

Only later, looking at the photo, did I wonder what would have happened if the snake being sooked in was longer than the one doing the sooking.

3. THE BATTLE SITE

Jbel Bou Gafer is a rugged mountain embedded in the southern Jbel Sahro (Sahara Atlas) of Morocco. In 1933 the mountain was the setting for the final battle in France's subjugation of Morocco (the Protectorate had been set up in 1912), when the tough Berbers in their southern mountains were finally subdued in a bloody month long encounter. Around a thousand men, armed with antique long-barrelled guns, faced 83,000 French and colonial troops using artillery and machine guns, as well as aerial bombardment by four air squadrons. On visits to the crags, gorges and screes of the mountain I have picked up battle souvenirs – like the base plate of a shell, a flattened tin plate and a rusty tin marked *boeuf assaisonné* (a corned beef equivalent). They now sit in my cabinet of curiosities.

My first visit to the Jbel Sahro was forty years ago, a holiday break with a trekking company which I enjoyed, partly, for once having no responsibilities. Our local guide was a lean old man of the local Aït Atta, always dressed in sheeps' wool *djellaba* and white turban. His face was deeply lined but there was always a twinkle in his eye. His name was Ali Ll'sch. He was tireless on his feet and always good fun – once at my expense. One evening he 'borrowed' my brolly (out there it was *parasol* not *parapluie*) and proceeded to walk round the camp doing a perfect imitation of my characteristic pace during a hot ascent, a brilliant parody that had us all laughing.

A day or two later Ali and I stood on a clifftop looking over to barren Bou Gafer: soaring pinnacles and ridges, a pockmarking of caves, and screes sloping down to a trickle of water in a rocky bed. Ali began to describe the battle with remarkable detail, pointing out where the French had positioned machine guns to kill anyone sneaking down to try and reach water, the goat path up the gorge cliffs to allow a night raid on French sentries (the only way in the end the Berbers could obtain ammunition), the routes the biplanes followed to twist into the valley to bomb any position picked out through French binoculars. Sheltering in caves were women and children too, all without food, and water only collected at night until even that became an exercise too far. Half the Aït Atta died, the 'Spartans of the Atlas,' and however brave, there could only be one end.

Ali fell silent, the twinkle gone from his eye, looking old and inestimably sad. With something like awe I knew. I put my arm round his shoulder.

'You were there.'

He nodded.

NOMADS PASSING

Why should they not be proud, aloof,
These survivors, these men of men,
Who have made the great journey
Again and again, who travel
From desert plains to biting heights
Year after year, a cycle of life and death
That cracks like the frosted rocks
Or flames with the pains of sun?
Their values are basic; primitive
Some would say, but where in all
Civilisation's concrete waste
Are embedded virtues of honour, faith,
Loyalty and knowledge based on life
That dares not make mistakes?
When the nomad caravan went by
I wanted to grab one of the beasts
And ride beyond my known horizons.
Instead, I'll fly home, with a plastic meal
Feeding the choked dreams I knew.

RAGBAG

THE 1978 BLIZZARD

> 'The surprising thing about weather is that it can still surprise us.'
>
> *(Glasgow Herald)*

> 'Snow can be an inconvenience.'
>
> *(The Scotsman)*

January 1978 will be remembered in many parts of Scotland as the month of the Great Storm. I was made to realise my age during it, because of the comparisons that were made with 1947; people either knew that earlier epic, or they were too young to remember it. It does show how far back we had to go to find like conditions.

I was just a laddie in 1947. Going through to the Alloa Baths on a Saturday morning from Dollar, I remember sitting on the top deck of a double-decker and just being able to look over the edge of the canyon of snow. What skating we seemed to have then! They did not salt the roads at that time, and it packed down so hard that I was able to skate down for the rolls and papers before breakfast: *down* was the operative word, and a right pech it was back *up* the Muckhart Road to home!

Perhaps the most enjoyable skating I have ever had was one winter on Rannoch Moor. We were staying at Blackrock, the Ladies Scottish Climbing Club Hut on the edge of the moor, and three of us had optimistically brought skates. Our faith was rewarded with a long deep freeze, followed by an overnight sprinkling of snow. Through this powder we scored our fancy patterns against the superb silvered background of the hills of Coire Ba. That night the storms came lashing back and the ice vanished under drifts.

In 1978 it was not as simple as that. Whole areas were cut off for days. When even trains cannot win through you know conditions are bad. I was in Strathspey – and there I had to stay. The week of blockage, and tragedy, was the result of a 24-hour blizzard; seldom can such chaos have come from so seemingly short a storm, a brief chuckling of snow and a wind swearing at the world.

I had had a dress rehearsal just ten days previously. Coming back from the North-West after five weeks of mountaineering activities over Christmas and Hogmanay, I was still managing day after day on the hill – hard work, as the snow was deep and powdery. When I left Loch Duich the roads north of there were blocked. I left Glen Garry with the hill road closing behind me. At Glen Coe the barriers were up. Superb day as it was at sea-level, a wind had sprung up and Rannoch Moor was being blasted in drift. We were told an articulated lorry had jack-knifed, blocking the road for fifty cars which the snow soon engulfed.

I spent the night in my dormobile at Carnoch – snug enough, though icicles dangled from bumpers and mirrors. Work by the ploughs went on through the night, and by next afternoon it was just possible to squeeze through. Though only aiming to go to Bridge of Orchy, I drove on to Crianlarich in order to take photographs of the haughty white hills of Ben More and Stobinian. Two days later you would hardly have known it had snowed, so sudden was the thaw.

Then, in January, I drove north one Friday morning. The road was fine, though in Drumochter a wind was sending the drift in waves along the new dual A9. After a few calls I went to Glenmore Lodge to visit friends. The forecast was pretty wild, so I needed little persuasion to stay. However, Saturday morning was promised fair, and as the ski road was open and I had a 10 a.m. reservation to teach a ski class, I went up. None of my class turned up, so I bought a day ticket and made the most of it. Slopes were quieter than usual as the A9 had been blocked. My clients had had car trouble and only reached Grantown at 3 a.m. And Grantown was to be cut off completely for several days.

I had a good day's skiing, but after lunch I went down to the dormobile to change into ski-climbing rig. It had been snowing for hours, and cars all carried roof blankets of white. In the Scottish Ski Club Hut I met the Langmuir family: Eric was for many years Principal at Glenmore Lodge. At the last tow my ticket was punched by Mollie Porter, leader of the local mountain rescue team. We were all glad the weather had not deteriorated as expected. Not yet anyway.

With skins I was able to ski straight up through the glare to the top of Cairn Gorm. In the lee of the weather station I took off my skins, adjusted the settings, and carefully set off down. The only thing visible was the faint shadow line of my own up-track and it was rapidly vanishing in drift. The wind was rising. Perhaps the storm was coming after all.

Back at the van I toasted cheese sandwiches and drank coffee till the general exodus was over, and then drove down into Aviemore. I left there at 5 p.m. It was snowing and there was a bit of wind. By Newtonmore I was thankful to stop. In that brief run the full fury had been unleashed and I'd had my share of excitement. Near Kincraig a car ahead of me suddenly went careering up the bank and then fell on its side. I pulled in beyond him, set the emergency flashers going, then raced back to see if anyone was hurt. The sole occupant climbed out of a door which had become a hatch, shaken but unhurt. Others joined us, and we bounced the car out and on to its wheels again. As I was blocking the way, I had to drive on. I needed ten minutes in the warm car to stop my shivering.

At times the drift was swirling up so that visibility went completely. I don't think I had ever seen such wildness. It was tempting just to pull into a layby and sit out the onslaught; after all, I was in a well-stocked dormobile. But I had promised to look in on a friend at Newtonmore. I pushed on slowly, groping through the flying clouds of snow or battering into drifts already laid across the road. Just before Newtonmore a car coming the other way began to waltz all over the road and went skidding past, missing me by a midge width. I drove down to the station and parked where I was near my friend's house, but out of the way of any snow-ploughs operating.

My friend Dave Morris was not in. He worked for the then Nature Conservancy Council, and I knew he had been to Deeside for a meeting, so I was not surprised. At ten o'clock I had just turned off the Tilley lamp (used for heat as well as light) in the van, when Dave knocked at the van door. He had got through, but his car was stuck a quarter of a mile outside Newtonmore. Few other people were to arrive anywhere that night. Dave had just got in when the police called him out to try to go through to Laggan; a climber was missing on Creag Meagaidh. The rescue team tried to press on, but even Land Rovers could not make it far out of the village. The climber had been left in a bivvy by his companions when he became exhausted and nobody gave much chance for his survival.

On the Sunday we went up to the village. Hardly a soul was to be seen. When a friend opened his door, only his head could be seen over the drifts. A band of snow completely concealed a car. The trees beyond the village were snapping under the grasping weight of snow. Dick Balharry joined us and we walked along a wall and over bare fields rather than the high, deep drifts of the road. Cows came bellowing up to us hopefully. A lorry was snow to its roof, the policeman's car next to it was half-covered, and beyond, where we knew there was a break-down vehicle, a road works pick-up and Dave's car, not a thing was to be seen; the cutting was filled and levelled off with snow.

We poked with broom handles and could not even hit a roof. The brooms were left marking the likely spot, and Dave returned home to dream of the big blower ploughing into his car and flinging it like confetti into the field. The storm died down, the 24-hour blast leaving incredible chaos in its wake. It took weeks in the end for life to return to normal. We sat glued to the radio.

Speyside was cut off: Newtonmore, Kingussie, Aviemore, Grantown – there was no link between them. To the north, Caithness and Sutherland had been overwhelmed, a bus was missing on the Ullapool road, Glen Shiel was impassable, Glen Coe blocked – yet when I rang home I was told Fife was snowless. It was fortunate the storm came on the Saturday night: Friday night or Sunday night would have seen thousands of skiers on the road and one shudders at the possible consequences. The toll of life was to be surprisingly small.

Monday morning was clear and still. I fished out my *langlauf* skis and with a shovel set off with Dave, who carried an avalanche probe, to where his car lay buried. There was a digger already biting its way forward, carving out a twelve-foot-deep canyon. People had just located Dave's car under his broom markers. I threw my spade over, and it was grabbed and used by a relay of willing workers. I spent a few minutes taking pictures. Several children from Kingussie went by, pulling baker's trays of bread and pies as if they were toboggans. Helicopters passed frequently on their vital missions, perhaps the greatest boon of all – there had been little such quick help in 1947. At one stage I had car, digger, the Chief Constable's helicopter and the first train to win through Drumochter all in my view finder – only to run out of film.

The Chief Constable, Donald Henderson, had landed by helicopter to check on the activity. He was relieved to be assured that no people were in the buried cars. The southern train was a welcome sight, opening up at least one exit route from Strathspey. Further north in Caithness the radio had announced the odd fact that a train had 'gone missing' – vanished as if someone had slipped it in their pocket and walked off. It had hit drifts and been derailed many miles from any road, and a relief train suffered the same fate. In the end helicopters airlifted seventy people from the scene.

The canyon was cut through to Dave's car and another, and after a bit of digging round they were pulled out like a couple of loose teeth. Inside, the engines were filled with snow, yet still started. By evening Newtonmore and Kingussie were linked by road again. The bad news began to come through; rescue parties were finding bodies in cars which had been overwhelmed. But there were odd miracles:

the climber on Creag Meagaidh was found alive after his night under the snow.

Tuesday saw the exodus begin. People from Newton-more were taking the train north to Aviemore in order to secure a seat south to Perth. The Slochd was still blocked so Aviemore was the temporary beginning of the line. Further north, a busload bound for Ullapool had been stopped by snow, fortuitously near the Aultguish Inn, whose walls bear pictures of past storms, which must have been much commented on by the refugees. Slowly this and that road were opened. The helicopters still flew long into the night, dropping food and medicine, lifting a heart case from a distant glen. Dave drove to Aviemore and found more helicopters than cars in its main street. One tall tale was going the rounds. A helicopter had spied a puff of smoke coming from a big drift, and investigation revealed a house completely overwhelmed. However, they were able to communicate – down the chimney. A voice from inside replied 'Who is that outside?' The rescuers shouted back 'This is the Red Cross,' only to hear 'Ach, go away. We gave last week.'

On Tuesday night the last known missing person was found. Willie Sutherland, in his sixties, had spent eighty hours under the snow yet was able to *walk* into hospital: a fine case of morale seeing a man through. To keep warm he had wrapped himself in women's tights (he was a sales rep. with boxes and boxes of them in his car). A wedding reception near Inverness went into its fifth day as Wednesday dawned. No doubt a merry time was had by all.

The radio said there was little chance of the A9 at Drumochter opening before Friday, so having a meeting at home that day, I joined the exodus by train. They were now operating from Inverness. Four engines pulled the

Clansman, and one passenger commented that on the Slochd the drifts had been as high as the train. The only break in the white scene was the colourful clutch of blowers and ploughs at work on the A9. Deer floundered across the slope and sheep stood forlornly. There must have been a heavy toll of wildlife.

Some good came out of the disastrous spell of blizzards. People helped and worked for each other in a way that seldom happens normally – and there is the residual awareness of just what can happen. Motorists and lonely households will have a greater respect for winter when they remember the blizzard of '78, just as we old stagers have always remembered the winter of '47.

What's In A Name

> *what is the best of the country?*
> blinkbonny! airgold! thundergay!
> *and the worst?*
> schrishven, shiskine, scrabster, and snizort.
> **Edwin Morgan**

Those lines are from the late weel-kent, weel-loved Glasgow poet. The poem's full title is 'Canedolia, (an off-concrete scotch fantasia)'; a cornucopia of Scottish placenames. Reading them has the names bouncing around like colourful snooker balls. When Edwin Morgan did a presentation at Pitlochry Festival Theatre it was the first thing asked for as an 'encore' from the audience – and I had my hand up too for the same request. The poem was a sure choice for my anthology, *Poems of the Scottish Hills*. I wonder how many map sheets produced the names. Any OS map sheet can give entertainment just looking at placenames, a useful game in tent, bothy or hut when the weather is unfriendly.

Walking across Scotland each spring on the Ultimate Challenge (now TGO Challenge) gives a fascinating ever-changing landscape, but the maps can also give a similar diversity in the place names. There is no likelihood of meeting Tipperty, Dillivaird, or Corsebauld west of the Great Glen, nor of coming across hill names like Bidean a' Choire Sheasgaich or Sgurr nan Ceathreamhnan in Angus or Fife.

Following down the River Avon in the Cairngorms on one crossing we stopped at Faindouran Bothy. In the bothy book stalkers mentioned going after hinds 'by the Spion rocks,' the map name not far above the bothy marking a characteristic Cairngorms granite tor. Having lived in South Africa and seen the prominent hill of Spion Kop, this set me wondering what could be the connection between a ferocious battle where the Boers defeated the inept British and a hillside in the Cairngorms. Then I found in the bothy an old tin trunk full of musty books which was labelled: 'O. Haig. 7th Hussars.' Now, if my link is correct, the 7th Hussars were in the Boer War, and as the Haigs once owned that estate, it seems likely that the *kopje* name was 'imported' to describe a distinctive tor in the Cairngorms.

We also found in the trunk a copy of Sir Herbert Maxwell's *Memories of the Months*, which contained articles about the fascination of names and their derivations. He was emphasising the simple solution in looking for derivations, rather than the fanciful. The part of Kinghorn where I lived is called Pettycur, the old ferry port for crossing the Forth, hence the Pettycur name on old milestones all across Fife to the Tay. The name comes from the *petty/pit* Pictish term for 'a portion of land' – and certainly not, as

I've seen suggested, from the French *petit coeur*. In those days the port of Pettycur and the village of Kinghorn were not contiguous, and our house stood on 'Crying-oot Hill' above the harbour. Lots of fancy derivations were offered, but it was probably just where some youth would scramble up to yell to the village that the ferry was coming and that passengers had better finish their drinks and get down to the *hynd*.

Hynd is an old Scots word for a harbour with only one arm. Along the coast is Buckhaven, but no local ever calls the town anything but Buckhynd, its older name happily preserved. On ancient maps I've seen it spelled that way or even as Hynd of Buck. As a Dollar lad I knew the River Devon well, the 'clear-winding Devon' of the poet Burns, but earlier it was the Dowan or Dovan, far lovelier names than the usurping anglicised one.

Names go on changing. The Cairngorms were once the Monadh Ruadh, and the Lairig Ghru was Lairig Ghrumach. Several names in the range seem to have been somewhat tampered with in Victorian times. Devil's Point is a euphemism for Devil's Penis, and balancing it, appeared the cringe-making Angel's Peak, a sorry exchange for the original, euphonic, apt Sgurr an Lochan Uaine, *peak of the green lochan*. Lochnagar's lumpy summit tors translate simply as 'big pile of shit' and 'small pile of shit'. Interestingly they are the wrong way round: Cac Carn Beag is higher than Cac Carn Mor. The Victorians didn't translate those names!

In the far North West, Loch an Nid, *loch of the nest*, led me, as a bird watcher, to one of my first eyries. More than once, going up a hill, I have carefully avoided a Garbh Choire (*rough corrie*), or planning a cross-country route over new country, taken a crossing by a Druim nam Bo (*ridge of the cows*) on the assumption the going would be easy – cows do not climb crags – and so it proved. Teasing out names can be fun. Maxwell, in his book at the bothy, suggests Gaelic was once spoken in Galloway because Gaelic names survive, like the headland indicated as Bhuidhe, *yellow*. In Munro's Tables the commonest mountain name is Ghabhar, *goat*, but there is not a sheep to be found, perhaps testimony to a change in status. The sheep came late to the Munros – take that how you will! English writers sometimes complain that Gaelic has six ways of saying white (there are actually more) but this is simply due to the richness of the Gaelic language. I bet it was a surveyor from Lancashire who turned Loch Ba on Rannoch Moor into *Loch Ball*. The notorious 'sportsman' Colonel Thornton managed to record Crianlarich as *Cree in la Roche*.

Many names leave riddles. Why a *smallpox peak* in the Cuillin? What tale is lost in the *ridge of the sword* or *the loch of the corpse*? Growing up with the Ochils as playground we made up location names for our own convenience, only to find that some of these have passed into 'common usage'. One study of local names suggested that our 'William's Stone' had perhaps a connection with William the Lion. But that is how names arrive and alas, become lost. When I visited a cousin living on Rousay (Orkney) she noted that nobody now knew the origins of local names (why *Mary's dyke* or *Ploughman's Folly*?) for there was not a single resident remaining with any local ancestral knowledge.

Walking across Scotland also gives interesting changes in people's accents. I recall once phoning from Speyside to Cock Bridge to book accommodation and the accent I heard was suddenly so very much of the north-east – quite a contrast to the accents soft as the weather at the walk's start at Achnashellach. Gaelic names faded very quickly after Cock Bridge but the east has its own splendid names – like Shank of Inchgrundle, Glensaugh, Tipperweir, Tillybreak, Kirktown of Fetteresso. Some leave one as bewildered as intrigued: Wairds of Alpity, Baudy Meg, Tigerton, Stankeye, Snob Cottage, Doup of Beckie, Bogjurgan, Feathers. There are plenty Bogbraes, Stony Muirs, Hillheads of course. Half of OS Sheet 45 had over 20 names with 'Bog' appearing.

That rainy night in Faindouran bothy we pored (poured?) over our maps of the country ahead, to find pleasing names. How would you like to farm at Titaboutie, Bonnyfleeces, Bennygray, Goosecruives, Balnamoon, Monboddo, Whistlebrae, Oldcake, Tillytoghills? And as for Blinkbonny – our next Challenge route was being planned to pass that name as we left the hills and made for the eastern sea. Once there, we will add a toast to Airgold and Thundergay.

THE CALENDAR ROUND

I can't now remember who challenged me, or when exactly, about the idea of a 'Calendar Round' of the Munros – that is, to have been up a Munro on every day of the year – a challenge which curiosity couldn't resist. In 1999 out came the ledger with all my Munro data.

The result was interesting. There were only nine gaps but these were scattered across the year in quite random fashion. There would be no quick one-week 'away' to roll up the list, but many day 'raids,' for whatever hills, at all seasons, something which made it an irresistible challenge. A pity the idea had not come earlier; by the end of the sixties something like 288 days of the year were already filled. The missing nine days were 18th, 29th, 30th January;

11th February; 14th March; 7th July; and 3rd, 11th, 17th September.

The winter-into-spring gaps were due to regularly working over the Festive Season, and then being out in Morocco for months on end. September had rather been a slack time in Scotland as I was often in Ireland. I'd need some careful planning for this logistical exercise – especially as I then promptly departed to the Atlas (pre-arranged) before Christmas, and only came home in March. I brought in the new Millennium on a peak in the sunny Anti-Atlas.

I flew Marrakech-London on 10th March, took the train to Scotland on the 11th, and climbed the Loch Lomondside Ben Vorlich on the 14th. My summary note on that day was, 'Night by the Falls of Falloch (campervan). Vile ascent. Nice after.' The only other gap filled that year was making a 7th July circuit of Coire Dhomhain at Drumochter, from A'Mharconaich round to the Sow of Atholl. I was back in Morocco over the September options. Only two in the year.

By making Morocco the following year, 2001, run from March to June I could surely fit in the clutter of January and September gaps, so Stob Ghabhar was done on 18th January 'Grey, driech, snowing much of the way.' I was then busy on a photographic stint on Speyside so grabbed the Monadhliath Geal Charn on 29th January, going 'up Glen Tarkie. Wintry. Met lad on top so down to Garva Bridge with him and lift to my van'. A chilly night in the camper and, next day, I set off up Ben More in good conditions but 'the glory goes and hellish, filthy mix to traverse to Stob Binnein and back by the Glen. Wouldn't have gone but for the Calendar Round'. Suddenly there were only four remaining.

Just back from a brief early February visit to Ireland (a cousin's 90th birthday), I had a wild night in my van at

Inveruglas before adding lowly Ben Vane on 11th February. All these hills had been chosen because they would add to the tally for my hoped-for eighth round of the Munros (now a lost cause); but I was decidedly scunnered (good Scots word) at the way the weather seemed to bear a grudge against any combination of efforts or being committed to specific days. I determined to finish off with easier days.

3rd September was a nice-enough day and I enjoyed cycling up beyond Derry Lodge to bag Beinn Bhreac (another 'eighth') and then added Carn a'Mhaim. A night in the van at Crathie, and Meall Alvie was climbed before heading home. On the 11th, Ben Vane as the lowest of all Munros lured me back (no longer an 'eighth') and I thought I'd made a good choice with this 'easier' regime in place, only to be ambushed on top. 'Soaker from summit' was an understatement. I descended river rather than road, had cramp, and ended shivering violently. Thank goodness for my bothy on wheels with a complete change of clothes and restorative hot drinks. (Dining with friends in Arrochar had been the real reason for choosing Ben Vane again.)

For the final gap a week later, 17th September, I went for the easiest of all Munros, declaring 'the weather can do its damnedest'. I had company for this occasion, though I did warn friend Jill that if things ran to form the weather would be vile. Incidentally, I've been on perhaps ten Munros being ascended for celebratory 'compleating' by friends, and on all but one the weather ranged from bad to diabolical. Being pinned to any precise date in the year seems to ask for trouble. The one glorious exception was taking the Devil's Ridge to Sgurr a'Mhaim for Jill's last Munro (described in *Walking the Song*).

Perhaps Jill has a line to the weather gods. Having chosen the Cairnwell for probably hell and high water we were granted a cloud-chasing, windy day of sunshine. In the lee of the summit wreckage we cringed to eat cake and drink a toast to this latest bit of fun in the Munro game. I just wish I could remember who made the challenge. May he have all the freezings and soakings I endured and, of course, the unchanging wonder and reward that we find on our Scottish hills and their beguiling Munros. And there was one potential awkwardness I never had to worry about: I had two February 29ths already in the bag.

Too Dull A River

Too dull a river to bother canoeing was the implication in this comment from a friend who heard I was planning to paddle the River Forth from Loch Ard home to Kinghorn's Pettycur harbour. This was another novelty in my tramping, with my dog Storm, from John o'Groats to Land's End. Ben Hope to Ben Lomond had foot-linked the north and south ends of Munrodom, and Ben Lomond had neatly completed a sixth round of the Munros.

On Ben Lomond I experienced something of a puzzle. There was a thick mist on top but in the forty minutes I spent by the trig, only one couple joined me, briefly: this on a fair-weather holiday Saturday in June. This is one of the most visited of Scotland's hills, always had been, long before Munro's list appeared, so where were the folk? Continuing, I headed round the rim and, at its other end where there was a rise and the path up from Loch Lomond joined this crest, I found the 'missing' crowds of people. Someone had stopped there on the assumption they had reached the summit and everyone else had just followed suit! I passed seventy more sweating up the slaistery tourist path (only the summit ridge was clouded) before swinging off for the Ben's lonely eastern face. My old canvas-on-wooden-frame canoe was with friends at the western end of Loch Ard. Storm enjoyed the company of their two dogs and assorted cats. After sweaty days on the trail I enjoyed a bath, not cooking my own supper, and good company.

The river is certainly not the most exciting, dropping just eighty feet in 37 miles, but worse, after a dry spell the water level was low, which set extra problems. At one stage I had to sit on a fallen tree trunk and manhandle the canoe over it, and there were plenty of groundings. Near Aberfoyle, after the Avondubh (from Loch Ard) and the Duchray Water joined to become the River Forth proper, I spied a bloated dead sheep caught up in the branches of a tree ten feet overhead – washed there in the last spate. (Water like that would have livened up the paddling. Knowing what the river can do, the Bailie Nicol Jarvie Hotel in Aberfoyle keeps a boat handy.) The real bane of the Forth is the way the river twists and turns and circles and loops, often almost coming back on itself: a lot of effort for little gain eastwards. The banks are so high there are seldom views and the sun smote remorselessly. Dull it was not. Just different. Most of the meanderings are across Flanders Moss.

I camped at the two extremities of this historical area, near farms called Offrins of Gartur and Kepdarroch. At one stage on the second day I gave up canoeing during the hottest hours of the day and just lay reading and snoozing on a shady spot on the bank. I had just passed Culmore and Culbeg (I kid you not) and began a favourite pastime of filling the margin of the map with interesting local place names: here were Faraway, Pendicles of Collymoon, Backside of Garden, Stock o' Broom, Goodie Water (from the

Lake of Menteith), Drip Moss, Kersebonny, Blackdub and Barbadoes.

Flanders Moss originally was forest but it was destroyed long ago, being a too-pernicious 'debatable land' between Highlands and Lowlands. Another of our pauses was at the Fords of Frew, one of the few crossings in ancient time, where James IV had battled across, Rob Roy had raided, and Montrose and the Young Pretender had led their forces over. Much of the moss's peat was thrown into the river and washed away downstream to create quality farmland but those high banks were needed to avoid flooding.

Nearing Stirling the rivers Teith and Allan joined our dark waters and Stirling Castle and the Wallace Monument reminded of other historical centuries. Passing under the old Stirling Bridge was a great deal more satisfying than passing under the bland M9. On tidal waters now, I put in, the castle looming overhead, to make use of the Cornton Camp and Caravan Park. The site proved to be well away from the river rather than on its bank, so everything from the canoe had to be carried over. I left the canoe upside down on the bank. We did little and then rested afterwards as the sun was remorselessly hot (sunburn is a regular feature of canoeing!). We had a comfortable night. But shocks lay ahead.

To make use of the tides I was back at the canoe at two o'clock in the morning, a nautical friend having given me completely wrong ebb tide times. I found my canoe in the river, full of water, and had a struggle to drain it and haul it ashore. Vandals had stuck a knife through the canvas in ten places along the bottom and then kicked a hole in it for bad measure. The frame was undamaged, however, and after an hour with scissors and tape we were off. Luckily the vandals had not seen the painter was tied to the bank or the canoe would have drifted away; and the paddles had been well hidden.

Stirling's history has been twinned with its geography for centuries, this being the 'lowest bridging point' on the Forth. The ebb bore us through it at a good rate, but the meanders – 'The Links o' Forth' – were then bigger than ever, to create a somewhat drunken geography as landmarks like the Wallace Monument popped up in varying positions. The Forth, alas, is a smelly, unappealing river for many miles with landing impossible on its wide, black gooey mudbanks. My first pause was at old South Alloa harbour (6.00 a.m.) where the folk from the only house insisted I went in for a cup of tea. A fisherman told me of a sunken ship here which defied salvaging until someone applied a brainwave: they filled the inside with barrels for buoyancy – but the pressure of the barrels then lifted the deck off the ship.

With the *leckie* (ebb) came wind, soon a dangerous, strong south flanker. I took breaks at Kincardine Bridge and on the seawall of Longannet Power Station. Nobody seemed to notice. Leaving, in a rough sea, I buckled the joint where my paddles fitted together and then, beyond Culross, well out to sea, I found skerries, wind and tide combining to make a sea of utter chaos. Spouts shot straight up all round us. In my struggles with these conditions the paddles broke. While bouncing about at the sea's mercy I grabbed sections of tent pole, cut off tent guylines and created a very bulky splint. Crombie pier offered no help as the canoe stuck in the mud, but not far on a big solid pier allowed easy access at this low tide and for re-launching on the next high tide. I carried the gear up to a grassy bank beside the wired-off hinterland. I made supper about six o'clock, but just could not stay awake in the westering sun thereafter and woke to a dewy midnight. I made a brew, then put the paddles against the fence, threw the tent over to make some shelter, and went back to sleep.

An hour later I was woken by flashing lights and found a policeman with an Alsatian regarding my bivvy with some incredulity. He called up a patrol car. A sergeant arrived. Things were becoming surreal. However it turned out the sergeant had a brother-in-law who had been on school expeditions with me so Storm the dog and I were recognised and vouched for. Yes, my story of *walking* John o'Groats to Land's End and just happening to land there on the Forth from a *canoe*, was very likely true. We had a good blether rather than me being arrested for landing at a high explosives depot with notices everywhere saying 'Keep Out' and 'No Naked Flames' – but none had faced the sea.

As the tide was already well-up, I pushed on and for several miles enjoyed a glittering display of phosphorescence. Storm was fascinated by the cascading diamonds stirred by my makeshift paddles. I had to go well out to round Kinniny Point, then passed a large floating dock and did the equivalent of tiptoeing through all the naval vessels off Rosyth (some NATO exercise). I went through them all unchallenged! After that it was a breakfast break ashore at North Queensferry and a wander round the impressive old abbey on Inchcolm before reaching home at Pettycur. Mother was not surprised, if not too pleased, to have me ringing the doorbell at 6.40 a.m.. No sooner inside, the weather let rip – for days of deluge. At noon I had a call from the Crombie police, 'just checking' we had made it home. So much for our days on the river that was supposedly too dull to bother paddling.

Taliban Among The Trees

A civilisation flourishes when people plant trees
beneath which they will never be sitting
Greek Proverb

It began with a dream. I came homing in on a great woodland which I knew – in my dream – as the site of the famous
cricket school funded by a millionaire who was determined
that Australian cricket should improve dramatically. The
Aussies had only once ever beaten England after all (not
true of course), even losing on one occasion by an innings
and 579 runs (which is true). But it was not cricket or its
pitches scattered like polka dots on the furry fabric of the
trees that my dream was to be about. The millionaire had
been passionate about trees as well, hence this setting. (I
liked the gentle irony that cricket bats come from trees.)

The man had collected trees the way small boys collect
stamps or marbles and had created probably the largest
arboretum in the world. The trees sprawled over the landscape in as natural a way as could be. That was important.
His was a friendly woodland and visitors were welcome
to share its pleasures. Every tree was carefully named and
described and he knew them all, so could rattle off generic
and specific name as if introducing friends. Trees may not
have been people, but they had personality.

In my dream I found myself gazing at a magnificent Atlas
cedar (*Cedrus atlantica*) while nearby I could hear young
voices and the clunk of bat on ball: the Class IV nets. The
millionaire had died and a committee, well, a Trust, now ran
the school and arboretum. All this in my dream of course.

As my eyes followed the up-sweeping pillars of the cedar to its spreading canopy above, I noticed a trembling and realised men with a large saw were at work on the trunk. They were felling the giant. I tried to shout out a protest but found myself speechless. One of the men stopped to wipe his brow and grinned at me. 'Got to go! All the non-natives, all the aliens. Only natives from now on.'

I exploded. 'But that's so stupid!' and in the shouting came to, woke up, and found myself as despairing awake as I had been in the dream. And if dreams are sparked off by some reality I could see this one as the result of local experiences – quite apart from looming Test Matches.

In the wooded hills behind our local villages I had planted various 'rescued' trees – some rowans, an ash, a couple of birch, an oak I'd grown from an acorn; and when I had a potted blue spruce, an *Abies* species, dumped on me I thought it might as well go on these slopes as well. Atop an open bank, my grandchildren might one day see the blue-grey-green giant in its stateliness. A few weeks later I found the young tree had gone. It had been yanked out; by vandals I presumed.

But I'm always amazed at the way word gets about. I learned that the tree had been removed by some local do-gooders who considered it an 'alien' and not right for a brae in Fife. No wonder I'd dreamed as I had. They had removed my gem from a woodland that is ninety per cent non-native sycamore – and *they* had planted a hedge of non-native beech to protect a viewpoint bench. Ignorance and arrogance is not a fruitful combination.

I was also criticised for planting 'alien' snowdrops on the braes. Nobody really knows when snowdrops arrived in Britain. Some suggest the easy-to-blame Romans, others the invasive Normans. Does it matter? They have blessed us for over a thousand years. How long do you have to be resident to become native? People of course face the same blind bigotry so we should not be surprised at the Brexiters of nature. Nothing growing, nothing living in Scotland, but didn't come from somewhere else. Let those who dug out my innocent tree send in their DNA for analysis and see just where they came from. I have just laughed at a newspaper feature which indicated that our Queen had an ancestor in the Prophet Mohammed, peace be unto them. We are all Jock Tamson's bairns. Taking these excluders' ideas to their logical conclusion would see a rather over-crowded Africa, from where I believe we all started. The very word 'alien' for a person, or a flower, or a tree is a sorry reflection of these attitudes. Buddha gained enlightenment sitting under a tree!

Many of our loved flowers and exotics came from far corners of the world. How much poorer gardens would be without begonia, fuchsia, dahlia, lobelia, forsythia, buddleia, montbretia, camellia, escallonia, hosta, kalmia, or even gunnera – all of which are named after people, not a few of whom were world-wanderers who found beauty and brought it home. Would those who dug up my tree destroy all rhododendrons (a good idea for one species perhaps), get rid of acers, cacti, the flower-graced Oriental cherries, wisteria, magnolia, London plane, sweet chestnut, giant redwood? Yet, I'll hazard, these narrow nationalists have no trouble drinking tea or coffee (with sugar?) and enjoying citrus fruits, bananas,[1] tomatoes, potatoes, and pepper. Of course there are rogue plants just as there are rogue animals and rogue humans. But we don't exterminate Germans because Hitler was vile. In reality we, in Britain, have been enriched by all the successive peoples who have come to our shores; and we were similarly enriched by the arrival of trees such as larch or beech. The glory of central Perthshire is its larch landscape, there are beech avenues and lime avenues which are as dramatic as any human structures, there are ancient sycamores (hundreds of years older than their critics) which stand in solitary magnificence, there are explosive laburnums lighting many corners of man-made dreariness, there are thriving giant redwoods that lift the hearts of all who see them. In themselves, trees are a rare magical perfection.

Beauty should be our only criterion. A fine tree has the same right to exist, anywhere, to be as admired as a Rembrandt or a Van Gogh (where, indeed, could you send a Van Gogh painting to, as *home*?) No wonder I woke from my dream shouting, 'That is so stupid!' I'm writing this in the café of our big local library, having walked up an avenue of deodar trees (*Cedrus deodara*) which are also beautiful beyond the praising of them. They too of course are incomers: welcome, enriching incomers. God protect them, and us, from the Taliban among our trees.

---

1 On namings: at a radio discussion someone from the south of England was complaining about Gaelic, that it needed so many intrusive, alien words. 'I mean, what is the Gaelic word for banana?' There was a brief pause, and then the Gaelic speaker replied, 'Just so, and what is the English word for banana?'

My Last Bivouac

Unlike the retrospective nature of most of the rest of this book, the following reports a recent escapade to show how aging's limitations don't mean less fun, or not accepting challenges. As Peter Sellars put it, 'We all need to be a little bit mad; it keeps us sane.' And why should

adventures, to bear that name, always be big? Gilbert
White of Selborne called his Sussex Downs 'that chain
of majestic mountains'.

Looking from my flat the view is over the green Burntisland
Links with the railway beyond as protection from the sea.
At low tide big sands appear and these dry out away past the
Black Rocks, a mile offshore. In Cromwell's time or when
Hessian dragoons were camped on the Links they used to
hold races, galloping over good ground all the way to the
Black Rocks, or Black Craigs as they were also called. The
sea has swallowed up all that land since then. From the shore
the rocks look very black, as if alive, and hungry; at low tide
they appear a stranded beast, at high tide, anchored out at
sea, looking very small, very lonely, very far away. For many
years I had intended spending a night on the Black Rocks to
experience the cycle of the tides.

I enjoy bivouacking though my last (then) bivvy (2017)
was only just bearable. A friend and I had walked in to
remote Peanmeanach Bothy in Moidart (on a previous visit
I'd arrived by canoe), looking forward to a quiet night after a
walk along the strand, a fine 'dropping of the daylight in the
west,' a good meal and a dram by the fire. Unfortunately we
were invaded by a dozen no-means-young yobbos from Ayr
whose only desire was to get roarin' fou, Hell for anyone
else. Having my Goretex bivvy bag with me I fled out along
the ruins to find a spot to sleep out. (By one ruin I found a
clump of rhubarb; we had it for supper next evening.) A
hard frost fell and wearing all my clothes inside the summer
sleeping bag I only just stuck it out. There's an art in lying
motionless and making believe one is warm.

At one o'clock I was shaken awake by my friend who
had packed up and was going to walk back over the hills to

his one-man campervan. Sleep had been impossible in the bothy. I thought that might have been my last bivvy but the next night, after we'd enjoyed a good hill day, I slept out above Loch Morar: cool, clear, no midges – bliss.

Driving from Kinghorn to Burntisland and looking over the miles of sand to the distant Black Rocks I suddenly recalled this lost bivvy intention. The tides would be perfect that night. Come on! Why not? The fun of doing daft things is really as necessary as eating or sleeping; after all, as Mallory of Everest affirmed, 'What we get from adventure is sheer joy'. So, an hour before dusk, rucksack on back, I tramped the mile out to the Black Rocks, wellies squelching the worm casts, and feet dodging the stranded jellyfish. I'd not been on the Black Rocks for a couple of years but picked the remembered best route up to the high point and realised there was a problem: the rock strata stood up like *sastrugi* on a glacier and only after a thorough search did I find a flattish place that would take the minimal level requirement for shoulders and hips when lying down. This sea rock was distinctly smelly, being liberally whitewashed: that I hadn't envisaged. I perched discreetly, for the tide was soon around the rocks and I'd no desire to be spotted by some worried walker and be 'rescued' by my local Kinghorn RNLI.

I had some tea and cake and enjoyed dusk's changing glitter on the little waves and the lights coming on in Edinburgh. Trains caterpillared along the shore, hardly heard at that distance, to vanish among the trees beyond the Kingswood Hotel and the cliffs where King Alexander III rode his horse over the edge. (If he hadn't done that you wouldn't be reading this right now.) The red lights on the Binn mast lit up. A friend, easily persuaded for a first bivvy, and I once went up to the summit of the Binn to watch the impressive fireworks display on the last night of the Edinburgh International Festival, and then bivvied up there. Even before getting out of my sleeping bag next morning I had the stove out and a dixie of water ready for brewing – and then found neither of us had a lighter or matches.

On the Black Rocks I was well and truly marooned by eight o'clock. There was not very much rock and a great deal of sea. I felt very isolated. When bedding down, the breeze died away and the smell of guano became overpowering. That made this bivvy unique if nothing else. Birds began to fly in to roost. I could have reached out a hand and grabbed an oystercatcher by its legs. A gull didn't recognize my green sleeping bag and landed wallop on my tummy before squawking off. The lap-lapping of the sea grew louder, and nearer, slightly scary, but my ledge was above high tide mark. Needing a pee in the middle of the night and without leaving my mat I was able to shoot directly into the sea. For some time I lay puzzling over something I'd seen on arrival: the Black Rocks were barnacle-studded but there wasn't any normal drapery of seaweed. Why?

I slept as well as usual under the solemn silence of the stars, and woke at the first smile of dawn. The quiet indicated the sea had retreated. The sun rose straight out of the sea, the blessed sun, the source of life, no wonder it was the earliest 'god' before mankind began creating gods in their own destructive image. We have done more wounding the world than worshipping it ever since.

When the sands appeared I could, like David Balfour on Erraid, escape my island, but first a brew, cereal and banana. On leaving it was very pleasant to breathe fresh air again! So that was my last bivvy.

Maybe.

NIGHT TRAIN

There tempts the night train:
A garland of light, brightly
Whistling a secret route
Through our derailed dreams.
Would I were on it, heading
For Tinga Maria, Rishi Kot,
Samarkand or Marrakech,
Instead of sitting, timetable on lap,
In a forgotten siding, signals
All set at red, indefinitely delayed.

JUST SO; STORIES

About The Stories

Some years ago I sent an editor a story which then appeared in the magazine and led to some correspondence on the topic covered: an unusual, creepy experience on the hills. When I mentioned mine was fiction the editor was not amused. 'I don't use fiction.'

This has happened more than once, as I mention with Schiehallion below, but I feel it flattering in a way as it shows that background descriptions or facts are correct. Naturally I have been to all the places mentioned in these stories but, as to what happens, readers will have to guess the veracity. Several people who had read Walking the Song asked me why I'd not included some fiction (and poems) so I've taken this chance to do so. I hope my choice is agreeable!

Sgurr Thuilm appeared in the *Scottish Mountaineering Club Journal* and won the W. H. Murray Literary Prize. *Sgurr Thuilm* and *Bothy Nights at Shenavall* appeared in the magazine *Loose Scree*. *Bothy Nights* was first told at Shenavall to my own Braehead School party, but has had various reincarnations, the most recent in Aberdeen's *Leopard* Magazine. The story was also read at one of the

'Feerlie Nights' at Pitlochry Festival Theatre's 'Winter Words Festival'. *Schiehallion*, from *The Last Hundred* (Mainstream 1994), was to have a curious sequel: I received a letter from a Sir Alistair Munro in America asking if the figure appearing in the story was the imagined Sir Hugh Munro of Tables fame – his grandfather. Alas, no; more in mind was the first Munroist, the Rev. A. E. Robertson who had been minister in Kinloch Rannoch. As for children, Braehead School had a bothy in the Black Wood of Rannoch so scores of boys and girls ascended the mountain. *The Frog Prince of Lochnagar* was written just before the shocking death of Princes Diana in 1997, so could hardly be published at that time, and the story lay forgotten till now.

Sgurr Thuilm

I met Bonnie Prince Charlie on top of Sgurr Thuilm. He blinked at my appearance and fingered my Goretex jacket with interest. I only let him do so as I – then – thought he was some weirdo who might react violently to any hint of aggression on my part. After all, he was an unprepossessing sight and, in the afternoon's westerly breeze, didn't smell so good either.

In my pocket I had a tube of Smarties which I'd saved for the summit (my 239th Munro) so I offered them. A grubby hand was held out and the gaudy sweets were studied carefully. When I popped some into my mouth there was a gasp. Two or three other disreputable characters had come up unnoticed and they grabbed the tube from me. Both ends popped out so Smarties scattered over the schisty rocks and they were, all, down, snatching and popping the sweets into their mouths. What a lot of savages I thought. They must have escaped from some loony bin. When another ragged character in a dirty kilt came peching up, dropped on his knee before the young one, and said, 'News, your Highness,' I began to wonder just who was going bonkers.

'Macmillan of Glen Pean has managed to get away and will be up betimes to take you northwards: doon tae Glen Pean and over Carn Mor.'

'Corbett' I commented, almost without knowing I'd spoken.

'Corbett?' several voices asked suspiciously.

'Aye, him that listed all the hills over 2,500 feet. J. Rooke Corbett.'

'A Sassenach?'

'Aye, but you can't hold that against him. He spent all the time possible up in the Highlands. Must have known them as well as anybody – A. E. Robertson, Munro and the rest.'

'Sound like a lot of spies to me,' a shaggy lad sneered.

'Or maybe they'd be useful guides. Are you in touch?'

'Well, yes, but only a photocopy of this area. Section 10. I'm not lugging the two books about all the time. Look.'

I produced my photocopies. They went from hand to hand. I suspect one or two had learning difficulties as they held the damned things upside down. The young lad who seemed in charge could read. He said what sounded like 'Merde' which, I suppose, might have been Gaelic.

'Did you steal these?' he asked.

'No I copied them. The Late Shop has a 5p copier.'

'And you'll guide us?'

My mouth fell open. 'What! Over Carn Mor?'

'Yes.'

'But I've done it. I want Sgurr nan Coireachan now,' and

I nodded west. I don't want to drag all the way up from Strathan again just for a Munro I can do today.'

There was a bit of muttering in which the name Munro came up once or twice. Someone mentioned a Colonel Munro. 'Effing Munro's regiment ... Cut the Frasers to pieces on Drumossie Moor.' I quickly interjected to point out this was the list of Sir Hugh Munro, Bart. of Lindertis in Angus, a most pacific gentleman only interested in finding his way up all the Highland hills. It was a bit of a speech.

'He spends all his time climbing mountains? Like this one?' The young one sounded incredulous.

'Aye.'

'What for?'

'Fun – I suppose.'

'Fun!' he grimaced. 'The man's mad.'

There were times I rather thought the same about Munro-bagging – but I wasn't going to admit that to this lot of scruffs. I launched into a somewhat long-winded defence of Munros, Corbetts *et al.*, how it gave one good exercise, got one away from life's ordinary pressures, taught self-reliance and gave an unrivalled knowledge of the Highlands.

There were some nods at the last anyway.

'Useful,' the young one smiled. 'My knowledge is growing by the day. This Sgurr Thuilm is a Munro then?'

'Yes.'

'And the next?'

He looked west.

'Sgurr nan Coireachan? Aye it's a Munro.'

Suddenly the young man smiled, which improved his looks somewhat. He suggested. 'Couldn't we walk – and talk – along to it then? Instead of skulking up here all day?'

There was an outcry at this. Movement was too easily seen. They might appear against the skyline. The cordon ran right along Glen Pean to Loch Morar. They'd made arrangements with Macmillan. And much more of the same.

The young man sighed.

'Your pressures may be at home, mine, alas, are always with me. Can I keep these delineations?' He held up my photocopies of Section 10.

I was about to ask for them back but I recalled a situation in Primary 3 when the big boys got our football and I asked for it back. This lot might deliver more than a bloody nose. So I took my leave.

'See you.'

'You going along there?' someone demanded.

'Why not? It's not the stalking season.'

'What if he's seen?' the man asked their leader.

He smiled and just waved me away. Condescending sod. As I left I heard the word 'decoy' whispered.

It's a right in and out, up and down ridge, but I got the second Munro for the day. In peace.

It was in the bothy that night I really began to think about this encounter. Just what had happened. Nobody was busy filming John Prebble or D. K. Broster. Those yobbos were authentically dirty (and smelly) and, besides, I'd been there at tea break time and nobody had knocked-off for a helicopter ride off for refreshment. It was all a bit strange, and it became even stranger as my imagination worked on it over the months, and years, following. I didn't ever mention my encounter to the boys. Nor the wife. Especially not the wife. She made snide enough comments when I began to read lots of books about the '45 and sat, headphones on, over several nights, listening to the Talking Book of Nigel Tranter's *Highness in Hiding*, the story of his wanderings after Culloden. It was awful, read by an Englishman who could pronounce nothing correctly (Benbecula became Ben Beculiar) but one thing did become clear from my researches eventually. Bonnie Prince Charlie had been on top of Sgurr Thuilm. Several books give details of his route. That made things all very peculiar indeed.

The years passed. The Corbetts were added to my Munros round and plans laid for going Furth of Scotland. I'd almost forgotten Sgurr Thuilm or I tried to convince myself I had. I was heading home early one Sunday, (the weather a complete wash-out), and turned off at Perth to get milk and bread at Tesco. I saw there was a car boot sale next door so I had a nosey round it. I usually pick up a few books if nothing else.

I found a cheap copy of one of John Buchan's short-story collections, one I'd had from the library and had been fascinated to find in it an account of Dr Johnson having an encounter with the dispirited and debauched Bonnie Prince when Johnson was wandering on the continent. Then I found a real treasure. It cost me all of 50p, being a hardback. It was Alexander Kirkwood's *True Records of the Rising of 1745 in sundry original documents by persons concerned therein, containing* ... containing another twenty lines of just what there was: letters, reports, autobiographical accounts, all in packed small print, 680 pages of it. And no index.

I went back into Tesco for a coffee and flicked through my find, reading a bit here, a bit there, till arrested by the name Dr. Samuel Johnson leaping out from another wordy section title. This told of his wanderings in France and Switzerland in 1776. I wonder if Buchan used this text as his source? The setting was the same: an inn at Thiers.

The ponderous doctor had made his guess at who the wino next door was and was rather sad. Ever since his wanderings with Boswell round the Highlands and Islands he'd had a sneaking softness for the sorry Jacobite saga. His own unchancy health and ungainly body was no joy, but to see the prince who had once set the heather afire reduced to such a state was dismal.

Being who he was however he set his table near the wall and noted down the snatches of talk that came through the thin partition that separated their rooms. (Bugging becomes history, it seems, as Kirkwood duly included the sage's notes.) Some of the talk did not make much sense, for which the meticulous doctor apologised ('methinks his erratic articulation at times arose from the distress of ancient remembrances') but there was one bit made me gasp so heads turned. Listen.

'*P. C.*: I once delighted in physical exertion.'

'*Companion* [too soft to note] ... march to Derby, your Highness.'

'*P. C.*: That was but strolling, sir. It was in the hills I found my best days. Ma fois! But I was like a deer on the hill. [pause] Never like it since. [pause] My only regret is that I climbed but one Munro in that time.'

'*Companion*: And what might that be?'

'*P.C.* [with some vigour]: Sgurr Thuilm, sir, Sgurr Thuilm.'

Bothy Nights at Shenavall

My name is Colin-Angus Fraser Mackenzie, which was a bit of an embarrassment at school – such a mouthful – I was always just called CA.

The name said plenty about my ancestry I suppose. Mr Lamont suggested once that the combination of Fraser and

Mackenzie merely supported the suggestion of our being 'such a parcel of rogues in a nation'. That is a quote from Burns though I didn't get it at the time. He, Mr Lamont, Roddy, as we called him when off on trips, thought I was a bit fey at times but what happened in the glen beyond An Teallach wasn't just me. It was him and all. It was all of us. OK, Coinneach Odhar (the Brahan Seer) was some sort of ancestor/relative. Lot of good it did him. He got burnt in a tar barrel down the road there.

Anyway, Mr Lamont, see, was appointed as a special teacher, to take expeditions in to the wilds (what would become 'Outdoor Education' later) and Fortrose Academy was one of the first schools to have anything like that, and it was marvellous. I went off whenever I could and the harder the trip the better. *That* one was a hard trek, a big Torridon Munro first before heading north. In snow. I'd 67 Munros when I left school.

We started at Kinlochewe and tramped round Loch Maree and up a glen to camp and then do Slioch. Then we moved to Loch an Nid and did the one with a long name I forget, Sgurr something, no, Mullach Coire Mhic Fhearchair. Unbelievable country, bulging up from deep glens to crags and screes. We saw an eagle every day.

We were washed out of our tents at Loch an Nid so we squelched along to stay in a bothy and dry out. It was called Shenavall. We seemed to spend the day collecting the bogwood needed to dry the clothes we got wet collecting bogwood. Sometimes it snowed. We made spotted dick at the fire.

We had a great supper. The apple rings we'd soaked all day swelled so much we had to put a rock on the lid to keep them in when cooking. We'd soup and a hooch. Roddy Lamont made us all into foodies. Gourmet campers. Later on we'd have a singsong or tell creepy stories and then have drinking chocolate and Ma Lamont's cake before getting into our sleeping bags.

I loved the whole routine. We were learning all the time and didn't even know it. Isn't that how education should be? One of that gang became a chef in Buckingham Palace – because he learned about cooking on a primus stove.

We soon settled down. Roddy had the wee back room to himself. He said all we lot did was fart and snore or yell in our sleep or keep traipsing out to make yellow snow. We did too. The trip before at Gorton bothy the lad next me had a nightmare and gave me a whack in the face.

I was still awake after everyone else was asleep. I don't go to sleep quickly. I liked to think things. Imagine things. Make up stories about us. But what happened then was shocking true. Even if it was only me – well, the first night anyway.

After an hour in my pit I became aware of a sort of rustling. Shenavall had mice and it wasn't them (all our food was hung up out of reach.) It was as if the room had people in it, moving about, doing things, sort of hurrying. Someone was sobbing. Not one of us. Sounded like a girl. All very quiet. Urgent. As if happening a long way away yet filling the room, all round, very urgent. They, they were packing, that's what it was. Voices whispering. Urgent. The door opened – and that was real. Had to be. I could suddenly see the moonlight. I grabbed Jimmy next to me, shook him, wanted to shout 'Wake up! Wake up!' but only croaked like I'd a bad cold. *They* were going. Hurrying out. But nothing showed against the sky. They weren't real. But they had to be, hadn't they?

Jimmy sat up. Asked what the f was going on. Got his torch. Shone it round. Shone it on the closed door. Shone it on the others still sleeping. Shone it on me. Dropped it. 'God, CA, you've the horrors on you!' which was one way of putting it.

I gabbled out what I'd seen and there was a knock on the partition at our heads. Roddy had woken.

'Whisper, CA.'

I did, urgently, not wanting to be the only one seeing things. But I didn't see them, not like seeing ordinary things. But real. People packed up in a panic and went. The door opened – for sure. And it was shut again when Jimmy shone his torch about. He did that again. There was nothing unto-ward. Just the worn old wooden walls with smoky graffiti and our belongings hanging on hooks and nails. Jimmy said the waterproofs and things looked like dead people hanging on the wall. Really comforting. He said I'd just had a night-mare. And I was a pest. Having woken up he was going to have to go out for a pee.

'Coming?'

I wouldn't have gone out that door for anything and held Jimmy back but he just shook my hand off, slipped his feet into his boots, tucked in the laces and clumped out. *His* exit and entry was plain enough. Quite unremarkable. He stuck out his tongue at me as he wiggled back into his sleeping bag, switched off his torch and gave a great fart as if to say what he thought about me and my imagination. But it wasn't. It wasn't. Things had happened in that room, unchancy, unhappy things that had cried out in the pain of night.

— — — — — — —

When the alarm went off it was still black night – and freezing – but poor Eck and Alan had their turn to get up first to light the lamp, put on the stoves and get tea water and porridge going while the rest of us relished being snug a while longer. Routine again. Crafty Roddy. You felt extra comfy knowing two others weren't.

I took the chance to whisper to Jimmy again about what had happened, threatened him dire murder if he breathed a word to anyone. It took a two Mars Bar bribe.

— — — — — — —

You have to get up in the dark to have a full day on the hills in winter. There's so little daylight. It's a hell till you're well on the way. 'Like warming a diesel engine,' Roddy used to say. We are just engines and so needed our fuel and warm-up too.

We were lucky it was so cold: the river was iced up enough so we could cross without paddling. The winter before a shepherd had given us a hint on that. You know how before any challenge you always seem to want a pee, well, you hold off till you've done the freezing paddling *then* you pee on your toes to warm them again. It works.

We did Beinn a' Chlaidheimh which is about the lowest Munro of all but the snow was frozen hard higher up so we had to put on crampons. I'd have gladly peed on my fingers; they froze struggling with the straps. Agony warming them up again under me oxters.

The sky was clear so it was a very cold day. The snow squeaked. Ice axes left blue holes in the snow. The scenery was like pictures of the Alps. An Teallach was magnificent but Roddy said its traverse was too difficult for this visit. We could do Beinn Dearg Mòr though. It looked nearly as spectacular even if not a Munro.

— — — — — — —

Back home, well, back in the bothy, I kept catching Jimmy's eye and he'd wink or smirk so I wanted to thump him. But he'd also said, 'I believe you; thousands wouldn't'. I could not be sure if he really meant it. Yet we were pals. Told each other things – as best friends do. As the evening wore on he seemed to grow quiet. Later he told me he was seeing my scared face in his torchlight again. That had been real, whatever I had told him. He knew I was a deep one; a Mackenzie after all.

There was a bit of larking about as we got ready for bed. 'Bumping.' You crouched down and hopped about to bump each other to see who you could knock over. Warmed you up beautifully. But neither Jimmy nor I had much enthusiasm for larking about. We were first into our sleeping bags and the last to switch off our torches. It was cold again, but had at least stopped snowing when we all had trooped out last thing.

Would we ever get to sleep? As it proved we didn't. Any of us. We *all* began to hear something.

'CA, do you hear what I hear?' Jimmy whispered.

'Voices?'

'Yes.'

I could feel him shaking. But it was someone else who, quite naturally, sang out, 'Voices'.

Someone said, 'Shit'.

'They'll be coming in and making a mess. Our stuff's all over the place.'

'Should we get a brew on?' asked a more sociably inclined lad. We heard Roddy stir.

Conversation died. We listened. There were voices indeed, nearing, raucous voices with an edge to them and other, puzzling sounds, sort of creakings and the sounds of metal on metal. Someone said, 'That's horses'.

'Don't be daft.' (No keeper would be out in the middle of the night.)

But it did sound like harness creaking. And the sort of tramp of determined purpose, not like others arriving late to a bothy on a climbing trip. Weird. As the party, whoever they were, came nearer, I noticed Roddy was standing in his long johns at the wee room's opening. Looking puzzled. Jimmy and I were looking at each other in sheer horror. Everyone was expecting a party to come bursting into the bothy but we sensed something other. The voices were wrong too somehow, the cadences were not familiar.

'Foreigners?' a voice suggested.

Jimmy and I gripped hands like bairns. Shivered. Then the strangest thing happened. There was a pause, a quietness outside. Jimmy said I was going 'No! No! No! They mustn't come in'.

He asked, 'Is it what went out last night coming back? In?'

No, the night before had been like a family in fear, fleeing, this was more military, antagonistic. Evil.

I was still shouting, 'It mustn't come in! It mustn't come in!' But I think the others were as much curious as concerned. Just folk arriving, even if rather funny; funny peculiar. CA off his head again.

Someone lit a candle which sent shadows across the walls. It was almost like a signal. There was a renewal of movement and sounds again outside, definitely men and beasts, armed men, with rancour in their tones – but moving on. Fading.

'Not after us then,' someone cracked.

'Weird.'

'What on earth was that?'

'No' nice.'

We looked at Roddy but he stood looking as perplexed as the rest. He's not often stumped.

'Let's have a brew,' he suggested.

He got the stove going and worked the fire into a blaze, while we crowded round, still in our sleeping bags, perched on stones and an old bench.

'You'd better tell,' Jimmy said.

So I mentioned how I'd had the uncomfy scene played out the previous night. Like how there were people packing up in a hurry; fleeing.

'From them?' Jimmy suggested.

He was as fey as I was!

'But we all heard it. Them! This time,' I said.

'We can't all hallucinate at the same time, can we, sir?'

Sir just shook his head.

Roddy did however open the door and look out on the bright, moonlit, snow world. Not a sound. He slipped his feet into his boos, tucked in the laces, and shuffled out with an attempt at humour: 'I may be gone some time'. One or two others had to follow. And all came in smartish. 'It's f-ing cold out there'. That practical necessity somehow broke the spell and we were ready enough for Roddy's, 'Off to bed everyone'.

Whoever – whatever – had passed in the night was heading down towards Loch na Sealga and that was the direction we headed for Beinn Dearg Mòr hoping we could cross the frozen burn where it shallowed on entering the loch. We did. Nobody got wet feet and we had a magical day on the hill, as good as any Munro. And giving plenty to think about all the time so the events of the night were not discussed, if not quite forgotten. Till after supper.

And I was the one who whispered in the after-supper bloat, 'Just what was going on in those nights?'

There was something of a swarm of suggestions and ideas, everyone speaking at once and all talking nonsense. Suddenly I jerked up and, according to Jimmy, went pale as death again. My gasp had all eyes turned to me.

'What is it, Colin-Angus?'

'When we went to kip last night, sir, it had stopped snowing, hadn't it?'

'Aye.'

'And we walked that way this morning...?'

'Aye.'

'Towards the loch?'

'Aye.'

In my eye I could see the pristine glen again, reaching away to the frozen loch between the mountains. I was right behind Roddy.

'We left plenty of footprints going and coming back, didn't we?'

'Yes.'

Some saw what I was getting at. Froze.

Taut silence.

Then Roddy whispered, 'There were no footprints in the snow'.

SCHIEHALLION

> And what was the toast?
> Schiehallion! Schiehallion! Schiehallion!
> **Edwin Morgan:** '*Canedolia*'

My mother's mother came from Kinloch Rannoch so we inherited the house. During the war and just afterwards nobody wanted to buy property in the Highlands and then it became the economic place to go for holidays. The house was called *Schiehallion*.

Schiehallion, the peak, dominated the village and the name translated as something like the *fairy hill of the Caledonians*. We came to regard it very much as *our* hill for, unlike most visitors and nearly all residents, our family actually climbed the hill. I made my first ascent when I was seven, the indulged youngest, which had Tom, three years older, complaining and Margaret, several years older again, acting the very grand lady.

The climb took all day, as we started and finished from home in Kinloch Rannoch – for at that time there was no big car park halfway up the hill by the Maskelyne memorial and a beaten trail up the long east ridge. We went up from Tempar always, after a four mile road walk. On the way we would seek out rabbits from the hedgerows with the dog or learn the names of flowers and birds. On the way back we collected mushrooms or brambles in season.

We often had cousins along too and other grown-ups or friends. I suppose the Schiehallion expeditions were saved for good days for we always had tremendous panoramas from the top and we seemed to spend half the day in the Tempar Burn. No climb would have been complete without a swim. On the way home at the last pool everyone went in, for the cottage could not cope with cleaning gangs of sweaty walkers. It was all very casual, the gaggle of kids strung out for miles, never a map or compass in sight. Later, I realised father always had these along and he kept a wary eye on all of us, however free we felt. But that was the way to treat the hills. We all loved our Schiehallion climbs. My last count showed I've been up 27 times and Margaret I know still takes her children up. I just wish I could join them more often for, though I became the Munro-bagger of the family, I ended up working abroad and visits home had to be carefully planned for new ticks in the Tables. Pity I can't swap a surplus of Schiehallions for a few remoter Munros.

Not that I've been up Schiehallion for a few years now. Though I try not to think so, maybe the last visit has affected me more than I'd like to admit. Perhaps I should be heading for the peak next time I'm in Scotland. See what happens. I'd have to do it again in winter or late autumn to have the line of white above the 2,500-level, since that was how it was last time. That time. Time to confess.

Rannochside in late autumn! Can anything beat it with the golden birch set in a world of dark pine greens? It hadn't taken much to lure me back that time and I'll swear the hired car swung up the hill at Trinafour of its own accord. I'd every intention of heading up Glen Lyon for Stuchd an Lochain, instead there I was twisting up the old, familiar way, turning off at Loch Kinardochy to pass the Braes farm and down by the little reedy lochan. I parked by the Tempar Burn bridge.

People sometimes say 'How can you keep going up a hill by the same way? Isn't it boring?' Of course it isn't! Especially with Schiehallion, *our* Schiehallion. Every yard seemed to bring back memories. Such as 'Tom's cairn,' our private name, recalling where my big brother on one occasion suddenly stopped his talkative ascent and spewed spectacularly for no obvious reason, or 'Maggie's mire' as we'd nicknamed a green sphagnum pool. Chuntering down, Margaret had turned to warn the rest of us, 'Be careful now. There's a horrible pool somewhere here' – and turned to go straight into it up to her waist.

The wintry sun glittered on the pools up Gleann Mor that moats Schiehallion to the south, a green glen as it marks an intrusive band of limestone. What days we had exploring its length with pools, caves and a bothy for rare nights out. As I climbed on, the whole length of Loch Rannoch lay a-glitter, a highway leading the eye away out over the great moor to the guardian peaks of Glen Etive and Glen Coe. I hadn't realized how much I loved that bit of country till then. Starting in the centre of Scotland, how could one *not* become a Munro-bagger. Wasn't this, too, the parish of Rev A. E. Robertson, the first Munroist nearly a century ago?

Schiehallion's top rocks were all covered in snow, a white sugar still in crisp freshness. The well-remembered height: 3,547 ft. I reeled off names of visible friends, from Macdui to Ben Lui, from the Lomonds to Ben Alder, rubbing hands together, partly in glee, partly because they were freezing cold! My eye was ranging over the Beinn a' Ghlo humps when I sensed rather than heard a footstep behind me. I turned to find another climber arriving at the trig point.

'Aye,' I greeted him.

He smiled back.

'Fantastic view, isn't it?'

He followed my sweeping arm, the smile broadening across his face, a kindly face, trim moustache and that glow of healthy living. Hardly talkative though.

Too chilly to linger I set off down the west ridge, by which we'd both come up, giving the other a nod and a grin. He barely noticed. Or perhaps the sun dazzled him. I think he was telling off the hills of memory too, away in that golden west. I stopped several times just to gaze along the loch towards the sunset lands. Just before leaving the snow level where the rough going over rocks ended and the snow lay on a kindlier surface, I noticed a set of footprints paralleling my own upward tracks. What astonished me was to see the clear marks of nails.

For goodness sake! Nails went out just after the war. A few old fogies kept on using them till they either died off, or their boots did, and nobody stocked them any more. Crampons now scratched rock, not nails. I chortled over this as I brushed through the heather down to the stile and the row of oaks back to the bridge. It was only on the tedious drive along the A9 to Stirling that I began to recall other odd details of our encounter.

The man's presence had been relaxed but I'd really hardly looked him over. What came back was strange. He had been wearing a tie. And tweeds. OK, plenty of keepers wear tweeds but not cut like that; his was a gentleman's suit, from God knows what vintage, grey-green with a gentle check of heather brown. Damn! Why hadn't I looked at his footwear? Why hadn't I *really* looked at him? But why should I have? He was just another climber enjoying the sparkling autumn afternoon on one of the best of Munros. We don't barge in on each other in such circumstances. Still, I'd recognize him if we were to meet again, on or off the hill. Pity I wasn't heading for Kinloch. The locals at the 'Bun' might have answered questions about the antiquely-equipped bloke. I switched on the radio and let the matter drift out of my mind. Back to Tom's house at Kirkie.

But things kept coming back over the rest of the holiday. I left Scotland with a useful 22 new Munros from the fortnight (only 17 to go!), had a week in the head office in London and was soon sweating it out in the Gulf once more.

One of my treasured possessions is a complete set of the *Scottish Mountaineering Club Journal*. (Munro's *Tables* appeared first of all in an 1891 number.) Though I wasn't a great climber I'd been elected to the club a decade earlier and had picked up early bound volumes from a club sale.

Others came in dribs and drabs from dealers and book-shops. I felt over the moon when the last numbers turned up. The first ten volumes were beautifully bound in leather but the dry heat means they leave a dust on my hands whenever I look at them. I don't very often. Too busy. Silly lifestyle.

However, the local *Mouloud* holiday gave me a free evening and, after I'd written a couple of dutiful letters, I pulled out a few early volumes of the SMCJ. It was always amusing to compare their accounts of days over Munros I'd done recently. Like Sir Hugh having the ice scraped off his back after a tussle on the hills above the A9. Heavens! He tackled such in tweeds (or kilt) and the big hobnailers of the club song.

Nails! In a flash the figure I'd met on top of Schiehallion was smiling at me. In the mind's eye. He'd been dressed in that sort of garb. Had the snow been old and icy he'd have sported an ice axe five feet long! I was letting my mind go wild. But . . . 'But me no buts'.

I tried to shake the picture away, went and poured a surreptitious G & T, took journals and drink out on to the verandah. A pattern of railings fell on the pages as the low sun spread shadows that would bring a blessed coolness. I was soon carried away to the hills of home as I dipped and browsed through those dusty tomes.

I'd carried out three volumes and, when I opened the last at random, it showed a picture of a group at the Ben Nevis Observatory in 1897, the three figures in their tweeds, draped with ropes and, sure enough, mighty ice axes. I smiled. Then the bloody phone rang so I perforce had to deal with some business – business that was *not* supposed to follow me home from the office. After several calls I ordered supper and ate in rather distracted fashion, my mind half on what had cropped up and half on something or other connected with what I was doing earlier, something to do with the SMC journals.

Abd el Ali had carried them in when drawing the curtains. He carried my glass off with a grimace. So I went through the scene on the terrace again in my imagination, trying to jog the tired old memory. Ah, yes; it came back. I'd just come on an interesting photograph when the phone rang. Suddenly I saw the photo plainly again in the remembering and the hair on my neck rose like a cat's. One gentlemanly face in the Nevis photograph of 1897 had been the face I had seen on top of Schiehallion in 1979.

THE FROG PRINCE OF LOCHNAGAR

Once upon sometime there was this Prince, heir to the kingdom, the most eligible bachelor in the whole wide world. Girls longed to win his hand but he gave little sign of wanting to marry anyone. He'd rather be out in the country, in his number two kilt and wellies, talking to his flowers, doing a spot of watercolour painting or making up stories about Lochnagar. Marriage with someone like that would never be easy. His mum was beginning to panic, and his grannie promised him a fairy castle to stay in if he married a nice girl. At long last he fell for a beautiful, beautiful Princess and everyone began to say this was romance for sure. She was the sweetest young thing. Even the press went daft about her, even the wrinkly monarch looked pleased: then – then the Prince disappeared!

Completely disappeared. 'You can't just disappear in the Palace!' everyone said, but he had. They searched every-where, from inside wardrobes (in case he'd gone Narnia) to unzipping the stuffed elephant sent from Zimbabwe. There was consternation as you can imagine. And wild speculation in the press. Even *The Times*. But nobody claimed responsibility, there were no ransom demands and the Prince didn't turn up at any of the second, or twenty-second, homes the family occupied occasionally. Weeks went by before there was 'the faintest glimmer of a clue' as whatshisname put it on the ITV news. Somebody must have leaked something from the palace.

The Prince had been having his portrait painted at the time of his disappearance. Royals always do that for important occasions, as if a photographer wouldn't do as well. The picture was on an easel in his old playroom where he kept his rocking horse and all the toys he couldn't bear to send to a charity shop or car boot sale. The painting was almost complete, so much so that many thought it was, that being the sort of work that gets by these days. It even had its signature except it wasn't a proper signature but it had been signed, so to speak, by painting a little frog. Very neatly done too, the frog half-hiding in the grass.

A little green frog it was which only one old white-haired lady had noticed, the daily who did the Prince's room. She was curious and, when emptying her dustpan outside the kitchen, she asked who the artist was. 'John Rana,' she was told, which didn't really convey anything to her. But it sounded eastern. 'Was he Indian?' 'No,' came the reply, but another voice piped up that *Rana* was the Latin family name for some frog species. The shocked old dear nearly put her mop through a pile of Sèvres dishes on the kitchen table, and poured herself a glass to recover. 'Too much imagination is my trouble,' she thought, but she clattered back upstairs for another close look at the painting.

Sure enough the signature was *frog* (so to speak) and as

she walked past the picture it somehow changed, a bit like those hologram pictures on a banker's card, and the Prince (full-length, in his best kilt) wobbled opaquely and stood out suddenly as a frog, then changed back to the human figure. She walked back and forwards, back and forwards and it happened each time: Prince, frog, Prince, frog, Prince ...

She blabbed of course and word worked its way up through the hierarchy of palace staff and from floor to floor. In the words of one delighted old sea dog, 'The balloon went up!'

The By Appointment magician was suspected but he had an alibi. Eventually, after interviewing the char and offering her an MBE, they realised it had to be something to do with the artist. With a name like Rana, I ask you. They hauled him in. He held out for a long time but eventually he broke under torture. Oh yes, torture. None of your thumbscrews and the rack. Much more modern, and subtle, leaving no marks on the victim: sleep deprivation. He was made to stand at the Bar of the House of Commons and listen to every debate, every Question Time, every word, for a week, non-stop, and when they weren't sitting he had to watch every party political broadcast in the BBC archives over and over again.

He cracked on the seventh day. He would have confessed anything by then. He gabbled out: 'Yes, I used magic to turn the Prince into a frog... he was a hopeless sitter, always moving and always talking about things he thought he was expert about.' Then what mattered: 'I took him to Lochnagar in Scotland,' and 'No, I can't change him back. Only the kiss of a Princess can do that'.

Well at least they had the Princess.

The next few weeks were interesting. When climbers came down from Lochnagar (the hill) saying big engineering works were going on round Lochnagar (the loch) there was an outcry from all the conservation bodies. There didn't seem to be any planning permission. Concern grew into direct action when the contractors started to drain the dark waters of the loch. When it leaked out the objective was to recover all the frogs in the loch questions were raised in every capital in Europe, not just Westminster. When Britain's National Security was given as a reason for not answering questions it led to such a hullabaloo the government was forced to resign and there was a General Election. Scotland looked like declaring independence, and the monarchy itself was under threat. A dreadful time. Another *annus horribilis*. (By one of those weird co-incidences it just happened to be the Chinese *Year of the Frog*.) Nobody was amused and the Princess grew thin – well, thinner – without her 'princely poppet' (*The Sun*).

The whole of the Lochnagar range – a huge area taking in a dozen Munros – was ringed by security forces and every inch searched by Mountaineering Scotland volunteers from the clubs, Scottish Natural Heritage, Forest Enterprise, the Mountain Rescue teams and, eventually, most of the Army. They collected 12,675 frogs in their sweep searches. When Lochnagar (the loch) was finally emptied they removed another, rather disappointing, 27 frogs from the sludgy mess – and six members of Greenpeace.

So that made, er, 12,702 frogs. The Royal Train was brought into service to hurry the loch's 27 frogs to the palace where the princess went through the motions of kissing them. Nothing happened, except that reporters and the TV lot all did well on overtime. The remaining frogs, as you can imagine, created quite a logistical problem. Frogs are rather jumpy things and don't keep still. I think every house in Deeside donated a chamber pot. *Any* receptacle to hold a few frogs was welcomed. Several barrels were sent from the Spey distilleries which had the effect of stilling several thousand frogs; they were all inebriated. Tankers from Dounreay were politely refused, and it was mostly milk tankers that eventually took the 12,675 frogs to Aberdeen where they were transferred to tanks requisitioned from every sea life centre in the country.

There they were loaded on a special train to King's Cross, in modified carriages to carry the hundreds of open tanks containing the frogs. They had been very thorough and just hoped they hadn't missed the one which would prove to be the Prince. The Archbishop of Canterbury and the Moderator of the Church of Scotland put up a joint prayer as the train headed off south.

The Princess didn't like the idea of having to kiss *any* frog, not after the twenty seven, even if it was an enchanted frog which would turn into her handsome Prince whom she could then marry and live happily ever after. That only happens in fairy stories after all.

The Princess hadn't been told about this reserve stock of course. Well, how would you like to break the news? She was bracing herself to kiss one or two more frogs, not 12,675 (or however many before the Prince magically reappeared). Sir David Attaboy on the BBC didn't help. He said frogs were all slobbery and tasted ghastly, like over-boiled cabbage.

The Princess rather lost her cool when she found there were 12,675 frogs to kiss. She refused. 'Not even for him,' she cried, 'Why, at one a minute, I'd be kissing for more than a week. Think of my lipstick!'

The slow train eventually crept up to the buffers at King's Cross. A 'frogs on line' suggestion on the way didn't please the Scottish-London commuters. Fantastic security of course; utter disruption for the public. The frog tanks were loaded onto those trolley things and they buzzed in and out with them to a waiting line of army trucks. Then disaster. Two of these trolley lines nearly collided and the one that was full of heavily loaded tanks of frogs swerved – and went straight down the pedestrian stairs into the Underground. Water and frogs splashed out all over the place but the train of tanks somehow kept upright and bounced down and along into the big hall. The driver had to swerve again to avoid the central kiosks and that was fatal. Over went the lot at the top of the escalators for the Northern and Piccadilly Lines. Water poured down to gush along all the passages to different platforms. Frogs everywhere. A week later one even popped out at Cockfosters and was rushed to the palace. Not that it mattered any more. By that time they'd locked up the Princess where she couldn't harm herself. She was quite batty by then. That was the general 'frognosis' anyway (*The Scotsman*).

They'd set up such an efficient system too, her break-down was such a shame. They reckoned she could manage three a minute over six hour shifts but the accident upset everything. The whole Underground system was hotching with frogs. The FFLG (Free Frogs Liberation Group) was rescuing them and throwing them in the Serpentine so an emergency operation had to be set up to drain it. Then some were thrown in the Thames. That was the last straw. The Princess had her nervous breakdown, the new Government was in trouble, the City in a panic, London at a standstill, and the Emergency Powers Act was put into operation, the monarchy the laughing stock of the world. A lady living in a council house in Pumpherston wrote a frog song which shot to the top of the charts. The royals were not amused.

They estimate the potty Princess had kissed about 9,628 frogs in that week but an accurate figure can't be given as the computer in the palace had a nervous breakdown too. Anyway, not one frog had proved to be the enchanted

Prince. The Princess, quite rightly I'd say, rather went off frogs. The country could only hold its breath and hold its breath and – wait.

A few months later the old lady who did the Prince's rooms found a solemn frog sitting beside the portrait. She picked it up in her palms and nattered away at it, all 'Ootsy-tootsy, supposing you're the Prince, what about giving me a kiss then dearie?' and she playfully gave it a smacker on its mouth. (It *was* slobbery and tasted of over-boiled cabbage.)

The result was spectacular. There was a big flash-bang! and the Prince was back. And he of course fell violently in love with the old lady. He couldn't help it. Magic! The cleaning lady played all coy and then got bleeding mad and socked the pushy Prince on one of his big ears. There was a constitutional crisis (you can't have a prince marrying a charlady) but the problem resolved itself when the enchantment ran its natural course. Having been refused for a month and a day (they did give her the MBE for that) the Prince suddenly turned back into a frog.

Luckily his private secretary, his personal psychologist and an elderly guru were there at the time to witness the transformation. They grabbed the frog and rushed along to the Princess in her darkened room. They knew they had the right one this time. Just one more frog to kiss. 'Please! Please!' The princess closed her eyes, grimaced, and kissed the frog they knew was the prince.

The outcome was disastrous. Seeing the future only lay in frogs the stock market collapsed, the monarchy was finally pensioned off and Scotland took its independence. As there was no death penalty John Rana was made an academician. EC funding allowed Lochnagar to become a Class I sanctuary and they roofed over the cliffs to make a

National Climbing Centre for Scotland. They run regular trips up from Deeside's Balmoral Heritage Park.

And all because of that last grudging kiss. The Princess had taken a lot of persuading but eventually, screwing up her face, she had given the frog Prince a peck on his neb. There was another flash-bang! And there, sitting on the table, were *two frogs*. In the middle of the very next night two Scottish students broke into the palace and carried off the sweety jar with the royal frogs in it. Where to take this symbol? Why, Lochnagar of course.

Presumably all those in Lochnagar (the loch) are their vivacious progeny. There's a survey going on at present to count the numbers of the aptly named *Rana regalia*.

COUNTING SHEEP

Sleep is postponed
When words sheep over
the gates of the mind.
It is too late, past dawn,
to gather wool from thorns
and barbed-wire fences.
The beasts have to be grabbed,
dipped and disinfected,
sheared in an hour while fighting
awake
hung-over from day.

Who would be a shepherd
with flocks of words loose
on the fells of the mind
in March moonlight?
I would wash my mind
of the stinking fold
but I cannot sleep
till I count my sheep.

ACKNOWLEDGEMENTS

Selected pieces, prose or poems, have appeared in the *Scotsman* and *Glasgow Herald* (for whom I wrote regular features in the Eighties and Nineties); in the *Scots Magazine* (over a forty year period); *Scottish Field, Countryman,* the *Great Outdoors; High; Climber; Loose Scree; Scottish Mountaineer;* journals of the Alpine Club, the Scottish Mountaineering Club, The Munro Society, the Mountain Bothies Association; *St Andrews in Focus.* I am also indebted to my local helpful Burntisland Library (endless photocopying), the Central Library in Edinburgh, and the National Library of Scotland, which houses my 'archive' of logbooks, articles, stories and other manuscripts (NLS reference Acc. 13060 and 13518). They also hold an archive of Braehead School interest. Many individuals helped along the way: Richard Cormack, Peter Willimott, David Steane, Adrian Snowball and, above all, Robert Aitken, useful critic, who helped improve the text into something much better as well as seeing it into its final form; also Margaret Higgins who also 'computerised' parts, invaluable labour, from comments to commas; Robert Davidson of Sandstone Press who, having published *Walking the Song*, made *Chasing the Dreams* a reality; and Rachel Nordstrom and Jane Campbell of St Andrews University Library Special Collections (which has my photographic archive) for scanning images from which the cover was prepared. Thanks to them all.

HAMISH BROWN
WALKING
THE SONG
by the author of HAMISH'S MOUNTAIN WALK

'Inimitable... some
of his best writing.'
MARTIN MORAN

'Eloquent and evocative.'
KEITH PARTRIDGE

Hamish Brown has contributed articles and essays to many
journals throughout his many years as an outdoorsman. This
selection presents a very personal record of many journeys and
interests from his 'dancing days of spring' to his present, very
active, later life.

Walking the Song
Paperback. RRP: £8.99
ISBN: 978-1-910-985-58-8

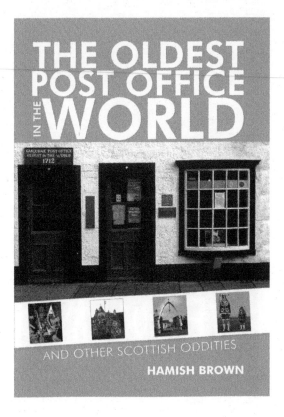

Hamish Brown, veteran outdoor and travel author, takes
us on a tour of ninety-four of the oddest locations located
throughout Scotland from the White Wife in Shetland to the
Oldest Post Office in the World in Galloway by way of all of
Scotland's regions and the strange things to be found.

The Oldest Post Office in the World and other Scottish Oddities
Paperback. RRP: £11.99
ISBN: 978-1-905-207-95-4

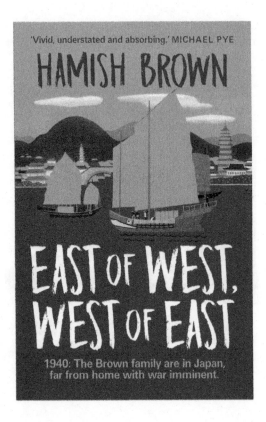

'Vivid, understated and absorbing.' MICHAEL PYE

HAMISH BROWN

EAST OF WEST, WEST OF EAST

1940: The Brown family are in Japan, far from home with war imminent.

This extraordinary book tells the story of a remarkable family caught in Japan at the outbreak of the Second World War in the Pacific. Brings the era to life with letters, journal extracts and notes from Hamish Brown's parents, as well as his own recollections.

East of West, West of East
Paperback. RRP: £9.99
ISBN: 978-1-912-240-25-8

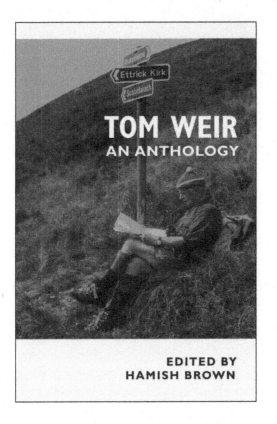

From his early years Tom Weir MBE was set on making his way as an explorer, writer and photographer. This collection of Tom Weir's writing has been selected by Hamish Brown from the whole body of his life's work.

Tom Weir: an anthology
Paperback. RRP: £14.99
ISBN: 978-1-908-737-28-1

www.sandstonepress.com

 facebook.com/SandstonePress/

 @SandstonePress